AF527907

Dalit Movement and Radical Left

Dalit Movement and Radical Left

A Study in Telangana

Rajesh Kota

RAWAT PUBLICATIONS

Jaipur • New Delhi • Bangalore • Guwahati • Kolkata

ISBN 978-81-316-1007-7

© Author, 2019

No part of this book may be reproduced or transmitted in any form or by any means, electronic or mechanical, including photocopying, recording or by any information storage and retrieval system, without permission in writing from the publishers.

Published by
Prem Rawat for **Rawat Publications**
Satyam Apts., Sector 3, Jawahar Nagar, Jaipur 302 004 (India)
Phone: 0141 265 1748 / 7006 Fax: 0141 265 1748
E-mail: info@rawatbooks.com
Website: www.rawatbooks.com

New Delhi Office
4858/24, Ansari Road, Daryaganj, New Delhi 110 002
Phone: 011-23263290

Also at *Bangalore, Guwahati* and *Kolkata*

Typeset by Rawat Computers, Jaipur
Printed at Nice Printing Press, New Delhi

Dedicated to my Teacher
Late Professor Gaddam Krishna Reddy

Contents

Acknowledgements

It has been a long, difficult and doubtful journey from social welfare hostel to Arts College, Osmania University and to submit a PhD thesis is a dream comes true. I had to try hard to make myself believe that I have done it! If I look back in time through hardships, I see many faces that have helped me to overcome difficult times. Unfortunately, due to constraints of time and space, I could not name them all here, but I can sincerely say 'I shall be extremely grateful to all of YOU always.'

When it comes to achieving difficult tasks, very few people believe in us. Professor G. Krishna Reddy happens to be one of those very few people who believed in me, not only that, he also made me believe that I could write. He has planted the idea of PhD and took all the care to see it flower and bear fruit. It is his continued encouragement, invaluable suggestions and able guidance which made this work possible. No amounts of thanks would suffice when it comes to acknowledge his help and guidance. I am deeply indebted to him. In my pursuit of knowledge he continues to be my source of inspiration.

After going through the harsh conditions of my school and college days, the place where I experienced the care and affection of teachers for the first time in my life as a student is in my PG.

They introduced me to the new definition of student-teacher relations–cordial relations have created a congenial atmosphere for learning. So, here I proudly take the pleasure of mentioning my PG teachers' names to whom I remain indebted and whom I remember forever. They are: Professor G. Ram Reddy, Y.V. Yoga Jyostna, Professor K. Laxmi, Professor G. Gopalreddy and Mr Chandru.

Department of Political Science, Osmania University has given me an opportunity to reinvent myself. I owe much to the Department for what I am now. It consists of not only intellectual stalwarts but also social activists of different fields. It is this unique nature of the department which helped me to understand and analyse both theory and practice with equal academic rigour, which I do not think would have been possible elsewhere. The affection they shower on the students is equally noteworthy.

As everybody knows OU is always academically active and politically charged. The political circumstances prevalent on campus have prompted me to zero in on my topic of research. When I joined the university, a serious debate was going on Dalit issues within Left organizations. Being a political science student I naturally got attracted to those discussions and debates. And this research is just another attempt to understand the Dalit and Left interface in depth and in detail. So, I feel, I also owe much to OU campus for the space it has given to explore myself and the society.

I owe a debt of gratitude to my faculty members, Professor D. Ravinder, Professor M. Chenna Basavaiah, Professor Naidu Ashok, Professor M. Brahamanandam, Professor J. Musalaiah, A.V. Satish Chandra, Goka, Ajay and Dr Ch. Venkateswarlu for their concern, care and timely suggestions.

I express my deep felt sincere gratitude to Professor D. Chennappa for his concern and continue guidance towards my academic career.

This study has given me a rare opportunity of meeting many great people. I express my heartfelt thanks and gratitude to Balladeer Gaddar, Manda Krishna Madiga, Ganta Chakrapani, Varavara Rao, Bojja Tharakam, Kura Rajanna, Amar, Chalapathi Rao, Duddu Prabhakar, U. Sambashiva Rao, Mallepalli Laxmaiah, G. Ramulu. These interactions have helped me to understand the limitations of ideology when it is put to practice. These intellectually inspiring interactions have enriched my study.

My special thanks to Professor K. Srinivasulu, Professor Kancha Ilaiah, Professor M. Kodanda Ram, Dr Chinnaiah Jangam, Professor K.Y. Rathnam, Professor Arun Kumar Patnaik, Professor Ajay Gudavarthy, Dr K. Balagopal, Professor K. Satyanarayana, Professor Adapa Satyanarayana, and Comrade Maroju Veeranna for their writings on Dalit, Left and Social Movements in Telangana and Andhra Pradesh, which have helped me immensely in carrying forward my research.

I thank Centre for Advanced Studies (CAS), Department of Political Science, OU for selecting me as a project fellow. This has helped me to carry out my research without any financial difficulties. This has also helped to meet and interact with academic intellectuals from all over the country and abroad.

I remember with deep feeling of gratitude my school teacher Koppula Venkataiah, who has taught me my first letters of alphabet without knowing he was making a PhD scholar, and my lecturers Achyut and Venkanna who inspired me to do MA in Political Science.

I am grateful to my uncles (my father's younger brothers) Mr David and Mr Francis for their love and affection and wholehearted support towards my academic career from the beginning to this date. I also must thank my friends Mr M. Bhaskar and E. Upender.

My special thanks to Progressive Democratic Students Union (PDSU), one of the leading Left student organization, for helping me to evolve as a human being. My close association with PDSU has helped me to understand society and politics in a better way. It has also given an opportunity to work with different students organizations which in turn helped me to understand ideological differences and conflicts.

I also thank my senior PhD scholar and friend Dr Nagam Kumaraswamy for his sincere advice, and flawless friendship. I thank my co-scholars Dr Sudershan Balaboina.

I am very much grateful to Dr Konda Nageswar Rao, Dr Jacab Kale, Dr Samunnatha, Nalamasa Krishna, Dr G. Srinivas Rao, Dr Chandraiah Gopani for their wholehearted support and for guiding me in the right direction. My special thanks to Mohan Dharavat, Shankar Sampangi from EFLU, Praveen Thallapalli, Mani from JNU for their continuous support.

I owe a lot to my OU friends for the love and affection they showered on me. They have made my OU days memorable and these people constitute my emotional support system. They are: Stalin, David, Mandala Bhaskar, Duragam Bhaskar, Mani, Shilpa, Ranjith, Azad and Aswat.

I am fortunate to meet and interact with many great people on various occasions like seminars and workshops. I have really benefited a lot from those interactions. Their observations and suggestions helped a lot in writing this thesis. So, I also express my gratitude to Dr Gaurav, Arundathi Roy, Dr Gopal Guru, Dr Anand Teltumbede, Dr Gail Omvedt, Dr Kaka, Dr Sudhpai, Dr Haragopal, Dr Dag Erick Berg, and Dr Danial C. Bach.

I owe a debt beyond measure when it comes to my parents and family members; especially my father Basavaiah and my mother Mariyamma. Being the eldest son I saw the troubles and the difficulties they have faced in bringing us to this stage. Nothing would have been possible without their love, affection, care and efforts. My thanks to my brothers, Sudhakar, Babi, and their families for their love and affection. I also thank my brother-in-law, Dr Aruri Sudhakar and my sister Balarani. I also express my gratitude to my aunt Laxmi Durga and her family for their support and concern.

I wish to acknowledge the efforts of my friends N. Shama Rao and K. Susheel Kumar. No words will be sufficient to express my gratitude to them, particularly Sham, who has been with me from the beginning of my project till I finished it, helping me with proofreading, editing and sometimes translating.

Finally my wife Raji, to thank her is to undermine her contributions. Due to my hectic and uncertain work schedules, with a baby girl to look after, she is the one who suffered a lot because of this research. She had even postponed her studies to see me finish my thesis. I will be ever grateful to her for bringing happiness into my life, for the unstinting support, for all the sacrifices she had made and for the immense faith she had in me. And my daughter Sadya has been the much necessary distraction from the long, tiresome and stressful work.

Glossary

Abkari	Toddy, liquor
Agraharas	Grants made to Hindu temples and brahmins without any revenue payment
Anaal Malik	Literally 'I am the King'
Andhra Jana Sangham	Andhra People's Association
Anna	Sixteenth part of a rupee in Indian Currency
Banjaras	Tribal community
Beedi	Local cigar made by tendu leaf
Bhoodan	Land donate
Chakali	Washermen
Chillara Kulhala Sangam	Lower caste organizations organized against landlordism in Telangana
Dalam	A communist fighting unit
Dandora	A traditional announcement by the Madiga men through Dappu in a village

Dandugalu	Arbitrary penal extractions
Deshmukh	Initially revenue collector turned landlord
Diwan	Prime Minister
Diwani	Revenue area directly under the control of the Diwan; also known as khalsa
Dora	'Master, Sir' title used for the Deshmukh landlords
Edureetha	Swim against the tides
Gaundlas	Toddy-tappers and liquor vendors
Girdavar	Revenue inspector
Golla	Shepherd community
Gonds	An adivasi community
Goonda	Anti-social element; villainous muscle man
Gram Sabha	A village level communist unit set up to look after village administration in the red areas
Gunta chutta	A kind of cigar
Harijan	Children of God, a term used by Mahatma Gandhi for members of the 'Untouchable' castes
Inam	Land grant made by the state in lieu of *vetti* services
Jaati	Caste or sub-caste; also used for nation
Jagir	A land grant given for services rendered to the Nizam
Jagirdar	Holder of a jagir
Jajmani	System of patron–client relationship
Jaithra yatra	Victory march
Jeetham	Farm-servant
Jogini	A type of socio-religious practise. That is in the form of servant of Hindu god. For this, mostly lower caste's women are drown into this system and they were forced to involved into the sexual exploitation by the dominant castes in Telangana.

Kalladars	Crop contactor
Kammari	Iron smith; blacksmith
Kapu	A peasant caste
Karnam	Village-level revenue official
Khalsa	Diwani
Koriwas (Sala)	Weavers
Kulanirmulana	Annihilation of caste
Kummari	Potter
Labour	Cooli
Madiga	An untouchable caste of leather workers
Mahasabha	Conference
Mala	A non-leather working ex-untouchable caste
Mamool	Gifts customarily demanded by the dora
Mangali	A barber community
Nalupu	Black
Paleru	A farm-servant
Patel	Hereditary village headman
Patta	Registered landholding
Pattadar	A registered landowner
Patwari	Hereditary village accountant and keeper of revenue records
Peshkar	Assistant
Pettandari	Landlordism
Police Patel	A village level official in-charge of general administration and law and order
Poramboku	Uncultivable waste (government) land
Pragathi Patham	Progressive path
Razakar	An activist of the Muslim communal organization known as Ittaehad-ul-Muslimeen headed by Kasim Razvi

Raktastruvulu	Tears of blood
Reddy	A landowning peasant caste though low in ritual hierarchy enjoys high status in the social hierarchy
Sarf-e-Khas	Crown lands of the Nizam of Hyderabad before 1949
Sarkar	Government
Shikmidar	Tenant
Shuddi	Purification ritual—the programme of reconversion of newly converts back to Hinduism
Shudra	The lowest rank in the four-fold Varna system
Shibiram	Camp
Subah	Province
Taluqdar	Collector
Taluq	A district sub-division
Telaga	A peasant caste
Vadla	Carpenter
Velama	A peasant caste
Vetti	Vetti chakiri or forced labour
Vetti Mandallu	Free manuring of the landlord's lands with the excreta of shepherds
Vetti Nagallu	Free tilling of the landlord's lands by the peasant castes

Abbreviations

AICCCR	All India Coordination Committee for the Communist Revolutionaries
APRCC	Andhra Pradesh Revolutionary Coordination Committee
AYS	Ambedkar Yuvajana Sangam
CCC	Committee of Concerned Citizens
CI	Circle Inspector
COC	Central Organizing Committee
CPGB	Communist Party of Great Britain
CPI	Communist Party of India
CPI (M)	Communist Party of India (Marxist)
CPI (ML)	Communist Party of India (Marxist Leninist)
CPUSI	Communist Party of United States of India
CRPC	Criminal Procedure Code
CRPF	Central Reserve Protection Force
CSP	Congress Socialist Party

DBSV	Dalita Bahujana Sramika Vimukthi
DCA	Depressed Classes Association
DMS	Dalit Mahasabha
JNM	Jana Natya Mandali
MIM	Majlis-i-Ittehad-ul-Mussulman
MRPS	Madiga Reservation Porata Samiti
NHRC	National Human Rights Committee
NTR	Nandamuri Taraka Rama Rao
OBC	Other Backward Caste/Class
PDF	Progressive Democratic Front
PDSU	Progressive Democratic Students Union
PUDR	Peoples Union Democratic Rights
PWG	People's War Group
RCS	Raitu Coolie Sangham
RSU	Radical Students Union
RYL	Radical Youth League
SC	Scheduled Caste
SCF	Scheduled Caste Federation
ST	Scheduled Tribe
TADA	Terrorist and Disruptive Activities (Prevention) Act
TDP	Telugu Desam Party
TRS	Telangana Rashtra Samithi
UCCRI (ML)	Unity Centre of Communist Revolutionaries India-Marxist Leninist

Introduction

India, the subcontinent of Asia, has some unique features with regard to political, economic, and cultural aspects. Among these, the social and cultural scenario of India is highly complicated. Caste system, a heinous social practice, exists nowhere in the world but for Indian subcontinent. As its origins are difficult to trace, its end also seems nowhere in near future. Dalits, who happen to be at the lowest rung of the caste system, are still fighting against the system through relentless struggles with undaunted spirit.

Caste in India was not simply produced by Hindu religious texts but shaped by ecologies, languages, religion, modes of production, and political system. The exploitation of the subordinate castes in India occurs through social relation rather than economic relation.[1] The caste issue occupies a central position in any discussion of social transformation in the Indian context. To a large extent the credit for focussing attention on caste goes to the Dalit movements. The Dalit movement specified the point that emancipation of the untouchables is not an isolated task. Similarly, social transformation cannot ignore the various layers of caste discrimination. A century-long anti-caste movement and the twentieth century Dalit movement in particular forced academia to take note of caste struggles in their analysis of social movements.

Telangana witnessed many socio-political and cultural movements such as adivasi movement, Telangana peasant movement, anti-arrack movement, Telangana statehood movement, Naxalite movement, tendu movement, civil rights movement, women's movement, students movement, and environmental movement. And in almost all the movements the role of Dalits is undeniable and also they played a crucial role in most of the movements. Arguably they played a major role in the transformation of the society as it is now.

The study has been restricted to Telangana state. Telangana region has a historical specificity of caste–class dynamics. A kind of solidarity between Dalits movement and Radical Left practice is found in this region, which is specific to this region.

This study begins with Telangana region of erstwhile Andhra Pradesh state as it used to be then. During the course of this research Telangana region acquired, through its relentless struggles, statehood. And, in all further discussions, the Telangana state is considered as Telangana region because the Left and Dalit movements which this study is going to analyse cannot be studied in isolation or can be restricted to strict geographical boundaries.

And also, this study focusses mainly on Radical Left politics rather than traditional Left politics. The reasons are: first, there is no noteworthy change in their (traditional Left parties) outlook towards Dalits and Dalit issues. Second, after the formation of the Andhra Pradesh state in 1956 the traditional Left party could not make a remarkable impact on state politics or could not influence the state government policies involving Dalit issues. In total, the traditional Left parties failed to recognize adequately the historicity of Dalit problem. On the other hand, the Radical Left parties were involved in the grassroots level of rural mobilization for the last four decades and have shown a greater degree of sensitivity to the concrete nature of the caste in the structures of dominance.

STATEMENT OF RESEARCH PROBLEM

The main assumption of this study is that given the Indian specificity, the caste question has to be central and integral to any Marxist understanding. In that sense caste is opposite to class, but dialectically related to it. Thus, the Dalit movement and Left movement are not two exclusive practices but signify historical continuum. It is the intention of the study to disregard the actualities of the perceived dichotomies such as class/caste, which in fact assume concrete forms in all political practices as it happens in the context of Dalit movement and Left politics. However, the effort is to overcome the problems posed by particular situations. This study thus attempts to contextualize source of the actual and real tensions between Dalit movement and Left politics.

CASTE SYSTEM AND ITS HISTORICAL BACKGROUND

Hindu social system is marked by a unique and unnatural division of labour which dehumanizes and degrades all those who come under this system. The Purusha Sukta in the Rigveda, the sacred text of caste Hindus, declares that the Brahmin, Kshatriya, Vaishya, and Shudra have come from different parts of the Creator Brahma's body. The Brahmins come from his mouth, the Kshatriyas from his arms, the Vaishyas from his thighs, and the Shudras from his foot, to perform societal functions, as priests, warriors, entrepreneurs, and the servile class. This arbitrary classification was named the *Varna* or caste system.[2] The rigid and congenital assignment of labour inevitably involved the legitimization of various mechanisms and ideological superimposition of Hindu sanctified dogmas of purity, pollution, and heredity, over and above the impersonal doctrine of Karma by the politico-religious power, and its incorporation as a rigid division of Hindu society.

Outside of this fourfold classification is a fifth class, which comes not from the body of Brahma but to serve the fourfold classes of Hindu society. Dehumanized, this fifth class, has constantly been subjected to change of nomenclature from epoch to epoch, as Pancharna, Nishad, Chandala, Pariah, and, currently, Dalits.

THE IDEA OF DALIT

Dalit as a word was used in the 1930s as a Hindi and Marathi translation of 'depressed class'; a term the British used for those who are now called the scheduled castes (SCs).[3] 'In 1970s The Dalit Panthers revived the term and expanded its reference to include scheduled tribes (STs), poor peasants, women, and all those being exploited politically, economically, and in the name of religion. So Dalit is not a caste but it is a social category'.

Etymologically, Dalit means what which is made of dal. According to the Sanskrit-English dictionary of Monier Williams, 'dal' means multi-sected, broken into pieces, fractured, violated, destroyed, subdued, exploited, kept disunited, and powerless. They are the Shudras and among them the Adi-shudras. They are called by different names by the dominant such as 'Avarnas', Outcastes, 'Panchamas' 'Dark-skinned Dasuya', 'Rakshasa', 'Nishidas', and 'Mlechas'. In the strict sense of state recognition, Dalits today mean the SC (the ex-untouchables) of our country.

CASTE AND ITS INTERFACE WITH LEFT POLITICS

The caste system is the historical specificity of Indian society. In the mainstream sociological perspectives which dominate social science thinking on caste and caste has been conceptualized as a traditional and pre-capitalist institution and as a primordial marker of social identity.[4] The implicit assumption here is that with the development of capitalism caste would lose its potency and become increasingly irrelevant.[5] But contrary to this assumption, caste has not declined in its importance but rather with modernization it proved to be more explosive than before. In fact it would be an exaggeration to state that with the process of modernization, caste has assumed a modern form and become part of modernization process itself. Therefore, the analysis of caste has to transcend the modernity-tradition perspective that has been influential in the study of the caste system.[6]

The main features of the caste that can be considered for our analysis are: first, caste system is an endogamous system; second, caste signifies a social hierarchy based on the principle of purity and pollution; and third, traditionally caste system characterized division of labour with a clear specification of occupation roles and specialization of social functions; and therefore, caste is an important structural aspect of socio-economic dominance-subordination.[7]

Apart from being a ritual category, caste also has been an important factor determining landownership and control on the one hand and labour process on the other. It is these dynamics of caste which are crucial to this present analysis. What adds complexity to the caste system, according to Dr B.R. Ambedkar, is the fact that caste has not only been the site of division of labour but also division of labourers. Because of this, the unity of labourers on caste basis becomes difficult. This is a challenge to the social movements that have been centred around or articulated caste as an important question.

Caste system thus constitutes a crucial challenge to any project of social transformation for social relations of production, and structures of domination have been crucially determined by this caste system. Any such project has to theoretically address, practically deal with, caste as a structure of inequality and discrimination.

The failure of the Left in India on this question is quite clear. The mainstream Left as part of dominant practice of parliamentary electoral politics has not distinguished itself from the bourgeois political parties in its perspective on and treatment of caste as a consideration in the electoral calculus. The CPI (ML) groups, having been involved in the grassroots rural mobilization for the last four decades, have shown a greater degree of sensitivity to the concrete nature of caste in the structures of dominance and its dynamics in the process of resistance to them.[8] Yet there is a wide gap between the theory and practice of the Left including the CPI (ML) groups on the caste question, while in practice, the CPI (ML) groups, in contrast to the parliamentary Left, have displayed a greater sensitivity in articulation to the caste question, but there is no corresponding theoretical reflection.

LEFT MOVEMENT AND ITS IDEOLOGICAL STANCE

The 1920s saw the emergence of Marxism, asserting a new theory of exploitation and liberation, claiming to have a total analysis applicable to India as to any society. It was rapidly picked up by a group of young, educated, and mostly upper caste radical nationalists searching for a mass base of the movement and eventually founding new communist and socialist parties. It also began to assert a powerful influence on the thinking of Left Congressmen such as Nehru and his colleagues.

'Marxism' as a theory and ideology came into India and existed for 70 years (with the solitary exception of D.D. Kosambi)[9] in a fairly mechanical, vulgarized form; its contribution to all liberation movement was its firm assertion that social system and relations are *historical* (they have come into existence, change, and will come to an end), *material* (they have a solid base in production and collective, non-ideal social forces), and characterized by *conflict*, *contradiction*, and *exploitation*. Its disadvantage was that it took the overriding reality of 'class' and 'class-struggle' so strongly as to assert the fundamental irrelevance of every other sociological category.[10] Indeed, at first the power of the 'class' metaphor seemed so strong both for analysis and as a guide to action that it was easy for the proponent of Marxism and socialism to treat family, kinship, the state, gender, and Indian of course caste, as not only secondary but practically non-existent factors. Its influence lay in its seductive strength, and it was an influence exerted not only on Indian activities but also on academics, to the extent that a large number of the Marxist-influenced theoretical and empirical studies even during the 1970s and 1980s identified their radicalism with their assertion that behind the apparent reality of caste ultimately lay class and its dialectics, a 'class content to a caste' form.

OBJECTIVES, SCOPE, AND LIMITATIONS OF THE STUDY

The objective is to understand the dynamics of caste and class in Dalit movement and the Left politics and to study the impact of the both movements mutually and their consequences on Telangana politics. The aim of the study is to know whether the Left intervention opens any possibility for Dalit's emancipation. Finally to know the interplay of class and caste factors in India society. The study titled *Dalit Movement and Left Practice: A Study in Telangana* is an empirical study. It also, some times, analyses Dalit and Left movement as the cognitive praxis.

The study is limited to just Telangana region. As we can see the presence of Radical Left parties and Dalits across the country, the scope of this study is huge. And it will be interesting to study the interface in states such as Kerala and West Bengal where the parliamentary Left parties are strong. This study has limitations when it comes to women's participation in general and Dalit women's participation in particular in Radical Left, Dalit, and sub-caste movements.

Though the title says it is the study of Dalit movements and Left movements in Telangana, it focusses mainly on Radical Left parties. The reasons are mentioned in the introductory paragraphs. Therefore, it also fails when it comes to the interface, however less, between parliamentary Left practices and Dalit movements.

Methodology

The thesis is an interpretative exercise which seeks to explore research questions, that is search for interface between Dalit movement and Radical Left practice. This study traces the interface through different movements such as Telangana peasant movement, Naxalite movement, Dandora movement, and Telangana separate statehood movement. The material for the present study has been gathered from primary as well as secondary sources. The primary sources comprise government reports, first person accounts of the Communist and Dalit leaders of the struggle, memoirs of nationalists, historical accounts based on primary documents, mainly the Report of Commissioner for SCs and STs, and the Andhra Pradesh State Assembly debates. For secondary source, it would like to explore a vast literature that is already emerging on the Dalit and Left movements. Books and published articles as also publicity material issued by the Dalit organizations and Left movement in the state were used extensively as both primary and the secondary sources.

Extensive field work has been done to understand the influences of Left parties on Dalits and Dalit organizations influence on Left parties. The districts that were chosen are Warangal, Medak, Hyderabad, and Ranga Reddy. Karimnagar and Nizamabad are selected to study Ambedkar Yuvajana Sangam (AYS) and Ambedkar statues.

For collecting the resource material extensively, face-to-face personal interviews were conducted with Dalit and Left movement leaders. Focussed group interview method has been followed. It includes not only contemporary leaders and activists but also veterans who participated in yesteryear movements. Conversational mode of interviewing has been adopted to allow the interviewee to say what they felt about the sensitive issues such as 'caste' from within and outside the movements. The interviews were held in Telugu. The study, to some extent, uses participant observation and open-ended questionnaire to understand the issue at hand from different perspectives.

Brief Chapterization

The present study comprises five chapters excluding 'Introduction' and 'Conclusion' and the following is the synopsis of each chapter.

Introduction

This chapter deals with a general introduction to Dalits movement and Left movement in Telangana region. It discusses historical background of both Dalit movement and Left movement. It briefly introduces to the idea of Dalits. It discusses, briefly, how these movements got shaped up and engaged with one another in an effort to transform the society. It briefly discusses role of Dalits in Communist movement, non-Brahmin movement, Telangana peasant struggles, and Telangana movement hinting the detailed discussion and analysis of these movements in the following chapters. It also states different modes of Dalit articulations in a century-long struggle for casteless society. It also introduces to sub-caste movement within the Dalit movement for equal share of reservation benefits that the Constitution has guaranteed to the Dalits. It touches up on the role of people in general and Dalits in particular in Left movement and the way in which Left movement accommodated and dealt with Dalits in the process of its struggle to establish socialist society. Apart from these, it also states statement of research problem. The significance of study, aims and objectives of the study, hypothesis, methodology, and sources are also covered in this introduction.

Dalit Movement in Telangana

This chapter traces the history of Dalit movement in Telangana from twentieth century to present day with its political roots and implication. It moves to Dalit movement via Bhakti movement and Reformist movement. Dalit movement in Telangana can be categorized into different phases. It began with reformist mode, trying to transform the way Dalits lived. Then it moved on to address the more specific caste-related atrocities such as abolition of *vetti* and *jogini* practices. Then it realized that lack of education was the main reason for Dalits deplorable condition, so it fought for the establishment of educational institutions for the enlightenment of Dalits. With the entry of Dr B.R. Ambedkar into Dalit politics, the movement has taken a drastic transformation which this chapter discusses in detail.

Depending upon the mode and method of the movement and also for the convenience of discussion and analysis, the movement is discussed in three phases. From 1906 to 1930s is considered as the first phase which the chapter argues as the beginning of the Dalit movement in Telangana region. The period from 1930s to 1950s is treated as the second phase of Dalit movement, which is termed as 'the phase of turmoil' in Dalit movement. And the third phase starts from 1950s, which is when the Dalit movements in Telangana began to recede. In this phase, special emphasis is laid on AYS.

This chapter also focusses on sub-caste movement, limiting itself to only Madiga Dandora movement. This chapter argues that Dandora movement brought to the front the discrimination within Dalits and raised the curtains for sub-caste movements. This chapter also argued that Telangana Dalit movement never disassociated itself with Radical Left movement, and also the class conscious generated by Radical Left movement has helped the Dalits to introspect and see the class differences within the Dalit communities, which in turn has led to the formation of Madiga Dandora movement.

Telangana Peasant Insurrection: A Historical Study

This chapter traces the trajectory of the Telangana peasant movement in Telangana in detail: from the beginning including the conditions that laid the foundations for the rise of Left movement via Library movement, Andhra Mahasabha (AMS) through a wide range of primary sources. It includes first person accounts of the communist leaders of the struggle, memoirs of nationalists, historical accounts based on primary documents, sociological analysis of the insurgent villages, and oral histories. This chapter discusses the history in different phases from 1947 to 1967. First, it gives detailed description of geographical features; second, it discusses economic and political conditions that led to the social settings that have finally favoured the Leftist movement, and finally the Telangana Peasant movement.

Radical Left Movement in Telangana

This chapter discusses the Naxalite Movement in quite detail including Naxalite movement specific to certain geographical regions such as Peddapalli and Sircilla. It seeks to describe the nature of the movement and how it progressed over the years; and finally, to draw parallels and contrasts between the Telangana Naxalite movement and the Naxalite movements of the late 1960s. Naxalite movement, this chapter argues, is the result of state's failure to bring about any substantial change in agrarian social relations and social life in the rural areas in spite of its progressive agrarian legislations.

This chapter also discusses the state's response to Naxalite movement and the role of Civil Liberty movement in addressing the problem. And the chapter concludes with Peace Talks.

Mapping Caste–Class Debate

The debates on caste–class relationships and social versus political changes which were initiated in the Ambedkar era are being carried forward even today. This chapter attempts to map the class and caste debate to understand how these two concepts are understood in relation to one another in trying to understand the society. The relationship between caste and class has been perceived by various intellectuals and activists in diverse viewpoints. These different perspectives on class and caste debate are considered in this chapter by broadly classifying them into four categories. First is the Marxist perspective on class and caste; second, the Ambedkarite perspective on class and class; third, class–caste perspective; and the fourth is liberal perspective on class and caste.

Through these four perspectives, this chapter presents broad spectra of the debate on class and caste.

The Interface Between Dalit Movement and Left Practice in Telangana

This chapter discusses the interface between caste and class. I could see the Telangana Dalit movement never disassociated itself with Radical Left. This chapter covers the caste–class interface in Peasant movement, Naxalite movement, Dandora movement, and present Telangana movement. It argues that the first phase of Left movement focussed on the class-based issues. In the 1967, Naxalite parties emerged to overcome this problem. They started taking up Dalit and adivasi issues without directly hinting at the caste but not taking up of issues directly related to caste. As almost all of the agricultural *coolis* and people involved in the bonded labour are Dalits, they could directly relate themselves to the Naxalite parties.

This chapter argues that post Ambedkarite Dalit movements in Telangana has got its roots in Radical Left movement of this region. Left movement has successfully exposed the hegemony of upper castes on Dalits and gave Dalits a cause and reason for united struggle against the oppressive regime. This consciousness has helped the Dalit in furthering their cause and fight for the social justice. Madiga Dandora movement is a contemporary example which has shaped up and supports my arguments. Even the huge support base of Dalits and their active participation in separate Telangana state could be viewed from this perspective. In Telangana, there a solidarity between Left movement and Dalit movement which is specific to this region.

Conclusion

Both the movements at their regional specifications have a long and cherished history of political struggles and in raising demands for social equality and economic freedom. It will be hegemonic and undemocratic to argue that one set of political ideology is more valuable in promoting the emancipation of deprived and oppressed. However, both the movements operated with a conscious aggression about their own ideological merits and hardly built any systematic dialogical relation with the other about the strategies for the defence of the oppressed sections.

With all these ideological differences and limitation, I have argued in this study that post-Ambedkarite Dalit movements in Telangana has got its roots in Radical Left movement in this region. Left movement has successfully exposed the hegemony of upper castes on Dalits and gave Dalits a cause and reason for united struggle against the oppressive regime. This consciousness has helped the Dalit in furthering their cause and fight for the social justice. Madiga Dandora movement is a contemporary example which has shaped up and supports my arguments. Even the huge support base of Dalits and their active participation in separate Telangana state can be viewed from this perspective.

Finally a consensus, or even an agreement, between these two forces of changes can only be built if both manage to move beyond the contestations of the past and also liberate themselves from their specific ideological canons to be open to constructing new radical alternatives. For both the Dalits and the Marxists, there is need to rethink their theoretical model based on the doctrines of Ambedkar and Marx.

Notes

1. Yagati Chinna Rao. *Dalits Struggle for Identity*. New Delhi: Kaniska Publications, 2006. pp. 45–46.
2. B.R. Ambedkar. *Caste in India: Their Mechanism, Genesis and Development*. New Delhi: Critical Quest, 2013. pp. 1–31.
3. Sagarika Ghose. "The Dalit in India", *Social Research*, Vol. 70, No. 1, Pariah Minorities, Spring 2003, 83–109.
4. Sudipta Kaviraj. "Caste and Class", *Politics in India*. New Delhi: Oxford University Press, 1997. pp. 172–173.
5. Gopal Guru. "Dalit Movement and Mainstream Sociology." *Economic and Political Weekly*, Vol. XXXVIII. No. 14, April 1993.
6. Eleanor Zelliot. *From Untouchable to Dalit: Essays on Ambedkar Movement*. New Delhi: Manohar Publications, 1992.
7. Surender S. Jodhka. *Caste*. New Delhi: Oxford University Press, 2012. pp. 10–11.
8. Ajay Gudavarthy. *Maoism, Democracy and Globalisation: Cross-Currents in Indian Politics*. New Delhi: Sage Publications, 2014. pp. 44–66.
9. Irfan Habib. "Kosambi, Marxism and Indian History", *Economic and Political Weekly*, Vol. 43, No. 30, July 26–August 1, 2008, 85–88.
10. Gail Omvedt. *Dalits and the Democratic Revolution: Dr. Ambedkar and the Dalit Movement in Colonial India*. New Delhi: Sage Publications, 1994. pp. 122–126.

I

Dalit Movement in Telangana

For many reasons, Dalit movement in Telangana occupies a special place in the history of Dalit politics in India. First, it is one of the foremost movements in India for the emancipation of Dalits from the clutches of brahmanical Hindu ideology. Second, it started a decade before Dr B.R. Ambedkar's arrival into Dalit politics. Third, it began in one of the princely states of British India where the effect of colonial modernism is least. Fourth, it was autonomous, urban, and to some extent radicalized movement in Telangana when compared to Dalit movement in Andhra. Dalit movement in Hyderabad began with the establishment of Jagan Mitra Mandali in 1906 by Bhagya Reddy Varma.

This chapter traces the history of Dalit movement in Telangana from twentieth century to present day with its political roots and implication. This chapter moves to Dalit movement via Bhakti movement and Reformist movement. Dalit movement in Telangana can be categorized into different phases. It began with reformist mode, trying to transform the way Dalits lived. Then it moved on to address the more specific caste-related atrocities such as abolition of *vetti* and *jogini* practices.[1] Then it realized that illiteracy was the main reason for Dalits deplorable condition, so it fought for the establishment of educational institutions for the enlightenment of Dalits. And then with the advent of Ambedkar into the Dalit movement, it fought for political space in the state.

SOCIAL CONDITIONS IN TELANGANA

Social conditions of the region are important to understand the social practices and social position of communities in India, which are directly related to caste. The identity of the region is, indeed, strongly rooted in its social landscape and vice versa. Caste in India was not simply produced by Hindu religious texts but shaped by ecologies, languages, religion, modes of production, and political system. In this sense, caste in Telangana is different from the other regions as the regions in India are conditioned by particular socio-economic and political practices. The socio-economic life of the Telangana region is generally characterized by feudal practices, which involve ruthless exploitation of masses through the caste relation. The exploitation of the subordinate castes in India occurs through social relation rather than economic relation. One is exploited and made poor and subordinated perpetually because of low status of his/her caste. There was a continuous conflict between castes and communities. A range of autonomous castes and communities were subordinated by the dominant castes throughout the history of Telangana. The dominant castes further imposed a series of restriction and humiliating practices on the subordinated castes to ensure the subordination perpetually.[2]

Telangana has been basically a region of adivasis, nomads and pastoral communities, and service and artisans castes. The geographical setting of the region, indeed, provided home to many such communities. It has occupied almost the centre of the Deccan plateau. The Sahyadri hills that run along the north were home to rich forests. Karimnagar, Adilabad, Warangal, Khammam, Nalgonda, and Mahbubnagar districts were particularly covered to a large extent by forest. These forests were found at the source of the rivers Godavari, Krishna, Tungabhadra, Manjira, Maner, Wardha, and Pranhita. Adivasi and pastoral and service communities such as Gonds, Rajgonds, Kolams, Nayakpods, Kondareddis, Koyas, Chenchus, Gollas, Kurmas, and Waddiras.

The Velamas came from the north of the Narmada River in search of settlements. Initially they worked as army men and local chiefs under the Kakatiyas.[3] Almost around the same period the Reddy Nayaks came from the coastal county in search of land, owing to widespread intra-community conflicts in the Andhra region and became powerful local chiefs under the Kakatiyas. After the collapse of the Kakatiyas, the Velamas and Reddys emerged as independent rulers at Rachakonda and Kondavidu, respectively, and had control over large parts of the Telugu-speaking areas.[4] Further under the Qutub Shahis, they consolidated as ruling aristocracy of powerful chiefs and magnates blending the required Hindu and Muslim ways of life. They were given ruling positions and titles and used to not only control the masses but also bring waste land into cultivation by forming new villages.[5] When it comes to Nizam rule, they transformed into modern landlords (locally called doras) with legal rights under, the ryotwari system. The Reddys and Velamas who were acting as *deshmukhs*, *deshpandyas*, *maktadars*, and other revenue agents in the old system were parcelled huge amount of lands by the state when their watan right was abolished by the new revenue policy. Beside this they also grabbed vast tracts of land in the villages using their nexus with officials. Many of them also honoured with village police *patel* and *karnam*. From the early twentieth century, the Kammas (another dominant peasant caste) of the Andhra also began settling down in Telangana as big landlords occupying vast tracts of land in the Godavari areas.[6]

The Shudra upper caste immigration thus had developed a distinctive social and economic system in Telangana which was rooted in brahmanical values. Although the presence of the Brahmin caste in the region was minimal, the caste practices were very much widespread in the region. The Dalits of Telangana were worst victims of these practices. Particularly *vetti*, *bhagela/ jeetham*, and *jogini* practices reduced the Dalits to a sub-human position. *Vetti* practice was in existence from medieval period in Telangana. Under the regimes of the doras, almost all the castes were subjected to *vetti* including Brahmins. However, the Dalits were worst victims of this practice. Each Dalit family was forced to send one person to do *vetti* in the houses of doras and village officials. Their jobs includes cleaning of houses of *patels*, *patwari*, *mali-patel*, or *deshmukh*, carrying reports to police stations and taluq office, keeping watch on the village chavadi and the poundage, cleaning the village chavadi, and serving the official on their visit to village. The Dalits involved in shoe making, tanning of leather, and making of leather accessories for agricultural purposes were forced to supply these to the landlords free of cost, while the other castes had to be paid for their services.[7]

Another practice attached to Dalits was *bhagela* or *jeethagadu*. It is difficult to translate precisely what these terms mean. It signifies a sort of bonded labour with limited freedom. A large number of Dalits were employed on these terms. Every landholder maintained a number of *jeethagadu* depending upon the land area and workload. This institution had been in existence for a long time in the state. Remuneration was generally yearly and in kind, besides interest-free advances on occasions such as children's marriages and festivals, and for daily needs such as clothing and *gunta chutta* (a kind of cigar). The practice was that once a *jeethagadu* registered with a landholder it was difficult for him to extract himself; sometimes the bond extended to his children.[8] Each landlord would have ten to fifty *bhagelas*—the larger the number of *bhagelas*, the higher their status and influence in society. Pratap Reddy of Ghanpur village of Mulug taluka in Warangal district had forty-three *bhagelas* on his one thousand or more acres of land.[9]

Jogini/murali (devadasi) was another heinous practice in the Dalit communities. Unmarried Dalit girls were dedicated to local goddess, and they were being used by the caste-Hindus. This practice existed from the medieval period. *Joginis* were leading a disgraceful life of prostitution.[10] The important atrocious practice imposed on Dalits across the subcontinent was untouchability. The Dalits of Hyderabad had begun waging war against these practices. The modern education was crucial in creating such a consciousness.

EDUCATIONAL DEVELOPMENT AND SOCIAL AWAKENING

From the late nineteenth century, Hyderabad state began to pay more attention to the general welfare of the people, although serious political reforms were initiated only at the end of the Nizam's regime. The last Nizam, Mir Osman Ali Khan, played a crucial role for the development of education in the state. Unlike the British colonial ruler, the Nizam endeavoured to develop an indigenous education system in the state combining both English and Deccan cultural values. Importantly it was a synthesis of both old and new. Although the medium of instruction was in Urdu, which was official language of the state, English was taught as second language from the school level. The last Nizam, indeed, paid special attention to get all the important science and engineering books translated into Urdu. In this sense, one can see a true nationalist in him.[11]

From the 1880s onwards, many educational institutions were established in the state. The total number of schools in the state in 1872–1873 was 141 in the districts and 14 in Hyderabad city.[12] Over the following decades, there was a remarkable growth, and by the end of the first decade of the twentieth century the number of schools were 1,000 and this rose to 4,500 by 1936, while the aggregate number of pupils had risen from 65,000 to 3,27,000. When the last Nizam, Mir Osman Ali Khan, ascended the throne in 1911 the total expenditure on education was 9.5 lakh and this was increased to over a crore by 1936.[13]

In the beginning, the dominant peasant castes began taking advantage of the educational opportunities. However, the subaltern castes also later on began realizing the importance of education and sent their children to school. Indeed the last Nizam had put special efforts to spread education among them. Apart from the general school, special schools were established for women, tribal, and depressed castes.[14]

There were 97 depressed castes or Harijan castes according to 1931 census in the state. Out of the 20,02,290 total Dalit populations in the state, 10,65,153 were in Telangana.[15] Hyderabad city had 1,00,450 Dalit population in 1941.[16] The Nizam government established a trust for the development of education and welfare of the depressed castes, which was chaired by the finance minister. Out of the eight members of the trust, four were representatives of depressed castes.[17] It is reported that more than ₹ 2.5 crore were spent for the welfare and educational development of depressed castes annually during the last years of the Nizam rule. In 1945, there were 186 special depressed class schools in the state, in which medium of instruction was Telugu. In the same year, 8,764 boys from depressed class were studying in these special schools and another 7,500 in the general schools.

Education was generally provided free of cost till primary level to all. However, for tribal and depressed communities, it was provided free of cost from primary to university level. Besides this, they were also provided with hostel facility and scholarship in order to encourage them in education.[18] The students from depressed caste were also awarded scholarship to study abroad.[19]

This rapid growth in education occurred against a backdrop of what was known in Hyderabad state as the *mulki* (local) and non-*mulki* (non-local) controversy. The *mulkis* were local people of the state and the non-*mulkis* were outsiders—men brought into reform the Hyderabad government. The *mulki* and non-*mulki* percentage of civil officers (total 476) in 1886 was 52 and 42 per cent respectively, and 5 per cent were European officials. A considerable number of non-*mulkis* were imported into the state during the prime ministership of Salar Jung I from north India, particularly from the United Provinces. Until the late nineteenth century, non-*mulkis* had no access to political power, but later on they became quite influential in the state and began holding political posts as well. The local Muslims as well as the Hindus were not prepared to tolerate this.[20] The growth of education had by the early years of the twentieth century produced increasing numbers of unemployed youth in the state who blamed their failure on the alleged discrimination by the state against *mulki*. The educated youth of the dominant peasant castes, particularly the Reddy, Velama, and Kapu, formed their own caste associations from the beginning of the twentieth century, and these identified themselves with the *mulki* agenda.[21]

The establishment of Osmania University in 1918 led to an escalation in these conflicts and also opened doors for communal politics. Both Hindus and non-*mulkis* opposed the introduction of Urdu-medium classes in the university as they felt that this was done deliberately to encourage local Muslims to fill administrative posts. In the process, Muslims were denied access to them.[22] A new dimension was added to these conflicts when the Arya Samaj supported the caste-Hindu peasants. The Arya Samaj was established in the state in 1891 and converted itself into a political platform from the beginning of the twentieth century in order to protect the interests of the Hindus.[23] This gradually encouraged communal conflict in the state. In response to the Arya Samaj, the Ittehad-ul-Mussulman (generally called the Razakars) came into being in 1927 to protect the local Muslims interest. These interlinked conflicting groups and communities had support from across and beyond the state and various groups began entering the state in support of their own religious communities and castes.[24]

Interestingly these developments led to the emergence of identity politics in the state. As mentioned in the preceding paragraph the dominant castes were organizing and forming their caste association from the beginning of the twentieth century, whereas the subordinate castes had started organizing themselves only from the 1920s. However, the depressed caste movements were more widespread in the state than in the Telugu-speaking areas of Madras Presidency. The last Nizam recognizing the importance of preservation of the history and culture of these communities had encouraged them with lavish donations for organizing their community meetings. Many community associations were running schools for their community children with the government aid, beside articulating and representing community aspirations and demands.[25]

These were the social and political conditions that actually led the movements that we can properly term as Dalit movements. However, the consciousness such as Dalit or depressed classes or to be precise the non-Brahmin identity has its roots in tenth century AD with the rise of Bhakti movement, which I will discuss briefly in the next section. Then the social reform movements such as Arya Samaj and Brahmo Samaj further strengthened Dalit identity that led to the fight for the share in the political space.

BHAKTI MOVEMENT AND NON-BRAHMIN CONSCIOUSNESS

Bhakti movement started in thirteenth century AD. The Bhakti poets questioned the religious restrictions on worship, in a way directly questioned the Brahmanical hegemony on religion and religious practices. By preaching all are equal before God, they created a split in the Hindu social order. They brought in Brahmin and non-Brahmin identity. Dalits who were denied entry into the temples naturally took to these people.

> The first phase of the identity formation of dalits may be said to be the Bhakti movement, which helped construct an identity in

> opposition to the Brahmin identity. The mystics who led the Bhakti movement include Ramananada and Radias in the north, Chaitanya and Chandidas in the east, Eknath, Choka Mela, Thukaram and Narsinha Mehata in the west and Ramanuja, Nimbaraka and Basava in the south. Their contribution to the anti Brahmin thought lies in opposing caste distinctions and asserting equality before God. M.G. Ranade called the Bhakti movement being unbrahminical.[26]

Bhakti poets paved the way for Dalits to identify themselves as anti-brahmanical, thereby created a new non-Brahmin identity consciousness.

SOCIAL REFORM MOVEMENTS AND AWAKENING OF DALIT CONSCIOUSNESS

Social reform movements have helped to bring a change in the way caste parameters operated in the late nineteenth century and early twentieth century. Some of the principles of Arya Samaj and Brahmo Samaj greatly influenced the Dalit leaders such as Bhagya Reddy Varma and Arige Ramaswamy in Hyderabad. In fact, Bhagya Reddy Varma, in the beginning, worked on the lines of thoughts of Arya Samaj and Brahmo Samaj. They propagated ideas such as stopping the sacrifice of animals before the Gods, stopping the drinking habits among Dalits, and avoiding eating meat.

> Another significant characteristic during this phase was centrality endowed to temperance, reform itself evidence of the influence of Arya Samaj and Brahmo Samaj ideology on the emerging outcaste intelligentsia. Bhagya Reddy Varma (1888–1939) laid the foundation for Dalit Movement in the region. He was actively associated with the caste-Hindu organisations especially the Brahmo Samaj, which were to have a decisive impact on his own ideology and agenda of action.[27]

It was the Arya Samaj which conferred on him the title 'Varma' in an annual function in 1913 for the social service he rendered to the society. Thus, he became Bhagya Reddy Varma.[28]

Arya Samaj was founded by Maharshi Dayanand Saraswati in 1875 at Bombay. The advocates of Arya Samaj in Hyderabad took pledge to devote their free service to the poor Hindus in their struggle to restore the civil and religious liberties. It has been hailed as one of the most potential and dynamic socio-religious movements of the day. It had a great impact on the life and thinking of the people particularly of the Hindus in the nineteenth and twentieth centuries. It propagated the message of Arya Samaj: (a) Equality of all human beings, (b) Condemnation of caste system, (c) Equal opportunities of education and refinement, and (d) 'Back to Vedas' and 'India for Indians'.[29]

The Arya Samaj in Hyderabad state was founded in 1880 in Dharur taluk of Beed district, which acted as head office to guide its activities. In 1892, the Arya Samaj of Hyderabad was started in Residency area, later renamed as Sultan Bazar. The first president was Pandit Kamata Prasadji Misra, and he continued to remain at its helm till 1932. He infused great vigour into the activities of Arya Samaj. He established many branches of Arya Samaj throughout the state and helped the spread of education through libraries and schools.

Though their objectives were high, it seems they never really worked for the equality of all human beings especially within the Hindu religion. They worked to create an ideal Hindu religion. Their interests were more political than social.

> The autocratic Nizam regime also effectively repressed political developments. The Congress and communists alike hardly made a beginning, even through front organisations, until late 1930s. Instead the Arya Samaj took on political importance, and fed into the Congress movement to give it a Hindu nationalist tenor.[30]

The Nizam's government efforts to increase the number of minority by proselytizing majority was questioned and checked by the Arya Samaj. Thus, the Nizam's government changed their attitude towards Arya Samaj and began to place a number of impediments before it. It grew so much that the normal functioning of Arya Samaj had become impossible.[31]

Brahmo Samaj was established in 1828 in West Bengal by Raja Ram Mohan Roy. The Samaj aimed at reformation of the Hindu society and the religious beliefs. The Samaj not only focussed on Sati, child marriage, and other social issues related to dominant castes but also chalked out programmes for depressed castes. The programmes were mainly focussed on openings schools for Dalits and also supporting their amelioration.

Hence, it has become the welcoming shelter for Dalits who tried to escape from the cruel practice of discrimination in the name of caste. Dalits strongly believed and supported its sincere objective in building a casteless society. Bhagya Reddy Varma, Arige Ramaswamy, and Kusuma Dharmanna were among the active workers during 1920s.[32]

Bhagya Reddy Varma being a preacher and leader of the 'untouchables' was the first person to be brought in contact with the reformers of the Brahmo Samaj movement. He rendered very valuable service in spreading this movement in Hyderabad city.[33]

Though these reform movements helped to bring a change in the consciousness of Dalits, present day Dalit critiques such as Adapa Satyanarayana strongly opine that these reform movements such as Brahmo Samaj and Arya Samaj were formed to reform and strengthen Hindu religion.[34] They never really wanted or worked for the upliftment of depressed classes or eradication of caste system. And one cannot deny their opinion when we see that though Bhagya Reddy Varma and Arige Ramaswamy followed Brahmo Samaj, they never advocated their brethren to follow them in this particular case. P.R. Venkataswamy, who was instrumental in keeping the Telangana Dalit history alive, also writes that our Dalit leaders had their own reservations in joining those organizations.

> He (Bhagya Reddy Verma) became a Brahmo but he did not advocate its adoption by 'untouchables'. Had he done it there would not have been the need for the existence of the organisation of the 'untouchables' and his leadership. So, to gain their favour and support he was with the Brahmos and helped them in their propaganda.[35]

Further, Yagati Chinna Rao says:

> Though Ramaswamy had faith in 'Achal Siddanth' and Brahmo Samaj, he firmly believed that Dalits were separate from Hindus.[36]

EMERGENCE OF DALIT POLITICS

As already mentioned in the beginning, this chapter studies the Dalit movement chronologically in detail by dividing the movement into five phases. We can say that the Dalit movement in Telangana began in the year 1906 because this was the year in which Bhagya Reddy Varma started his Jagan Mitra Mandali, which we can call as the first Dalit organization that worked for the Dalit cause.

Beginning of Dalit Movement: 1906–1930s

The Dalit movement in Hyderabad started with the establishment of Jagan Mitra Mandali in 1906, an organization of untouchable, by Madari Bhagya Reddy Varma.[37] It started the work of reform and awakening social consciousness among the untouchables. As part of the Mandali's activities, Bhagya Reddy Varma organized *Harikatha Kalakshepams* regularly at the end or beginning of which he used to speak to Dalits. In these meetings, Bhagya Reddy Varma spoke eloquently about Dalit's social and economic conditions and the ways to overcome their miseries. During these meetings, he told them that they were the original inhabitants of the country, and that the others had migrated from Central Asia for their livelihood and the main reason for their backwardness was their ignorance and illiteracy and Hinduism's treachery. Jagan Mitra Mandali, by its name and activities, was really a friend of the poor and uneducated masses which tried to educate the untouchables about their social maladies.[38]

Its members believed in Buddha's humanist philosophy and were against the Vedic dharma, the *varna* system, and offering animals to appease deities, and preached vegetarianism. Buddha Jayanti was celebrated every year on 'Vaisakhi poornima' day from 1913 until 1938. They also organized inter-dining called *preeti bhojanam* among all untouchables. This gave a possibility for a feeling of oneness and brought them together to fight for betterment of their brethren.[39]

In 1910, Bhagya Reddy Varma founded 'Dharma Pracharini Sabha' as a branch to Jagan Mitra Mandali. Through this organization, he tried to enlighten Dalits by explaining them that the root cause of Dalits deplorable condition is Hinduism's treachery. He also published and distributed books and pamphlets to educate and enlighten Dalits.[40]

Bhagya Reddy Varma founded the Manya Sangam in 1911. Through this organization, he worked against animal sacrifice, drinking alcohol, and *devadasi/jogini* tradition. The principal aims and objectives of Manya Sangam were as follows:

1. To educate all children of the untouchables;

2. To eradicate child marriages;
3. To prohibit non-vegetarian food and intoxicants in marriages and other auspicious functions;
4. To eliminate the 'Devadasi' known as *jogini* or *murali* or *basavi* tradition widespread in the community.

At the general committee meeting held on 19 January 1913, Sangam elected an executive body to fulfil their aims and objectives. The Manya Sangam was established with members including Vellati Seshaiah, a building contractor, Jakkula Muthaiah, owner of a bakery, Venkataram, the superintendent, M.L. Audiah of public works department, and other employees of the Hyderabad public gardens.[41]

He also founded *Adi Hindu Murali Nivarana Mandali* specifically to fight against the practices such as *jogini*, *devadasi*, and *basavi* in the name of God. He also urged the government to help in eradicating this evil tradition.

He also founded Ahimsa Samaj in 1912 to propagate vegetarianism among Dalits. Since Dalits are blamed for eating dead animals and to uplift them from this social disgrace, he founded this organization. This organization changed its name in 1915 to *Jeevaraksha Gyana Prachaara Mandali.*

In 1912, Bhagya Reddy Varma organized the Swastik Dal with the help of 35 Dalit volunteers. It was based on the activities of Humanitarian League of which Bhagya Reddy Varma was a full-time preacher. They worked on parallel lines to that of the Red Cross Society, but their symbol was an orange Swastik, the Buddhism symbol. This band of passionate volunteers did yeomen services during the epidemic days when plague and cholera broke out in and around Hyderabad. In 1925, when plague broke out again the epidemic took a serious toll in Hyderabad. The Swastik Dal volunteers served the desolate, tended the unwell, and cremated the dead bodies. Their actions and timely services were recognized and awarded accordingly. These volunteers participated in various activities of local organizations and rendered services to many others, including the Indian National Congress meeting at Kakinada and the cow conference at Gudiwada.[42]

With the establishment of Suneethi Bala Samaajamu in 1912, another great leader Arige Ramaswamy entered into Dalit movement. He started this organization with the principle object of temperance. He caught hold of some of his friends, reformed them, and carried on his work of social reform among Dalits with the help of his reformed friends.[43]

Ramaswamy had belief in *Achal siddantham* and Brahmo Samaj, yet he firmly believed that Dalits were a separate identity from the Hindus. He formed an Adi-Hindu Jatiyonnati Sabha in 1922, with Konda Venkataswamy as president and Arige Ramaswamy as vice president and J. Papaiah as its secretary.[44] Since its beginning, it received huge support and existed as a substitute organization to the Adi-Hindu Social Service League.

In 1912, another Dalit leader, Madari Audiah, under the influence of the activities of Bhagya Reddy Varma, started another Manya Sangam of Ghasmandy and carried on his activities in Kummaraguda, a locality in Secunderabad where he lived. The object of his organization was mainly based on Manya Sangam of Bhagya Reddy Varma. He urged his brothers to abandon liquor and preached against animal sacrifice and child marriage. It was very tough job in the initial stage to stop the age-old custom of drinking, eating meat in social functions, and in matrimonial and funeral ceremonies. There was a strong opposition from the 'orthodox' section of the community but he continued his activities in a serious and effective way.[45]

M.L. Audiah founded another reform association known as Sanghabhivruddi Samajam. Though oriented towards social reform, the members of the organization developed a community spirit by involving and assisting people during their social functions, particularly ritual ceremonies such as marriage and death.[46]

However, for Hyderabad, the crucial year was 1922. Almost immediately afterwards the Madras government accepted request of the Dalits to be addressed by their regional name prefixing Adi, that is, Adi-Andhra and Adi-Dravida. The Manya Sangam established in 1911 by Bhagya Reddy Varma was renamed Adi-Hindu Social Service League in 1922. He organized the first All India Adi-Hindu Social Conference in Hyderabad, under the presidentship of T.J. Papanna of Belgaum in the Bombay presidency,[47] with M.L. Audiah as chairman of the reception committee.

This conference was held for three days (29–31 March 1922) and attended by Dalits from regions including Bombay, Pune, Karachi, Akola, Amaravati, Nagpur, and Raipur which gave an all

India look to the meeting. Many delegates from the coastal Andhra region of Madras presidency participated.[48] The first two days of the session was allocated only for the Dalits and the third was an open session for all Adi-Hindus, caste-Hindus, and others. Many Hindu reformers and philanthropists, such as Justice Rai, C. Balamukund, Pandit Kesava Rao, Seth Lalsji Meghji Jain, Narayan Govind Wellinkar, and R.E. Reporter spoke on the occasion.[49] The Manya Sangam became the main organization of the Dalits in Hyderabad.

In 1922, Arige Ramaswamy founded another organization called Adi-Hindu Jatiyonnati Sabha.[50] He felt the need of an organization to counteract the authority and influence of the caste-Hindus on the Panchayat Board and to establish a parallel Panchayat system. He conducted weekly meeting regularly at the residence of Konday Venkataswamy at Kummarguda, which were addressed by Arige Ramaswamy and Bhagya Reddy Varma. He invited members of the community to attend the meetings and the members also looked up to the sabha as a symbol of their hopes and aspirations and a corporate body to which they could represent their grievances for redressal. The main object of the sabha being social reform, the poor people of the community sought the help and cooperation of the members of the sabha in their social functions. There were number of enthusiastic young men in the sabha to render social service to the needy under the inspiring leadership of Arige Ramaswamy.[51]

This organization aimed at removing immoral appellations regarding the identity of Adi-Hindu and non-Aryan egalitarian traditions[52] along with the customary aims of internal reforms in Hyderabad state. In the 1920s and late 1930s, they organized many conferences in Hyderabad state but unlike the coastal regions with less rural support.

The year 1922 saw the emergence of another great Dalit leader, B.S. Venkata Rao, in Telangana Dalit history. In this year B.S. Venkata Rao with the cooperation of Madari Govindarajulu and Madari Venkataswamy started an organization under the name 'The Adi-Dravida Sangam' in Bangaru Basti, Gasmandy. This organization was an imitation of the Adi-Dravida Sangam of Madras Presidency. Its main objective was the removal of *devadasi* system which was rampant in Bangaru Basti.[53]

In 1925, Bhagya Reddy Varma organized an exhibition of handicrafts including paintings, sketches, and sculptural works. Another novel arrangement was made by the Adi-Hindu community at Residency Bazar (now known as Sultan Bazar), Hyderabad, which was inaugurated by Goswamy Rajah Dhanrajgiri Narsingirji.[54] The idea behind the exhibition was to illustrate that Dalits were in no way less skilled in fine arts and crafts even though they had no facilities and opportunities to develop their skills.[55] In 1925, the Manya Sangam organized Adi-Hindu youth gymnastics at Prem Theatre grounds under the presidentship of Kodi Ramamurti Naidu, the Indian heavy weight champion. He was very impressed by the well-disciplined presentation of skills in the use of ancient arms by the Dalit youth and remarked that it was a matter of pride that the Adi-Hindus have retained the art of using ancient weapons with excellent skill. He further noted that they were really the sons of 'Bharat Mata' who sacrificed everything and preserved Bharatiya culture.[56]

In 1927, B.S. Venkata Rao formed the Adi-Hindu Mahasabha along with C.S. Ethirajan, K. Ramaswamy, Arige Ramaswamy, and others and tried to bring a new awakening among Dalit masses. He also extended financial help for the opening of a library and reading room, which was called 'Adi-Hindu Library'. Worker of the community regularly met at the library to discuss their difficulties confronting them.[57]

The year 1931, we can argue, marked the split between Malas and Madigas of Telangana region, which ultimately culminated in the formation of Madiga Reservation Porata Samiti (MRPS) in 1994 about which I shall discuss briefly later in this chapter. In this year Arige Ramaswamy founded Arundathiya Mahasabha, a separate organization for Madigas with Madigas as working committee members. Only president and vice president were chosen from caste-Hindus who were pro-Dalits.

In the beginning, it appeared very harmless, as the two organizations were considered the two wings of the community. But the subsequent political changes in the state brought about a great change in their outlook and instead of community, they put forth their demands for sects. This resulted in the disruption of the solidarity of the community and weakened its position on the political map of Hyderabad. The formation of the new body, from the view point of divide and rule policy, produced deleterious effects on the body politic of the community.

Arige Ramaswamy's efforts to bridge the gap between Malas and Madigas did not become fruitful. Till then there was no separate organization within the Dalit community. It became evident that within the Dalits there were differences in opinions and certain sections within Dalits were not given equal importance. P.R. Venkataswamy says:

> The gulf of deference between Mala and Madiga was widening day by day … . He (Garikala Mallesh Rao) suggested a separate organisation for Madigas to achieve their legitimate rights. But Ramaswamy hesitated to take any hasty step in that direction lest it might cause a split in the community. So he went to Bhagya Reddy Varma and sincerely pleaded for the cause of the Madigas to give them a place of equality with the Malas. But Bhagya Reddy ridiculed his Utopian ideas. Ramaswamy warned him of the evil consequences of his short-sighted policy. Bhagya Reddy bluntly told him to have his own way and he was not in the least bothered about it.[58]

This new organization created a split between Adi-Hindu Social Service League led by Bhagya Reddy Varma and Adi-Hindu Mahasabha led by B.S. Venkata Rao. Arundathiya Mahasabha supported Adi-Hindu Mahasabha upsetting the balance of power.

A Phase of Political Turmoil: 1930–1950s

Though the Telangana Dalit movement was confined to Hyderabad, it was strong in terms of organizations and articulation of Dalit cause. However, the quickly changing political scenario at the national level has severely affected the Dalit movement in Hyderabad. The Hindu–Muslim tensions in the Nizam dominion have created a space for Dalits to organize and fight for their rights within the Hinduized society. The entry of Ambedkar into Dalit movement in Maharashtra has had a great effect on Dalit movement in Telangana. Many organizations have been founded based on Ambedkar ideology.

In 1936, B.S. Venkata Rao led the delegation to the Maharashtra Asprishya Youth's Conference at Pune. This conference was presided over by N. Shivaraj and addressed by

Dr Ambedkar.[59] Influenced by the speeches of Maharashtra Dalit leaders, they organized the youth league of Ambedkarites with Venkata Rao as president and Venkataswamy as secretary. Its aims were to organize the youth to support Ambedkar in leading the untouchables out of the Hindu fold, to enlighten the people of the troubles of Hinduism and to organize a dynamic campaign of socio-economic disabilities and deprivations.[60]

On the insistence of Ambedkar, Venkata Rao presided over the Bombay presidency Mahar conference at Bombay held on 30 May 1936.[61] Soon after, Venkata Rao was nominated to Hyderabad Municipal Corporation in 1937, for the defence council of Nizam in 1943. He was elected unconditionally in the Nizam's Legislative Assembly in 1946 and became the education minister under the leadership of Mirlaik Ali in 1947. A genius and an active personality, his followers conferred on him the title of Rao Saheb. He sacrificed all he had for the community and died as leader of the community.[62]

By the later part of the 1930s, disputes arose on pro-Muslim versus Ambedkarite reaction to the declaration of departure from Hinduism. The state branch of Harijan Sevak Sangh at Hyderabad was formed in 1933,[63] the Congress preparation to reconvert Dalits into Hindu religious fold which had only a minor impact and Ambedkar's decision to give up Hinduism was described as a real 'bombshell' in motivating immense debate on conversions throughout the country.[64] Several Dalit leaders and activists became active, including Kusuma Dharmanna, a great poet, in the coastal Andhra region. P. Veerani, a Hyderabad Dalit, confronted Gandhi in his 1935 visit and later became a propagandist for Islam under the name of P.V. Sardar Ali.[65] Shyam Sunder (1908–1973) was another pro-Muslim Dalit activist. After the intensified Hindu–Muslim clash of 1938–1939, B.S. Venkata Rao also began to work in this direction.

Venkata Rao was elected as president of the Depressed Classes Association (DCA) with K. Jagannadham as its secretary.[66] On 7 May 1938, the association sent a note to Akbar Hydari, the prime minister of Hyderabad, urging for separate electorates and demanded their representation in municipalities and local boards based on population.[67] This was followed by the declaration of constitutional reforms in July 1939 which not only polarized Dalit opinions but also formed divisions among Dalits leaders.

During these days of confusion, Bhagya Reddy Varma, an all-India Dalit leader from Hyderabad, passed away on 18 February 1939. This was a major loss to the community and the movement as a whole because his commitment to Dalits upliftment and relations with pan-Indian Dalit leaders caste-Hindus and Muslims organizations for Dalit cause was irredeemable.

Later leadership was marked by exhaustive competitive struggles. However, there were ideological and political differences even earlier in Hyderabad state for Dalit autonomous movement but in 1940s, these differences were more of a longing for power and leadership leading to occasional confrontations.[68]

Most of the young radicals, including J.H. Subbaiah and Venkata Rao, who were connected with the DCA, were involved in quarrels that reached its peak and led to a division in the organization. Subbaiah accused Venkata Rao of helping Kusuma Dharmanna in working towards propagation of Islam.[69] Later, he joined Arige Ramaswamy along with a major number of youth and started revitalizing the Hyderabad state Adi-Hindu Mahasabha. This split sustained until 1942, when both factions went to Nagpur to attend the founding meeting of the Scheduled Caste Federation (SCF) in July (18–20) 1942.[70]

Though they appealed to Dr Ambedkar to facilitate unity among the divided leaders of the Hyderabad state, the differences could not be patched and resulted in the formation of another SCF. Without an official attachment to the all India body, the revived Adi-Hindu Mahasabha was compounded in it. They chose Subbaiah as president and Venkataswamy as general secretary and adopted the Nagpur resolutions.[71] By this time, the personal competition of factions turned into organizational competitions between the DCA and SCF to lead the Dalit community in Hyderabad state. The DCA took a stand of pro-Muslim orientation and propaganda gained nourishment from the fact that the Nizam was actually implementing some reforms, including distributing wasteland to the Dalits, while the communists were under attack by the Nizam Razakars.

The use of the Indian army hampered the progress of these reformers, while the Congress progressed little in the state for Dalits, but emerged as a Hinduistic organization based exclusively on the representation from the Brahmins, landlords, middle-class peasantry, and the upper castes.

The Dalit organizations in Hyderabad were divided into six groups working all together until the late 1940s. With the British declaration of transfer of power in February 1947, the Dalit organizations were nonplussed. The state of Hyderabad issued a declaration of independence on 11 June 1949, which set off increased factionalism among the Dalits. The biggest groups were still the SCF led by Subbaiah and the DCA led by Venkata Rao. While the DCA approved the constitutional reforms, the SCF, along with the Congress and communists, discarded them.

Both the dominant organizations of Subbaiah and Venkata Rao, R.P. Venkataswamy and Shyam Sundar came together under the banner of the Independent-Scheduled Castes Federation that proposed conditional acceptance of the reforms,[72] whereas an Arundathiya Mahasabha, based primarily on Madigas, pressed for a separate electorate and conditional acceptance in the elections. Venkata Rao and Syam Sundar were elected, while five more members were nominated.[73] Both these elected leaders shaped their pro-Muslim position and appealed to the Dalits to extend their support to the Nizam's ruling classes of Hyderabad to sustain political power.[74]

In addition, the Adi-Hinduism Social Service League, later revived by M.B. Gautham, son of Bhagya Reddy Varma, also rejected the reforms, as did the Dalits grouped under Arige Ramaswamy and working in the fold of the Congress.[75]

Contrary to earlier Dalit movements and urban-based internal factional mobilizations of Dalit leaders, some of the local Dalit leaders organized several meetings at the grass-roots level in spite of the Dalit leaders' personalized politics on one hand and the Congress and Muslim co-optive attitudes on the other. For instance, Butti Rajaram (1911–1978) organized rural masses in Karimnagar district, and Kusuma Achalu in Nalgonda. Rajaram organized many public meetings under the presidentship of J.H. Subbaiah and K.R. Veeraswamy in the district.[76] Soon after, the Telangana armed movement dominated rural Telangana on one hand, while on the other, both the DCA and SCF Dalit groups conflicted with each other to mobilize Dalits on Ambedkar's ideology. However, by then Ambedkarites in Hyderabad state had become feeble both organizationally and politically.

Here, an interesting alliance was emerged between the Dalits and communists at the time of the 1952 elections in the state. Although it was against Ambedkar's liking, it was beneficial to the Dalits at least for a short period. The SCF allied with the Progressive Democratic Front (PDF) (the front organization of banned communists) and contested in the election. PDF won 36 seats out of the 45 contested seats in Telangana. Two of them were former members of SCF. In addition, ten socialist Dalits allied with PDF's own seats, while SCF itself won five assembly seats and one parliament seat with the help of PDF.[77] However, the merger of Telangana into Andhra State in 1956 had consolidated Reddy feudalism further, in the region. In the newly formed Andhra Pradesh, feudal Reddy leadership which blended with modern politics had not only crushed down the Communist Party but also Dalit politics in the state by the early 1960s. It was during this period many Dalits began sheltering in the Communist Party as grassroots activists since the electoral alliance had already set a stage for such migration, although a considerable number of Dalits had gone into the Congress fold.[78]

Diffusion of Dalit Movement in Telangana: 1950–1960s

However, the Dalit politics began fading owing to larger developments in the state as well as in India. Particularly the Indian government's police action on Hyderabad in 1948 had serious impacts on the Dalits movement. Following the police action, Dalits were subjected to serious repression by both armed forces and local landlords because of their pro-Nizam stand.[79] The landlords evicted the Dalits from their assigned lands distributed by the Nizam and took them back. Notwithstanding this repression, many Dalits took shelter in Congress or its affiliated Harijan associations. Venkata Rao was arrested. Shyam Sunder escaped the wrath of the military government as he was sent by the Nizam to Europe to represent Hyderabad's right to independence before the UN.

With this sort of political and factional disturbance, the Dalit masses in rural areas were being influenced into different ideologies without any clear direction and objectives. If the coastal Andhra Dalit movement ended in 1940s with the establishment of Brahmin-led Congress hegemony, the Hyderabad movement broke into pieces due to factional leadership and climaxed with the 'police action' on the Telangana movement, and integration of Hyderabad through police action into the Indian Union in 1948.[80]

Therefore, for the Dalit activists in the state, there was a strong need for an alternative ideological plank and to continue the fight against oppression and injustice. This unrest ultimately resulted in the establishment of AYS (Ambedkar Youth Leagues) at various places in the state

Ambedkar Yuvajana Sangams in Telangana

Bojja Tarakam became the moving force behind the founding of the first such Sangam in 1971 Nizamabad district and registering it. Tarakam, a lawyer by profession, was a staunch Ambedkarite and Naxalite sympathizer. Under the banner of Yuvajana Sangam, Tarakam started organizing the landless agricultural labourers, and daily wage workers in the beedi and cigar rolling industry. The Dalits and other working classes themselves approached him to redress their grievances. Tarakam prepared memoranda on their behalf, submitted them to the authorities concerned, arranged protest rallies, and argued the cases in court.[81] In the process, the sangam activities spread to several other districts such as Karimnagar, Medak, and Adilabad. Mallepally Laxmaiah, a Dalit activist, stated that more than a thousand AYSs got established between 1987 and 1990. This massive size of Dalit organizations have directly led to the formation of Bahujan Samajwadi Party (BSP) in Telangana. The Yuvajana Sangam along with the CPI (ML) Raitu Coolie Sangham (RCS) led many struggles against the upper caste landlords. Both the Sangams united in their demand for an increase in the wages of the landless agricultural labourers and the beedi and cigar industry workers and for better treatment of farm servants.

Legislation governing small-scale industries provided many benefits and welfare facilities to the beedi workers, but the indifference of government officials combined with the ignorance of these benefits by the workers led to their poor living conditions. Tarakam, after he was elected president of the beedi workers' union of Nizamabad, took up these issues and led many successful demonstrations and huge rallies and strikes against the lethargic bureaucracy and the state government. One of these strikes, lasting 25 days, demanding the implementation of the Beedi and Cigar Workers Act, resulted in its successful outcome.

The conscientization of the Dalits, however, led to general discontent and distrust against the upper caste Hindu establishment, adding to the general national crisis which culminated with the imposition of internal Emergency in 1975–1977. During this period, many Dalit leaders and activists were arrested. Tarakam was imprisoned.

The revocation of the Emergency in 1977 resulted in the massive resurrection of Yuvajana Sangam activities. Many new Yuvajana Sangams were formed and worked autonomously in their localities. It would not be exaggeration to say that each village has a sangam, which is systematically connected to the main body at the district level through mandal branches, the number of AYSs in Karimnagar district alone stood up to 1,200 by late 1990s.[82] Efforts were made to coordinate the work of these sangams and to form a state level association. The result was the formation and registration of the Andhra Pradesh AYS in 1977.[83] Thomas Rao was elected its president and S.S.R. Bhupathi became the general secretary. The other leaders associated with it were P.V. Rao, S. Ramakrishna, J. Rajgopal Rao, M. Prem Kumar, and J.B. Raju. The activities of the state level sangam were limited mainly to the state capital. The sangam along with the Scheduled Caste Employees Welfare Association started night schools for the Dalits, and nearly 220 slum dwellers were organized in Hyderabad city. P.V. Rao took up the *Jai Bheem Patrika* and opened a new column called 'Raktastruvulu' (Tears of Blood), chronicling the atrocities on Dalits.

Installation of Dr B.R. Ambedkar Statues

The making of modern statues appears to involve a double movement.[84] And AYSs have rightly chosen the path of erecting Ambedkar statues all over the state apart from the occasional, sometimes, spontaneous agitations. Stressing the importance of such statues, Robin Jeffrey says:

> Statues were a way of exalting a ruler or a representative of a particular group, of bringing him constantly into the public eye and of thereby inducing people to regard him as powerful, great and legitimate-people who should be supported, not overthrown.[85]

The campaign produced remarkable consciousness and identity among the Dalits in Andhra. In villages and towns, the statues were installed in the centre of Dalit colonies. In big cities, they were installed mainly at the city's crossroads. The statues, showing Ambedkar standing, symbolized self-realization and self-respect. His raised right hand would be pointing to the distant horizon, signifying the intended goal. His left hand held either his book *Kulanirmulana* (Annihilation of Caste) or the Indian Constitution. His keen eyes and broad forehead portrayed the maturity of his intellectual calibre. The statues were intended to create a strong effect not only on Dalits but also on every viewer, reminding them of Ambedkar's three mottoes: Educate, Agitate, and Organize.

The Dalit identity was asserted through erection of the statues. It could rally the Dalit sections, from illiterates to educated employees behind this issue, as there was a tremendous enthusiasm among them to reconfigure their leader. By mid-1980s, all the district headquarters and major towns had come to find the statues of Ambedkar being erected in central places. Subsequently, these statues have played a symbolic role in mobilizing the people. In all the districts including Hyderabad, these statues have become venues for the Dalit rallies.[86]

Ambedkar's statues also became a focal point in the celebration of Ambedkar's birth and death anniversaries. The statue at Tank band, Hyderabad, installed in 1968, became almost a pilgrimage every 14 April, which is Ambedkar's birth anniversary, the event being marked by a distinct festive mood. In 1978, Chief Minister Chenna Reddy made it an official function. Thereafter, the event is marked by two functions near the statue, one by the state officials with full state honours and the other by the Dalits themselves. Dalits from different districts and Taluks would pour into the city holding aloft banners, shouting triumphant slogans, and singing songs of solidarity, accompanied by dance. The cynosure of the cultural function would be Gaddar performance.[87]

Thus, the installations of Ambedkar statues have their own historical importance, which profoundly reveals the whole spectrum of sociocultural, political, and psychological dimensions of the Dalit movement. The statues have both subjective and objective expressions. They have been not only used as the devices for the expression of self-respect but also to communicate the social ideas. Moreover, they have been used as a powerful means of political agitation and reflect the publication of the future hope of the present oppressed Dalits. In many cases, experiences shown that the Dalits have an emotional symbolic attachment with the statues. Any kind of dishonour and defile of the statue would result in the display of unrestraint indignation and protest from the Dalits. Thus, the study about the installation of Ambedkar statues is a complex subject and comprises more than one factor, which had profound political implications for the Dalit consciousness and identity.

The eighties opened with a marked degree of Dalit assertion in Telangana. The Dalits expressed a distinctive, more active enthusiasm and participation to build up an effective youth and workers' movement. Their discontent was emphatically expressed by observing Independence Day and Republic Day as black days.

Under the Congress rule, atrocities on Dalits increased. Even the Congress Dalit leaders were publicly humiliated. The Congress Dalit MLA, Masala Veeranna, was denied entry into a temple, and Jagjivan Ram was denied the opportunity to become the Prime Minister. In protest, the Yuvajana Sangams along with all progressive and radical organizations gave a call to observe Republic Day of 1982 as a Black Day. Black flags were hoisted throughout the state on that day. In Hyderabad, nearly 50,000 people were mobilized and gathered at the Ambedkar statue near Tank band in a peaceful procession carrying black flags. Chief Minister, T. Anjaiah, was greeted with black flags when he went to attend the Republic Day parade. Shocked by this display, Anjaiah ordered the police to take action. The police, without prior intimation, lathi charged and tear gassed the peaceful demonstration. The lathi charge continued for nearly six hours. The fleeing Dalit men, women, and children were chased up to three kilometres.[88]

The increasing oppression of the Dalits under the Congress rule and the ruling party's indifference to their plight frustrated the Dalits who denounced the government. In the ensuing 1983 assembly elections, the Dalits played a crucial role in defeating the Congress party, which had hitherto ruled the state unopposed. The newly formed Telugu Desam Party (TDP) meanwhile made extravagant and attractive populist promises. The concept of pseudo-Telugu upper caste-dominated nationalism and Telugu pride was capitalized in the form of votes. Against the twenty-point programme of the Congress, the Telugu Desam formulated a fifteen-point programme called *Pragathi Patham* (Progressive Path), which mainly addressed the weaker sections. Thus, expecting a better future for them, the Dalits voted in favour of Telugu Desam.[89]

Satyashodhak Social Research Centre

In 1990s, Osmania University professors and other academicians started Satyashodhak: Centre for Social Research to respond to ongoing social process and people's experimentation therein, concentrating on questions raised by anti-caste, class, and gender initiatives.

One of their pamphlets defines their work as:

> Satyashodhak collective dissatisfied with the dominant perspectives and disciplinary specificities governing the protection of knowledge alternatively view the questions raised by the grassroot Dalit anti-caste, class and gender initiatives and articulations as constructing the point of departure for the basic social science research. Satyashodhak consider themselves equally responsible to disseminate the knowledge produced through dialogue with these movements in the larger social and intellectual milieu through seminars, workshops, awareness campaigns and publication of research material and through this wish to play a catalytic role in helping the popular initiatives to realise their historical potentialities.[90]

Thus, intellectuals also played a crucial role in sustaining and forwarding the Dalits and other oppressed peoples' cause.

Dandora Movement and Democratization of Dalit Politics: 1990–Present Day

The 1990s forms a crucial phase in the Dalit political history of Telangana. It is in this decade the internal tensions and contradictions between Dalit castes began to surface. The new government did not help the Dalit cause. It was viewed as a change in the regime—from Reddy Raj to Kamma Raj.[91] The formation of Madiga Reservation Porata Samiti (MRPS), popularly known as Dandora Movement in 1994, marks the split between Malas and

Madigas in Telangana. As mentioned earlier in this chapter, we can see the tensions between the two dominant castes within the Dalit community long back in 1933, which is when Arige Ramaswamy formed Arundathiya Mahasabha, an organization for Madigas. A series of incidents, one of which is a marriage ceremony between a Mala boy and a Madiga girl, which Bhagya Reddy Varma seriously opposed, led to the formation of this organization. Arige Ramaswamy pleaded Bhagya Reddy Varma to treat Madigas equally with Malas but Bhagya Reddy Varma did not heed to his suggestions. From this it becomes clear that Madigas were never treated equally with Malas even then. In one of his articles, Muthaiah states:

> Bhagya Reddy Verma, who was then the leader of Adi Hindu Social Service League, expelled the mala leaders Arige Ramaswamy, Adayya and P.R. Venkataswamy from the mala caste when they attended mala-madiga inter-caste wedding on the grounds that this went against mala tradition.

Bhagya Reddy Varma denied a share to madigas in the Adi Hindu Bhavan, built with donations from patrons, on the grounds that madigas did not contribute one paisa to its construction. Resenting this anti-madiga attitude of Bhagya Reddy Varma, the expelled leaders Arige Ramaswamy, P.R. Venkataswamy, Adayya and others established the Arundathiya Mahasabha in 1931.[92]

Had they addressed the differences, then there would not be this split between Malas and Madigas today. Assertion of Madiga identity and fight against the inequality meted out to them within the Dalit community started then and resurfaced when Sadalakshmi, a minister in Congress government, gave a memorandum regarding categorization of SCs to the then Chief Minister Jalagam Vengal Rao in 1972. She was the follower of Mudigonda Lakshmaiah who was the leader of Arundathiya Mathunga Mahasabha in 1940s. Again in 1992 in Adi Jambava Arundathi Mahasabha, she strongly argued for categorization of SC reservations. Her guidance and directions played a central role in the formation of MRPS.

The MRPS was founded by a few self-conscious assertive Madiga youth on 27 July 1994 at Edumudi village in Prakasam district. This is in stark contrast to the earlier Dalit organizations which were urban based and headed by well off educated Dalits.

Apart from the common caste and caste-related problems they addressed, there was very less for the common Dalits to relate themselves to their caste organization. But with MRPS, this has changed. It started in a village with a rural base of only 20 members under the charismatic leadership of Manda Krishna Madiga, and within a few months they were already a political force to be reckoned with at the state level.

> There always existed a gap between the rural uneducated Dalits and their leaders in urban areas. In contrast, the Madiga Dandora has produced new Dalit organic leaders who are semi-literates and rural based youth. For the first time in the history, this leadership has brought their community on the streets to raise their voice about their rights and plight.[93]

One of the main reasons of the movement was the seething discontent among Madigas over their relative backward status compared to Malas. The immediate factor was their contempt about the monopolization of resources and reservation facilities by Malas. They complained that though the Malas are relatively lesser in number than the Madigas they were benefited more by the reservation policy. As a result, they initiated a movement to fight for justice, popularly known as 'Madiga Dandora'.

The term 'Dandora' refers to their traditional profession. Traditionally, the drum 'Dappu' was used to make several public announcements in the village. MRPS leaders have used the cultural symbols extensively and effectively in their movement. The word 'Dandora' itself lost its common meaning and stood for strong assertion of Madiga identity and political rights. The whole movement became famous as Dandora Movement. Dappu became the symbol for Madiga identity and unity. Now, we don't see any rally or meeting without the use of this musical instrument. The sound of Dappu, before the movement, was associated with death of some member of the society. But after the movement, the sound of Dappu became the clarion call for Madigas to come out and fight for their just cause. In Jangam Chinaiah's words,

> the Madiga's cultural and productive symbols like drums, such as 'Aeree' and 'Gootam' have been brought into the mainstream, and they act as the symbols of revolution, which unite their community. So popularisation of cultural symbols and making

them the symbols of political assertion is a new facet, which has been brought about by the Madiga Dandora.[94]

The striking thing that Madigas did was add the prefix 'Madiga' to their movement and all related activities such as Madiga Dandora movement, Madiga Dandora rally, and Madiga Dandora meeting. Even they started suffixing their caste name to their name to assert their self-respect and confidence and to identify with their own caste men. This is a clever intentional subversion of meanings associated with certain words. Earlier the term Madiga was considered to be demeaning and was used abusively by the caste-Hindus. They began to add their caste name with pride. The leaders of MRPS began to call themselves as Krishna Madiga or Krupakar Madiga.[95] This tradition spread over to rank and file of MRPS across the state. K. Balagopal in his *EPW* article observes that:

> The first and most audacious thing the Madigas did was to suffix the caste tag to their names. Krishna became Krishna Madiga, Krupakar became Krupakar Madiga and so on down the line. In a society that addresses any number of Krishna Shastris and Krishna Reddys respectfully the discomfort this caused was most amusing to watch. As 'Madiga' has served as term of abuse, whether directed against a Madiga or otherwise, it was most discomforting to be confronted someone who wanted you to address him as 'Krishna Madiga'. And when people confessed to themselves that they found it embarrassingly absurd to think of someone as Krishna Madiga, they were forced to ask themselves why they did not find it absurd to think someone as Krishna Shastri, Krishna Reddy or Krishna Naidu.[96]

The leaders were successful in communicating effectively to their Madiga community. By explaining their history, culture, the position of reservation facilities, and their position in society, they made them conscious of their status. This provided a platform to the Madigas to unite and organize themselves. They used the elements of culture excellently and transformed them into political tools to play it on political arena.

Another important dimension of the success was that it was not identified or loyal to any political organization, at least in the beginning. The MRPS leadership instilled confidence among the Madigas by rejuvenating consciously and positively an earlier demeaning caste identity. Thus, elevating Madigas to a self-conscious position and making them proud of their 'new' identity. This facilitated mobilization and organization of the Madigas to fight for their demands for categorization of the existing reservation policy according to proportionate population.

The MRPS leadership has explicitly expressed that their demand for a reasonable share in the SCs reservation was justified, as Madigas were not benefited out of the reservations and have remained backward. On the contrary, it was argued that the Malas have availed benefits disproportionate to their population. Their contention is that all the sub-castes of SCs should receive benefits in proportion to their population. They further declare that there are certain sub-castes or *jatis* such as the Rellis, who are more backward than the Madigas. Therefore, such backward groups among the SCs should be provided their due share. This logical exposition of the Dandora leadership for the classification received wider acclaim. After securing from the grassroot level by organizing meetings, rallies, and padayatras, the MRPS was successful in mobilizing 1 lakh Madigas from all over the state. They proceeded to Hyderabad, the state capital, to demonstrate their strength and to press for their demand. Finally, the state government appointed a one-man commission on 10 September 1996, headed by a retired judge of Andhra Pradesh High Court, Justice Ramachandra Raju, to enquire into the issues of Dalit reservation in the state and the demand raised by the MRPS.

The commission has found that the SCs are a very heterogeneous group with wide disparities in social, economic, cultural, occupational, and educational levels. In such a situation, constitutional provisions and several Supreme Court judgements support the need for rational categorization to ensure equity and to rectify injustice.

The commission inferred that the Mala and Adi Andhra communities, both individually and the group of communities belonging to the Mala and Adi Andhra group, have so far been enjoying to a large extent a greater share in public employment than their percentage share of SC population.[97] According to the commission 'there is disproportionate distribution of reservation benefits in favour of the "Mala" group and "Adi Andhra" group of scheduled caste communities compared to their respective populations. Both the "Madiga" group and "Relli" group of communities are not adequately represented either in public appointments or in educational institutions compared to their respective populations'.[98]

The commission suggested 'categorization based on most backward to least backward among scheduled castes'.[99] Accordingly, the 'Relli' group of communities is the most backward among the SC communities. Thus, they were categorized as 'A' with percentage entitlement of 1 per cent both in public appointments and admission to educational institutions. The 'Madiga' group of communities is the next most backward among the SC communities. They are categorized as 'B' with percentage entitlement of 7 per cent both in public appointments and admission to educational institutions. The commission recommended that the 'Mala' group of communities is receiving the benefits of reservation wholly disproportionate to its population. They are categorized as 'C' with percentage entitlement of 6 per cent both in public appointments and admissions to educational institutions. The 'Adi Andhra' group of communities is receiving the benefits of reservations wholly disproportionate to their population. They are categorized as 'D' with percentage entitlement of 1 per cent both in public appointments and admission to educational institutions.

The commission also made clear that the categorization made into 'A', 'B', 'C', and 'D' groups does not apply to posts or admissions to educational institutions in the central government or in central government corporations or central government public sector undertakings.

Meanwhile the MRPS intensified its struggle throughout the Andhra Pradesh. The commission at last submitted its recommendations to the Andhra Pradesh government on 28 May 1997 for its executive action. The then TDP government immediately responded to the commission's recommendations and issued government order Numbers 68 and 69 classifying the SC reservations as 'A', 'B', 'C', and 'D' groups as recommended by the Justice Ramachandra Raju Commission. However, the Mala Mahanadu resumed an anti-categorization movement vehemently opposing the division and demanded that the government should withdraw the orders issued classifying the Dalits into four groups. It argued that the division of reservations is the divide and rule politics of dominant castes and Dalits should fight united against the caste annihilation.[100]

Unconvincingly, Mala Mahanadu raised two issues: one is regarding the reservation benefits by Malas attributed to their individual 'merit' and argues that although the Madigas have been oppressed by the upper castes, they are unforthcoming because of their marked occupancy, and the Madigas were expected to repeat the cycle of skill acquisition, improvement in competitive spirit, and 'merit' for any modern occupational ladder.

Any failure to do so on part of the Madigas is not the result of Mala betrayal. In fact, the Madigas are simply not willing to do the hard work that Malas did a generation ago in order to get the first leg up the ladder. Second, the division of reservations have been artificially induced by the upper castes in order to stimulate hostility and conflict and to prevent all exploited groups from joining together to end their mutual exploitation led by the Dalit movement in Andhra Pradesh.

With this understanding, the Mala Mahanadu challenged the government orders in the Andhra Pradesh High Court and the honourable Court suspended the government orders on technical reasons saying that the state legislature has no competence to make any law in regard to bifurcation of the Presidential List of SCs prepared under Article 341(1) of the Constitution. The legislation was bad because the Report of the National Commission on Scheduled Castes was not placed before the Legislature as required under Article 338(9) of the Constitution of India.[101]

However, considering the importance of the Dandora movement, the Andhra Pradesh government enacted Andhra Pradesh Scheduled Castes (Rationalization of Reservations) Act 20 of 2000 based on the Justice Ramachandra Raju commission's recommendations. Again Mala Mahanadu went to the Supreme Court challenging the Andhra Pradesh Scheduled Castes (Rationalization of Reservations) Act 20 of 2000.

The Supreme Court in its verdict said that the mini classification based on micro distinctions is false to the very egalitarian spirit of Indian Constitution and violates Articles 14, 15, and 16, which constitute the basic structure of the Indian Constitution.[102] Though there is a temporary impasse on the division of reservations as demanded by the Dandora movement, the movement has brought out yet other important questions before the Dalit movement as the democratization in Andhra Pradesh.

Notes

1. "Adi-Hindu Social Service League Shata Jayanthi Vuthsavalu", *Samaanthara*, May 2012, 36–37.
2. V.T. Rajashekar Shetty. *Dalit Movement in Karnataka*. Madras: The Diocesan Press, 1978. pp. 111–113.
3. Syed Siraj Ul Hassan. *The Castes and Tribes of H.E.H. The Nizam's Dominions*. New Delhi: Asian Educational Services, 1989. pp. 635–636.
4. H.K. Sherwani, P.M. Joshi. *History of Medieval Deccan*, Vol. I. Hyderabad: Andhra Pradesh Government Textbooks Press, 1973. pp. 520–522.
5. *Statement of Agenda for People's Telangana*. Hyderabad: People's Telangana Foundation, 2007. pp. 3–4.
6. Bhangya Bhukya. *Subjugated Nomads: The Lambadas under the Rule of the Nizams*. New Delhi: Orient Blackswan, 2010. pp. 62–63.
7. Puchalapalli Sundarayya. *Telangana People's Struggle and Its Lessons*. New Delhi: Foundation Books Publications, 1972. pp. 22–26.
8. S. Kesava Iyengar. *Economic Investigation in the Hyderabad State 1929–1930*, Vol 5. Hyderabad-Deccan: Government Central Press, 1931–1932.
9. Ibid., p. 202.
10. P.R. Venkataswamy. *Our Struggle for Emancipation*. Secunderabad: Universal Art Printers, 1955. pp. 24–26.
11. *Modern Hyderabad*, talk given on 10th March 1936 at the Indian State Broadcasting Station, New Delhi, by Sir Akar Hydari, Finance Member, the Nizam Government (published by Government of Hyderabad), 1937. p. 2.
12. Sheela Raj. *Medievalism to Modernism: Socio-Economic and Cultural History of Hyderabad 1869–1911*. Bombay: Popular Prakashan, 1987. p. 250.
13. Ibid., p. 4.
14. Ibid., p. 5.
15. Census of India 1931. *H.E.H. The Nizam's Dominions—Hyderabad State*. Vol. XXII, part II. Hyderabad-Deccan: The Government Central Press, 1933. p. 221.
16. Census of India 1941. *H.E.H. The Nizam's Dominions—Hyderabad State*. Vol. XXI, part III. Hyderabad-Deccan: The Government Central Press, 1945. p. 610.

17. P.R. Venkataswamy. *Our Struggle for Emancipation*. Secunderabad: Universal Art Printers, 1955, p. 386.
18. Grigson, W.V. *The Challenge of Backwardness.* Hyderabad: Government Press, 1947, p. 106.
19. P.R. Venkataswamy. *Our Struggle for Emancipation*. Secunderabad: Universal Art Printers, 1955, p. 224.
20. Leonard Karen. "Hyderabad: Mulki-Non-Mulki Conflict". Ed. By Robin Jeffrey, *People, Princes, and Paramount Power: Society and Politics in the Indian Princely State.* New Delhi: OUP, 1978. pp. 65–106.
21. G. Sudharshan Reddy. "Caste Associations and Social Change in Andhra 1900–1925". PhD Thesis, Osmania University of Hyderabad, 1986. pp. 68–69.
22. Leonard has argued that this was deliberately done by non-mulki officials in order to divert the *mulki*–non-*mulki* politics. See her *Hyderabad: Mulki-Non-Mulki Conflict*. pp. 65–106.
23. Hyderabad State Committee of Compilation of the History of Freedom Movement in Hyderabad. *The Freedom Struggle in Hyderabad, 1885–1920*. Vol. III. Hyderabad-Deccan: Hyderabad State Committee, 1957. pp. 54–60.
24. Ian Copland. "Communalism in Princely State: The Case of Hyderabad, 1930–1940", *Modern Asian Studies,* Vol. 22, No. 4, 1988, 794–794.
25. Bhukya Bhangya. *Subjugated Nomads. The Lambadas under the Rule of the Nizams.* New Delhi: Orient Blackswan, 2010. p. 52.
26. Braj Ranjan Mani. *Debrahmanising History: Dominance and Resistance in Indian Society.* New Delhi: Monetary, 2005. pp. 168–169.
27. M.B. Goutam. *Bhagyodayam: Maadiri Bhgyareddy Varma Life Sketch and Mission*. Hyderabad: Samaantara Book House, 2009. pp. 40–56.
28. To know more about him see the article written by Yagati Chinna Rao in *Samaanthara* Magazine published in May 2007.
29. Jaya Sree S. Prabha. "Arya Samaj Movement in Liberation of Hyderabad-Karnataka", *Indian Streams Research Journal*, Vol. 3, No. 4, 2013, 1–5.
30. Gail, Omvedt. *Dalits and the Democratic Revolution.* New Delhi: Sage Publications, 1994, p. 120.
31. Leonard Karen. "Hyderabad: The Mulki-non-Mulki Conflict". Ed. by Robin Jeffery, *People, Princes and Paramount Power: Society and Politics in the Indian Princely States.* New Delhi: OUP, 1978. pp. 65–106.

32. Tummapudi Bharati. *A History of Telugu Dalit Literature*. New Delhi: Kalpas Publications, 2008. pp. 31–36.
33. P.R. Venkataswamy. *Our Struggle for Emancipation,* Vol. 1. Secunderabad: University Art Printers, 1955. p. 7.
34. Personal Interview with Prof Adapa Satyanarayana, August 30, 2014.
35. P.R. Venkataswamy. *Our Struggle for Emancipation,* Vol. 1. Secunderabad: University Art Printers, 1955. p. 7.
36. Yagati Chinna Rao. *Dalit Struggle for Identity*. New Delhi: Kaniska Publications, 2003. p. 151.
37. Bhagya Reddy as the founder of the Mandali is subject to conflicting opinion. See Venkataswamy, P.R. *Our Struggle for Emancipation,* Vol. 1. Secunderabad: University Art Printers, 1955. p. 3.
38. P.V. Rao. "Tholi Suryudu—Bhagya Reddy Varma", *Samaantara* (A Telugu Monthly Journal), Vol. 3, No. 2, May 2009, 5–7.
39. Ibid.
40. M.B. Goutam. *Bhagyodayam: Bhagyareddy Varma Jivitadharsham-Aacharana* (Telugu). Hyderabad: Samaantara Publications, 2009. p. 7.
41. Gaddam Shankar. "Dalita Vudyamakarudu P.R. Venkataswamy Chirasmaraniyudu". *Samaantara* (A Telugu Monthly Journal,) Vol. 3, No. 4, July 2009, 9–10.
42. For more details see P.R. Venkataswamy. *Our Struggle for Emancipation*. Secunderabad: Universal Art Printers, 1955. p. 6.
43. P.R. Venkataswamy. *Our Struggle for Emancipation*. Secunderabad: Universal Art Printers, 1955. p. 4.
44. Ibid.
45. Ibid., p. 5.
46. Ibid., pp. 18–19.
47. Belgaum now in Karnataka state earlier belonged to the Bombay Presidency.
48. Yagati Chinna Rao. *Dalits Struggle for Identity*. New Delhi: Kaniska Publishers, 2003. p. 172.
49. "Adi-Hindu Social Service League Shata Jayanti Vuthsavala Committee 1911–2011". Pamphlet Published in Hyderabad: *Samaantara*, Vol. 6, No. 2, May 2012, 36–37.
50. There seems to be disagreements regarding year of founding of this organization.

51. For details see P.R. Venkataswamy. *Our Struggle for Emancipation*. Secunderabad: Universal Art Printers, 1955. pp. 13, 15, and 17.
52. Gail Omvedt. *Dalit Vision: The Anti-Caste Movements and the Construction of an Indian Identity*. Hyderabad: Orient Longman, 1995. pp. 34–42.
53. P.R. Venkataswamy. *Our Struggle for Emancipation*. Secunderabad: Universal Art Printers, 1955. p. 12.
54. M.B. Goutam. *Bhagyodayam: Madari Bhagya Reddy Verma: Life-sketch and Mission*. Hyderabad: Adi-Hindu Social Service League, 1991. pp. 20–21.
55. Yagati Chinna Rao. *Dalits Struggle for Identity*. New Delhi: Kaniska Publishers, 2003. p. 173.
56. Participation in that exhibition was predominantly from the youth belonging to the Madiga community. Madigas were traditionally leather workers in Andhra Pradesh. See Yagati Chinna Rao's *Dalits Struggle for Identity*. New Delhi: Kaniska Publishers, 2003. p. 196.
57. P.R. Venkataswamy. *Our Struggle for Emancipation*. Secunderabad: Universal Art Printers, 1955. p. 49.
58. Ibid., p. 51.
59. Ibid.
60. Ibid., pp. 80–101.
61. R. Surender. "Dalitodyama Tejam Aadharshaniyudu 'Hyderabad Ambedkar' B.S. Venkatrao", *Samaantara*, Vol. 3, No. 2, May 2009, 8–11.
62. P.R. Venkataswamy. *Our Struggle for Emancipation*. Secunderabad: Universal Art Printers, 1955. pp. 658–661.
63. Yagati Chinna Rao. *Dalits Struggle for Identity*. New Delhi: Kaniska Publishers, 2003. p. 181.
64. Gail Omvedt. *Dalits and Democratic Revolution: Dr. Ambedkar and the Dalit Movement in Colonial India*. New Delhi: Sage Publications, 1994. p. 296.
65. P.R. Venkataswamy. *Our Struggle for Emancipation*. Secunderabad: Universal Art Printers, 1955. p. 64.
66. Ibid., p. 654.
67. Y.B. Abbasayalu. *Sociology of Depressed Groups*. Hyderabad: Centre for Harijan Studies, Osmania University, 1978. p. 43.
68. P.R. Venkataswamy. *Our Struggle for Emancipation*. Secunderabad: Universal Art Printers, 1955. pp. 662–663.

69. Pamu Rammurthy. *Rashtra Harijana Nayakula Jivita Charita*. Kakinada, 1976. pp. 662–663.
70. Y.B. Abbasayalu. *Sociology of Depressed Groups*. Hyderabad: Centre for Harijan Studies, Osmania University (OU), 1979. p. 28.
71. S. Prakash Rao. "Nizam Rajyamlo Dalita Vudyama Nirmatha: P.R. Venkataswamy", *Samaantara*, Vol. 3, No. 4, July 2009, 24.
72. Gail Omvedt. *Dalits and Democratic Revolution: Dr. Ambedkar and the Dalit Movement in Colonial India*. New Delhi: Sage Publications, 1994. p. 304.
73. P.R. Venkataswamy. *Our Struggle for Emancipation*. Secunderabad: Universal Art Printers, 1955. pp. 359–360.
74. Ibid, pp. 386–387.
75. Yagati Chinna Rao. *Dalits Struggle for Identity*. New Delhi: Kaniska Publishers, 2003. p. 184.
76. R.K. Kshirasagar. *Dalit Movement and Its Leaders (1857–1956)*. New Delhi: MD Publications, 1994. pp. 190–191.
77. Gail Omvedt. *Dalits and the Democratic Revolution: Dr. Ambedkar and the Dalit Movement in Colonial India*. New Delhi: Sage Publications, 1994. pp. 313–316.
78. Inukonda Thirumali. *Telangana-Andhra: Castes, Regions and Politics in Andhra Pradesh*. New Delhi: Aakar Books, 2013. pp. 92–102.
79. Gogu Shyamala. *Nene Balanni: T.N. Sadhalaxmi Batuku Katha* (Telugu). Hyderabad: Hyderabad Book Trust Publications, 2011. pp. 32–33.
80. P.R. Venkataswamy. *Our Struggle for Emancipation*, Vol. 2. Secunderabad: Universal Art Printers, 1955. pp. 662–663.
81. K.Y. Ratnam. "Dalit Movement and Democratization in Andhra Pradesh". Working Paper. East West Centre, Washington, No. 13, December 2008, p. 16.
82. Gaddam Krishna Reddy. *Dalit Movement and Electoral Politics in Andhra Pradesh: A Study in the Interface*. Minor Research Report Submitted to the UGC in 1997, p. 27.
83. *Personal Interview* with Bojja Tarakam, October 8, 2014.
84. Shigeharu Tanabe and Charles F. Keyes (Ed.). *Cultural Crises and Social Memory: Modernity and Identity in Thailand*. London: Routledge Publications, 2002. p. 170.
85. Robin Jeffrey. "What This Statues Tell: The Politics of Choosing Symbols in Trivandrum", *Pacific Affairs*, Vol. 53. No. 3, 1980, 484–502.

86. Gaddam Krishna Reddy. *Dalit Movement and Electoral Politics in Andhra Pradesh: A study in the Interface.* Minor Research Report Submitted to the UGC in 1997, p. 24.
87. Personal Interview with Gaddar, 2 November 2014.
88. Personal Interview with Bojja Tarakam, 8 October 2014. Also see *Eenadu Newspaper.* 27 January 1982. Hyderabad.
89. For more information, see K. Srinivasulu Working Paper 179, G. Krishna Reddy. See K. Balagopal. op. cit.; A. Kohli. *Democracy and Discontent: India, Growing Crisis of Governability*. New Delhi: Cambridge University Press, 1992, Indian Edition. Chapter 4.
90. From, A position paper by Satyashodak Social Research Centre, Hyderabad.
91. Personal Interview with Krishna Madiga, 12 November 2014. (Krishna Madiga is the founder of the Madiga Dandora Movement which spearheaded the movement for sub-categorization of SC reservations.)
92. P. Muthaiah. "Why Categorisations of SC Reservations?", Ed. by Susie Tharu, K. Satyanarayana, *From those Stubs Steel Nibs Are Sprouting: New Dalit Writing from South India*. Noida: Harper Collins Publishers, 2013.
93. Yagati Chinna Rao (Ed.). *Dividing Dalits: Writing on Sub-Categorisation of Scheduled Castes.* Jaipur: Rawat Publication, 2009. p. 103.
94. Chinnaiah, Jangam. "Sub-Caste Consciousness: Challenges before Dalit Intellectuals", Ed. by Yagati Chinna Rao, *Dividing Dalits: Writings on Sub-Categorization of Scheduled Castes*. Jaipur: Rawat Publications, 2009. pp. 100–105.
95. K. Balagopal. "A Tangled Web: Subdivision of SC Reservations in AP", *Economic and Political Weekly*, Vol. 35, No. 13, 2000, 1075–1081.
96. Ibid.
97. See for details, "Report of Justice Sri P. Ramachandra Raju". Hyderabad: Social Welfare Department, Government of Andhra Pradesh, 1997.
98. Ibid.
99. Ibid.
100. See "Pamphlet", Mala Mahanadu Andhra Pradesh Committee, January 21, 2006.
101. Ibid.
102. Ibid.

II

Telangana Peasant Insurrection

A Historical Study

In the history of Left politics in India, the Telangana Armed Struggle of peasants against tyrannical, feudalistic, and autocratic rule of Nizam constitutes an indispensable chapter. This chapter traces the trajectory of the Left movement in Telangana from the beginning including the conditions that laid the foundations for the rise of Left movement through the wide range of primary sources. We have even first person accounts of the communist leaders of the struggle, memoirs of nationalists, historical accounts based on primary documents, sociological analysis of the insurgent villages, and oral histories.

Before the discussion on the movement led by the communists, and the conditions that have led to the movement, it is important to study the geographical character and socio-economic and political conditions of the erstwhile estate of Hyderabad. Agricultural farming was the main occupation of about 60–70 per cent of the people in the state; therefore, land becomes the central issue around which socio-political and economic conditions in the state depends. Hence, this chapter is organized accordingly; first, it gives detailed description of geographical features; second, it discusses economic and political conditions that led to the social settings that have finally favoured the Leftist movement.

GEOGRAPHIC FEATURES OF TELANGANA

Nizam's state was the biggest of all the 600 odd princely states in India. Telangana is the Telugu-speaking eastern part of the formerly princely state of Hyderabad. It is situated at an average height of 1250–1500 feet above the sea level.[1] Hyderabad encompasses an area of 82,700 square miles in south central India. It was divided into three linguistic regions: Marathwada with six districts, Karnataka with two, and Telangana with nine. When the States Reorganization Commission's recommendations were adopted in 1956, Telangana was merged with the Telugu-speaking areas of Madras Presidency to form the Andhra Pradesh.

Being hilly, Telangana was covered mostly with sandy soils, good for growing jawar and bajra (different kinds of millet). Some areas had fertile black soils, used mainly for dry cultivation. The average annual rainfall was about 30 inches but it fluctuated greatly from year to year. Most of it fell during the period from roughly June to September. The main food crops were jawar, bajra, rice, wheat, and pulses. The major cash crops were peanut, castor, linseed, sesame, tobacco, and sugarcane. Double cropping was commonly practiced, the crop being harvested in October and late January to early February. Jawar and bajra were the main crops in Mahboobnagar; Nalgonda was the chief source of castor and an important producer of rice; Warangal, benefitting from good irrigation and heavier rainfall, produced rice as well as peanuts and tobacco.

Irrigation was provided by tanks, wells, and canals. Telangana, where tanks were important, had 80 per cent of the state's irrigation facilities. The percentage of irrigated area to total cultivated area, though, was low in the Nizam's dominions, just 6 per cent in 1931 compared to 20 per cent for the country as a whole.[2] Rain water filled the tanks during the monsoons; by the end of the following summer they were dry. The river Godavari defining the eastern border of Telangana and the river Krishna demarcating the southern border are both rain fed. They too dried up during the summer. However, the torrential monsoons caused the rivers to swell. The current in the Godavari was particularly strong, making it virtually uncrossable.

All along the Godavari, between it and the plains of Warangal and Karimnagar where agriculture is the main occupation, were thick forests. That was not true, though, of the entire state, only 12 per cent of which was forested. Adilabad had even larger portions covered with dense forests. Here tigers and leopards, bears, antelopes, wild boar, many species of snakes, and various small animals were to be found. There were forests along the Krishna too, in the southern parts of Nalgonda and Mahboobnagar but these were smaller and less dense.

SOCIO-ECONOMIC STRUCTURE OF TELANGANA

Hyderabad state was divided for administrative reasons into four subahs—namely, Aurangabad, Gulbarga, Gulshanabad (Medak), and Warangal—headed by a subahdar each. These subahdars were entrusted with the responsibility of revenue collection and other duties according to the new system introduced in 1867 called 'Zilla Bandhi'. These subahs were further divided into 15 districts headed by the first Taluqdar (collector) with revenue as well as administrative functions. There was also one subdistrict with an Amaldar. These districts consisted of 101 (and later increased to 117 talukas) under a Taluqdar with a Peshkar (assistant) and a Girdavar (revenue inspector). The Department of Land Revenue and Survey Settlement set up in 1873 sought to streamline the land tenurial system.

As far as Telangana is concerned (in the two subahs of Warangal and Medak), the department of land settlement effected a 30 years tenancy settlement for four districts of Warangal, Nizamabad, Medak, and Mahboobnagar, a 15 years settlement in the four districts of Karimnagar and Nalgonda which were partly assessed. In the two remaining districts of Adilabad and the crown district of Atraf-i-Balda (Hyderabad), land was not surveyed at all.

In Hyderabad state, as a whole, broadly two land tenurial and revenue systems came into being one, Diwani (or Khalsa) lands and another non-Diwani comprising about 60 per cent and 40 per cent of the entire Hyderabad state respectively. Sarf-e-Khas or crown lands amounted to roughly about 50 lakh acres in about 3,335 villages of the state out of which 646 villages are in Telangana but mainly concentrated in the Hyderabad district. There were about 573 such villages in Hyderabad, 25 in Karimnagar, 15 in Nalgonda, 15 in Mahboobnagar, 13 in Medak, and 4 in Warangal districts, which contribute about ₹ 2 crore per annum in a state with a budget estimated at ₹ 20 crore.

Land revenue collected by the officials in these villages was sent to the Tehsil office from where it was deposited in the Nizam's treasury. This was extracted mainly from the 15 lakh peasants who occupied these lands.[3] Next in the list of the non-Diwani lands are Paigahs—lands granted by the Nizam to his close relatives (mainly through matrimonial ties) or his army commanders of a high rank. Paigah, hence meant 'prompt and high rank'. The land revenue in these estates amounted to ₹ 30–54 lakh. These covered an area of about 4,134 square miles of the state.[4]

Samsthanas and Jagirs are the other major aspects of the non-Diwani tenures. There are about 10 samsthanas located in Gadwal, Anegondi, Paloncha, Gopalpet, Wanaparty, Jatpole, Narayanapur, Medak, Amarchinta, and Gurgunta. There were former rulers (rajahs) in these territories that patched up with the Nizam and retained about 94 per cent of the gross income from the land. They pay a nominal peshkash to the Nizam. They also possess village grants on a fixed assessment.[5] Jagirs were granted by the Nizams to Pathans and Arab Jammandars and others for the services rendered to the state. The Jagirdars in turn are granted ownership rights in lieu of the payment of a Nazrana. These Jagirs acquired judicial and administrative powers. The number of the grants of these Jagirs increased from about 1,100 in 1992 to 1,500 in 1949 and so do the number of middlemen leading to the 'subinfeudation' process.

Some Jagirdars cultivated their land through forced labour or *vetti* and *Bhagela*.[6] These were Swantha Kamatham lands or *seri* lands. On the whole since the revenue to collect from the tenants was not mentioned in the grants, the land taxes and rents were exorbitant in these Jagirs in comparison to the land tax in the Diwani areas. There were as many as 40 such taxes in the Jagirs at times.

Thus, through rack-renting and exorbitant taxes, Jagirdars, Samsthandars, and others acquired considerable influence in the society. Ten families in this section acquired revenue and taxes worth ₹ 10 crore with the Nizam at its head with about ₹ 2 crore as rental income and a personal fortune worth $2 billion and thus become 'the richest person' in the world at that time.[7]

In the Diwani lands to the influence of Jagirdars, deshmukhs, and other can be seen. Though the settlement in these areas was known as Ryotwari, that is, the owner of the land is in direct relationship to the state on payment of a fixed land revenue—a variable tenure systems emerged, namely Pattadars, Jagirdars, Inamdars, Ljaradars, Banjardars, Sarbastadars, Agraharas, Maktadars, and so on.[8] The land occupancy of the Pattadars was dependent on the regular payment of the land revenue, but these Pattadars more often than not had partners called Shikmidars, from whom the former received a percentage of the agricultural produce depending on the agricultural inputs (implement, seeds, cattle, etc.). Shikmidars were permanent tenants, whereas another group of tenants called Asami-Shikmidars or Kashtakars were tenants-at-will. *Liara* (contract) lands were granted for the purpose of extending cultivation lands without the tag of any revenue payment for the first 30–40 years but gradually land rent increased after this period. There are about 465 villages in Telangana above of such grants which occupied about 95 lakh acres.[9]

Inam lands were granted to the non-cultivating classes for the services rendered to the state or for charitable purpose, either free of revenue or subject to a quit-rent. The patels and patwaris were the major beneficiaries of these lands at the local level.[10] Sarbastadars came into existence after Salar Jung abolished the system of revenue farming, the previous revenue farmers were given watans or Inams. Deshmukhs paid a fixed revenue to the state and here too the exact amount to be collected from the tenants was not mentioned, leaving deshmukhs free to employ force labour. Moneylenders too joined their ranks.

Makta resembles the jagirdari system, with the exception that the grant holder has to pay a fixed rent. This system prevailed in about 664 villages. Though the intention here was to make the actual cultivator a Pattadar, in practice the Maktadar retained the patta by evicting tenants at his will and so on. Agraharas were grants made to Hindu temples and Brahmins without any revenue payment. They numbered about 309. Banjardars cultivated the forest lands.[11]

These Jagirdars, Samsthandars, deshmukhs, Banjardars, and so on exerted formidable influence on the rural socio-economic structure. They have extensive powers in the villages including judicial and administrative functions. The small Jagirdars and deshmukhs indulged in moneylending, secured abkari (today, liquor) contracts. Even though they numbered about 0.5 per cent of the population, they as rent receivers and landholders trampled upon the rural folk by *vetti* and *bhagela*. However, there were many gradations within the landlord sections. For instance, on the one hand we see a Janna Reddy Pratap Reddy possessing as many as 1,50,000 acres of land, a Visnoor Ramachandra Reddy about 40,000 acres, a Suryapet deshmukh with 20,000 acres, and a Kallur family about 80,000 acres.[12]

The compilation of the name of the landlords possessing extensive lands is difficult. But a glimpse can also be had from the fact that about 77 holdings in Warangal district and 53 holdings in Karimnagar district ranged between 1,000 acres and 2,500 acres. About 10 holdings in Warangal and 7 in Karimnagar districts varied between 2,500 acres and 5,000 acres. On the other hand, we find small landlords with a few hundred acres who live in a single village who invariably indulged in moneylending (grain lending to be precise), land grabbing, and so on.

This was the social stratum which the Hyderabad state backed to the hilt. The state-sponsored reforms committee of 1938 said it in as many words: its report said that 'the heads of the Samsthanas, Jagirdars, Zamindars have permanent attachment with the state and the Royal House ... [their] loyalty to the Ruler and his Government, on which rests their stability, has always remained unshaken'. In the words of the Nizam himself:

> You Jagirdars belong to a class of gentry who stand in special and distinctive relations to the state of Hyderabad. My principle has always been that, as far as possible, Jagirs should be continued to be preserved and that they should be saved from extinction.[13]

Beneath these sections are the 'Lower' classes-agricultural workers, who constitute roughly about 10 per cent of the population (including farm servants and farm labourers but excluding those who perform general labour and earth work comprising about 13 per cent of the population), tenants of various gradation who pay a land rent to the landlords forming about 31 per cent and others, caste-wise break-up is according to the following pattern. There are about 21 castes and sub-castes; they were roughly Kapus or Kunbis (based on the land) numbering about 26 per cent of the population. Next in strength were Malas or Madigas in Telangana or Mangs in Marathwada comprising about 14 per cent of the population. The rest was occupied by other castes: Brahmin formed about 6.21 per cent, Vaishyas or Komtis (traders) 4.91 per cent, Gollas (shepherds) 7.47 per cent, Gaundlas (toddy-tappers and liquor vendors) 2.55 per cent, Koriwas 4.78 per cent, Salas (weavers) 3.8 per cent, Banjaras (gypsies) 1.54 per cent, Gonds (tribals) 0.49 per cent, and so in 1903. As population grew so did the numbers of these castes but almost in the same proportion.[14] When survey settlements were made, the state did provide lands to washermen, barbers, Malas, carpenters, blacksmiths, and others to perform labour for the villagers but without permanent rights over the land or disposable rights. These sections were the most vulnerable, as the dynamics of the countryside showed, to the exactions of the state landlords and moneylenders on the one hand, and famines and natural calamities on the other hand.

Hyderabad had a population of just over 16 million in 1941, at an average density of 198 people per square mile. Though this was far lower than the all-India average of 246, it represented a two-thirds increase over the last 60 years. In a predominantly agrarian economy where well over half the population depended on agriculture for their livelihood, population per square mile was a less important statistic than population per cultivated square mile. In this regard, in 1931, Telangana with 476 people per cultivated square mile was nearly twice as densely populated as neighbouring Marathwada which had 243 persons per cultivated square mile.[15]

As in the rest of the country, the rural population, about 89 per cent of the total population, lived in villages in the plains and in small hamlets in the forests. The major portion of the rural population either came from untouchable castes such as the Malas and the Madigas or tribal groups such as the Hill Reddis, Chenchus, Koyas, Lambadis, Banjaras, and further north the Gonds.[16]

The cattle population, at about 12.5 million, was almost as large as the human. The dominant breed was called the Deccani. The quality of the cattle can be gauged from two facts. A good pair of bullocks could cover just three-fourths of an acre of dry land and half an acre of land in a day. In Telangana, a cow yielded just over half a litre and a buffalo around 1.25 litres of milk a day. This was enough to provide a meagre 4.3 ounces of milk per day per head, whereas nutritionally minimum requirements were estimated at 10 ounces per day per person. Sometimes, as in the homes of some deshmukhs and Zamindars these cattle shared a roof with the families of the domestic servants of the household.

In such places, as elsewhere, hygiene was poor, medical facilities nearly non-existent, and epidemics of cholera and malaria frequently proved fatal to physiques already weakened by malnutrition. Life expectancy was a mere 25.9 years and had increased little over the 40 years since 1891. Tribal groups had an even lower average lower life expectancy.

But if health services were poor, 'infrastructural' development was worse. Warangal had boasted 443 miles of metalled road until 1950. Adilabad, sprawling over 7,000 square miles, had 307 total miles of roadway; Nalgonda had merely 300 miles of metalled roads.[17] These roads probably extended from one commercial centre to another; almost certainly, they led to the big train junctions that were the main vertical links through which trade was conducted. The postal service was minimal: one post office for each 48 square miles or 10,000 people. The entire state had just 64 telegraph and telephone services[18]. All these details may seem incidental; as we shall see, however, they were to shape in a critical way the content and nature of the armed struggle that followed.

POLITICAL ORGANIZATION IN HYDERABAD

Formally, the supreme authority was the Nizam, presiding over a 'political and social structure from medieval Muslim rule (that) had been preserved more or less intact' (Smith, 1950: 28). This was certainly true as far as the jagirs were concerned but it was also true in another respect: the Nizam had the equivalent of a royal retinue, consisting of big industrialists, administrators, and government officials. These were usually Muslims,[19] though Hyderabad's population was predominantly (81 per cent) Hindu.[20]

The Nizams of Hyderabad had ruled since 1723 when Asaf Jahi had founded the dynasty by breaking away from the Moghul Empire. They had retained close relations with the British who stationed a permanent force of 9,000 troops in Secunderabad, on the northern outskirts of the city of Hyderabad.

In the second quarter of this century, when British withdrawal from India was imminent, the Nizam was placed in a tenuous situation. His power base within the state was extremely narrow, limited to a small group of noblemen in the urban areas, a few Jagirdars in the countryside, and those Muslims in the city who benefitted directly from the state's Islamic character. On the other hand, the British were increasingly reluctant allies. The concerted efforts of the communal Majlis-e-Ittehadul- Mussulman (MIM)[21] to raise the slogan of Anaal Malik (literally 'I am the King') can be interpreted in this context.[22] With the Nizam's blessings, the Ittehad (as it was popularly called) was engaged in a last ditch legitimating campaign but it was to be too little too late.

In the last few years of the Nizam's rule, the Ittehad was to play an increasingly important political role, especially in the armed struggle. Thus, it might be useful to trace its origin and character.

It started in 1927 with a cultural organization called the Anjuman-e-Tabligh-ul-Islam, which engaged itself in converting untouchables to Islam.[23] The Arya Samaj[24] responded by converting (on the name of shuddi) them back; communal clashes resulted and both organizations were banned. Bahadur Yar Jung,[25] the leader of the Tabligh, then took over another social and cultural forum—the Ittehad. Under his leadership, the Ittehad became an aggressive political organization dedicated to the Nizam's rule. However, it was not until the lawyer Qasim Razvi became the leader of the organization that it attained its reputation for fanaticism. He created an armed wing called the Razakars, which became an informal army parallel to the Nizam's regular army. It was then that the Ittehad obtained the dubious distinction of being identified with autocracy, communalism, and fascism[26] at the same time.[27]

Religion was just one of the ways in which group loyalty was divided—there was class, culture, and caste, and there was language.[28] The Nizam patronized Urdu, making it the only medium of instruction in the state's schools.[29] Urdu and English were the official languages: while none of the other languages prospered, Telugu was singled out for derision.[30] Even among elite Hindus, Telugu was not favoured; resentful of the treatment of their native language in their own land, some of these people formed an organization called the Andhra Jana Sangham (literally 'Andhra People's Association'). Its objective was to secure 'a proper place for (the) Telugu language and culture in Hyderabad city'. In a couple of years by it had become a statewide organization and was given a new name—the Andhra Kendra Jana Sangham. The Jana Sangham in turn became an umbrella organization for other similar groups; finally, in March 1930, a new organization called the Andhra Mahasabha (literally 'Andhra Convention') was formed at a conference in Jogipet. The emergence of this organization is significant: it indicated some slippage of the Nizam's hegemony. Previously, there was strict control of libraries; public meetings, even of a literary nature, could only be organized with prior permission from the state; newspapers were closely regulated; and civil liberties were in general few. Composed largely of the urban petite-bourgeoisie, the prospering merchants and traders, and professionals such as lawyers, government officials, and teachers, the Mahasabha represented the lower strata of the ruling class, divided from the upper echelons by linguistic, cultural, and other factors. Its class composition was reflected in its concern,[31] which consisted of passing resolutions aimed at social reforms.[32]

From its inception, the AMS fused linguistic and regional concerns with cultural and later social ones. This is best seen from Ravi Narayan Reddy's description of the incident that started it:

> It was 1922. A Hindu social conference was held in Vivek Vardhini Theater where all the speeches were in Urdu and Marathi. Only one speaker tried to speak in Telugu but he was hooted and shouted down. The number of Maharashtrians in Hyderabad city was small, yet they exhibited their superiority in all walks of life.[33]

In the fourth conference at Sircilla, a resolution was passed requiring all speeches to be delivered in Telugu.[34] This orientation stayed with the Mahasabha well into the Telangana movement. At its sixth conference, the Mahasabha elected Ravi Narayan Reddy, already a secret member of the Communist Party, as secretary. By its eighth conference in 1941, the Mahasabha was well on its way to becoming a front organization for the communists. Before we go on, it would be helpful to take a brief look at the history of the Communist Party of India (CPI).

The CPI was founded at Tashkent in October 1920 by a group of Indians in exile headed by M.N. Roy; by July 1924, it had been admitted into the Communist International.[35] From the start, the Communist tradition has leaned very heavily on Moscow.

From a small base in the Indian intelligentsia, the illegal CPI working with the active participation, and under the influence of, the Communist Party of Great Britain (CPGB), convened an all-India conference in December 1928 of its 'front' organization, the Workers and Peasants Party. By this time, the Sixth Congress of the Comintern (an acronym for Communist International) had adopted its famous resolution entitled The Revolution and Movement of the Colonies and Semi-Colonies. The colonial thesis advocated an aggressive attitude towards the bourgeois national-reformist parties but did not rule out temporary agreements in the name of anti-imperialism. One year later, specifically addressing the CPI, the Comintern's tenth plenum discredited the two-class Workers and Peasants Party.[36]

On the Comintern's advice, the CPI denounced the nationalist movement. However, this only succeeded in isolating it from any mass following. In addition, 31 of the CPI's most important leaders were put into jail in the Meerut Conspiracy Case.[37] At the seventh Congress of the Communist International in August 1935, the CPI was severely criticized for its 'left, sectarian errors'. The CPI was urged to work with the nationalist movement to create an anti-imperialist united front.[38] The CPI politburo issued a statement:

> The concrete application to the present stage of the anti-imperialist movement in our country of the line of the Seventh Congress is a historic affair.[39]

A two-pronged strategy was decided upon: individual CPI members were to infiltrate the Congress; at the same time the party would continue to build a base of mass support. The communists' efforts to infiltrate the Congress were greatly aided by the Congress Socialist Party (CSP), the 'Left' group within the Congress. Working within the Congress gave the CPI access to the students and trade unions while freeing them from an 'outward-oriented' image. When the communists were finally expelled from the CSP in 1939, they already had significant backing. In Kerala, for example, the entire CSP cadre reconstituted itself as the CPI.[40]

The communists had been active in the coastal districts of Andhra since 1934; however, it was not until 1939 that some organization was established in Hyderabad. The Nizam State Communist Committee, which brought together four small groups, registered the nominal start of the CPI involvement. However, it was the AMS that provided the first substantial gain: in the eighth conference in 1941, Ravi Narayan Reddy was elected president. Resolutions were passed demanding the abolition of *vetti*, jagirdari, the tax on tapping toddy, and the eviction of tenants; the reduction of land taxes, rents, and compulsory survey settlements was proposed, as was the confirmation of land titles.[41] Before this time, the Mahasabha had done little to organize the peasantry; they were content to pass resolutions or at most make 'representations' to government officials.

Now they tried to devise campaigns around themes such as education and anti-forced labour. Their most effective action however was against the levy of food grains mentioned earlier.

Two other factors were important for the Mahasabha's increased popularity. The Congress had been banned in 1938 and was rendered virtually powerless, leaving the field to the Mahasabha. By contrast, the CPI, which had also been banned, was now allowed to operate legally.[42]

The reason for lifting the ban on the CPI was a remarkable about-turn in the party's policies. Sensing revolutionary opportunities at home and seeking to capitalize on Britain's preoccupation with the fighting in Europe, the CPI started vigorously opposing the British war effort, calling it an Imperialist War. In the face of the Congress' lukewarm opposition to the war, such activism greatly helped to win support for the CPI though inviting repression from the British, and in Hyderabad, from their loyal ally, the Nizam[43] (Masani, 1959: 79).

Then in June 1941, Nazi Germany invaded Russia, throwing the CPI into confusion. After some internal debate on the merits of the antiwar nationalist effort and considerable pressure from the international organization, the CPI decided to abandon its earlier position and support the People's War of the Soviet Union against the German aggressor. The CPI joined the war effort at the same time that the Congress was launching the Quit India Movement and popular opposition to British rule was growing.[44] While the

Congress was banned as a result, the CPI was encouraged in its activities.

With almost all the Congress leaders in jail, the CPI could consolidate its organizational gains; however, it had lost much of its credibility. Even Ravi Narayan Reddy, after giving a feeble justification for the switch, had to admit that

> The Communist Party committed certain mistakes in implementing the people's war policy. It recognized the danger of fascism but underestimated the imperialist danger. Therefore it made the mistake of characterizing many patriots as fifth columnists.[45]

Despite their mistakes the CPI 'grew substantially during the war period.'[46] This was evident at the eleventh conference of the Mahasabha at Bhongir in 1944 as membership fees which had earlier been reduced from ₹ 1 to four annas were further reduced to one anna.[47] A vigorous membership drive had been launched in the past year; 1,00,000 people had been recruited in the rural areas, 8,000–12,000 of whom had come to Bhongir. Faced with almost certain defeat, the 'Right' wing of the Mahasabha walked out. The CPI now had the organization to themselves and elected Ravi Narayan Reddy as president and Badam Yella Reddy as secretary.[48]

But the greatest gains of this period were to be found in the increase of grassroots organization: district, taluka, and village committees were formed and cadres were trained. Most of these initial cadres came from rich peasant backgrounds. To discourage armchair revolutionaries, they were asked first to organize against the landlords in their own villages. 'Training' was mostly intellectual. They discussed politics and read translations from Lenin, Stalin, Palme Dutt,[49] other Marxist classics, as well as Gorky's *Mother*, and a local novel on the oppression of untouchables, *Malapalli*.[50]

First the question of forced labour—*vetti*—and then problems of tenancy and eviction increasingly turned into minor skirmishes.[51] The Nalgonda District Committee, led by former student leaders not strongly influenced by Gandhi and Mahasabha-style reformism, was particularly truculent. This strategy worked very well against small landlords who were quite unable to meet cooperative resistance.

But why did the state and the big landlords allow these initial organizational attempts by the CPI to succeed? What did they do about it? The evidence here is very sketchy. 'The revolutionaries', according to D.V. Rao, 'had to face intense repression in the form of arrests and sentences of imprisonments'.[52] By this time in 1944, the CPI had not yet come out for the abolition of landlordism and the Nizam's rule. It even appealed for an interim government in which half the seats were reserved for the Ittehad.[53] The end of the war also witnessed a quickening of the pulse of the national Independence movement, forcing the Nizam to pay increasing attention to external events. These reasons are, however, not sufficient answers for the questions posed above.

The early success of the CPI was thus characterized by the following features: articulation of the long-standing grievances of the poorer peasants; action on issues which affected the economic conditions of these peasants in a direct fashion; an aggressive district committee in Nalgonda; the creation of a dedicated cadre; and most importantly mass participation. Reddy tells us that people joined the party because 'membership by payment of one anna was deemed by the people as a passport to their emancipation from these atrocities'.[54]

It was in this context of increased agitation that the incident described at the start of the chapter occurred. The Telangana movement was on its way to a prolonged period of armed struggle.

We have noted that the communists took control of the AMS from about 1940. The Mahasabha slowly gained strength and popularity in the rural areas. Step by step the movement took the form of a peasant upsurge culminating in a major uprising between 1947 and 1950. This period of upsurge could be conveniently analysed in three phases.

The First Phase: Mass Resistance and Upsurge

We have earlier described the socio-economic structure of the state of Hyderabad and the oppression to which the peasants were subjected, and how the middle classes as well as the lower classes in the rural and urban areas were made conscious of the injustice meted out to them by the Nizam's government and the feudal lords.

These were the days of Second World War. There was food shortage all around. The government introduced rationing on commodities such as sugar, cloth, wheat, rice, and kerosene. A system of levy on food grains was introduced. Under this system, each cultivator was required to give a certain quantity of food grains per acre to the government. While every cultivator was expected to perform this duty, the landlords managed to escape somehow or the other and the burden fell on the ordinary peasants. The price paid by the government was less than the market price. Merchants hoarded the daily necessities of life and sold them in the black market at a higher price. The government also forcibly collected money towards the war fund. All these measures seriously affected the peasants. At the same time, the big landlords and deshmukhs continued their exploitation of the tenants, agricultural labourers, and other service castes. Forced labour still continued. However, the masses were no longer as subservient as before and began to resist these exploitive measures.

The large-scale discontentment that gripped the middle classes and the poor peasants and workers was naturally favourable to the growth of the AMS and the Communist Party. In many villages of Nalgonda district, struggles between the peasants and the propertied classes began to take place. The big landlords and the police joined hands with one another to resist this on rushing tide of resentment. But the masses fought the police and the *goondas* (hooligans) hired by the landlords. Attacks by armed police on villages in the Nalgonda district became a regular feature. The houses of important AMS leaders were raided and many were arrested. Sundarayya and Ravi Narayana Reddy have provided detailed accounts of the methods which were adopted by the people to fight the Nizam's police and the types of clashes that took place in different villages.[55] It would be sufficient to say here that during this period the AMS and the Communist Party trained many volunteers to fight the police with *lathis* and slings. Women volunteers used to throw chilli powder, stones, and boiling water at the police.

Sundarayya writes that it was 'only when under the incessant armed police attacks, the first upsurge of the peasant masses was suppressed and our cadre were forced to scatter, and the police and their landlord agents started combing operations in villages and fields widely, that the party, with the sanction of the Politburo, allowed our cadre to arm themselves with muzzle-loaders and seize fire-arms (sporting guns, revolvers, and rifles) and allowed them to go in for armed self-defense'.[56]

Nonetheless the masses could not continue their fight against the army which established camps in many villages. The Nizam's government also banned the Communist Party in November 1946. Thus, the mass upsurge against the big landlords and the government came to a halt. But the ban on the state Congress unit had, however, been lifted by that time.

The Second Phase: Liberation Struggle

Soon after the ban was lifted in April 1946, the state Congress began to mobilize people in favour of a struggle for the freedom of Hyderabad state. It began to pressurize the Nizam of Hyderabad to join the Indian Union in the event of the British granting independence to India. On 11 June 1947, the Nizam announced his desire not to join either the Indian Union or Pakistan and to remain independent. He also imposed a ban on the hoisting of Indian national flag in the state of Hyderabad.

The state Congress adopted a resolution moved by late Shri Burugula Ramakrishna Rao protesting the decision of the Nizam and decided to launch a state-wide Satyagraha. On 7 August 1947, national flag was hoisted all over the state of Hyderabad. Thousands of Satyagrahis were arrested. India became independent on 15 August 1947, and on 27 August 1947, the Nizam declared his independence. People of all sections were deeply disappointed by this decision of the Nizam.

While all the political parties supported the accession of the state of Hyderabad to the Indian Union, the Ittehad-ul-Mussulman was opposed to this move. The Ittehad-ul-Mussulman developed a cadre of volunteers who were called Razakars and these Razakars began to rouse the feelings of Muslims against Hindus. Under these circumstances, political parties of all shades united under the leadership of the Congress led by Ramanand Tirth and planned state-wide non-cooperation and civil disobedience campaigns. Except for a small number of Hindu feudal lords, all the Hindus and some Muslims supported these activities.

The Communists, Congressites, and also socialists led the campaigns such as refusal to pay taxes on land and on palm and date trees, boycott of toddy shops, and non-payment of customs tax. Customs check-posts on the borders were burnt down. In view of the government's ban on it, the Communist Party functioned from Vijayawada.

The army and the Razakars resorted to large-scale terrorism and even took to methods such as murder, arson, and rape. In the beginning, the Congress and Communist squads worked hand in hand. The Congress set up its camps on the borders and from there made counter-raids on the police and the Razakars. While the communists squad mainly worked from within the state, a few were set up on the borders and particularly in the Munagala enclave situated in the district of Nalgonda. Students boycotted schools and colleges, many village officials ceased to cooperate with the government, and clashes between the people and police became frequent. During the day, the Razakars and police forced the people not to cooperate with the Congress and the communists and in the night the Congress and communist volunteers would force the villagers not to cooperate with the government.[57]

Not being able to put up with these pressures and counter-pressures, some big landlords migrated to towns and others migrated to neighbouring states of the Indian Union. Those who remained in the villages were mostly from among the middle class and the peasantry. The communists took the latter categories of people into confidence and with their help intensified attacks on the police. In fact, the communist leadership made a study of the whole situation and arrived at the conclusion that the field was fertile for armed insurrection and guerrilla type of warfare. They procured arms from various parts of the country and established regular, armed squads all over Telangana.

In addition, in keeping with its ideology, the Communist Party raised the slogan 'land to the tiller' and began to work against the landlords. Tenants were asked to occupy lands and government-owned waste land was distributed among the landless. The Andhra Communist Party extended its support to the Telangana movement in all possible ways. In a way, the Andhra leaders were really guiding the movement. By the end of 1947, it was estimated that the communists had succeeded in distributing the land of the rich landlords among the poor and established local rule in about 3,000 villages. Munshi refuted this claim but felt that the number of liberated villages could not be less than 2,000.[58]

This full-scale armed revolt was not supported by the Congress Party leadership at both the national and state levels. In January 1948, Ramanand Tirth dissociated the Congress from the armed clashes. Naturally, the talk of radical land reform and the sectarian policies of the communists antagonized the landlords. The Congress was in favour of agrarian reform but was certainly not in favour of a class conflict in any form. Consequently, the Congress, which initially worked along with the communists in resisting the Nizam, withdrew and left the communists all alone in the field. In fact, the communists and the Congress were involved in some kind of infighting. They even began to throw bombs at one another's camps. Despite this, the way in which the communists increased the number and the strength of their squads is noteworthy. Village squads 'with about 10,000 members and regular guerrilla squads with more than 2,000 members were formed'.[59] A field survey of eight villages in Suryapet taluk revealed that in each village between three and twenty-three members joined the village communist bands and a majority of them belonged to the lower caste peasant groups. Some also belonged to the locally dominant Reddy and Brahmin castes. In the liberated villages, Gramraj was established.

By about June 1948, civic life in Hyderabad state virtually came to a standstill. The Razakars terrorized the people. They killed a number of villagers who were suspected of anti-government activities. In one village, 19 Hindus and non-Muslims were made to stand in a line and (were) shot dead by the police.[60] Similar incidents took place in many villages. Fifteen people were shot dead in one village on the same day; and in four villages of Suryapet taluk of Nalgonda district, thirteen persons were killed. It was estimated that 'between April 1947 and March 1948 approximately 250 villages in the state had been looted or burnt. Four thousand houses set on fire, 500 persons killed or wounded and 450 women molested' by the Razakars.[61]

In the villages, the communist-inspired revolutionary spirit was on the increase and the influence of the Congress had waned. The communists killed seventeen persons in the seven villages studied by the author. All those killed were either rich peasants or supporters of the Nizam's government. Three out of the seventeen were Razakars. In all the villages, the landlords left villages and took refuge in the towns or in the border villages. In three villages, the lands belonging to the landlords were distributed among the tenants and poor peasants. A government report said that

> From the 15th August 1946 to 13th September 1948, they (the Communists) brutally murdered nearly 2,000 persons, attacked 22 police out-posts, seized and destroyed village records, manhandled a large number of village officials, burnt 'chawdis' and customs out-posts, captured 230 guns, looted or destroyed paddy and robbed cash and jewelers worth more than a million rupees.[62] They attempted large-scale disruption of communications and lines of supply and transport and steadily and systematically adopted the technique of guerrilla, fighting with the arms and resources at this disposal.[63]

Even so, the Hyderabad government lifted its ban on the communists and put many Congress leaders behind bars. This further led to the growth of communist power in the countryside. It was under these conditions that the Union government took police action in September 1948 against the Nizam and made the state of Hyderabad a part of the Indian Union.

The Third Phase: Armed Struggle and People's Resistance

It is now clear that during the first phase the peasant movement came under the influence of the Communist Party and the communist-led AMS; and in the second phase, after independence in 1947, the Communist and the Congress parties put up a joint front against the Nizam but soon the upsurge against the Nizam and the Razakars turned into an armed struggle against the Nizam's government led by the communists, while the Congress and the Communist Parties fell apart. The anti-Hindu behaviour and anti-people's stand of the government was also a factor which encouraged people of all classes to support the united front of the Congress and the communists. In both the phases, the communist-led upsurge which turned into a class struggle and this slowly alienated the communists from the landlords as also from rich peasants. It was also evident that the Congress government at the centre looked upon the communist-led armed struggle with resentment.

After the police action, military rule was established. The Razakar menace was curbed and the Razakar leaders, Kasim Razvi and others, were put behind bars. People supported the army in arresting the Razakars. Those who had temporarily migrated to the towns and border areas settled back in the villages. Landlords made efforts to take back their lands which the communists had distributed among the poor. The Congress Party was the main adviser to the military government and participated in the civil government established sometime later. This naturally went against the communists and their activities. Landlords and rich peasants began to support the Congress.[64]

All these developments went against the gains made by the Communist Party so far and the party, therefore, found itself in a strange situation. After serious deliberations, the Communist Party decided to revitalize its armed struggle against the new government with the avowed aim of consolidating the gains of their struggle in favour of the poor peasants and the rural labour force.

Guerrilla warfare again spread to different villages and communist squads took shelter in the villages in the plains and slowly moved to the forest-tribal areas as well. Consequently, the landlords and the village officials again moved to towns and cities for shelter.

But slowly the guerrilla squads found themselves in a helpless situation. The army made large-scale arrests and killed the communist guerrillas and their supporters in the villages and tribal areas. The Congress and the local leaders openly supported the army in its raids on communist hideouts and the arrest of Communist leaders.[65] The army intensified combing operations and tortured the communists and their supporters. The Communist Party had taken arms from the Razakars when they were surrendering themselves to the Indian army but the quantity was not sufficient for their task. Hence, the communists established their own centres of production of arms in the forest areas.[66] However, as the pressure from government increased and the people began to withdraw their support, it became impossible for the Communist Party to continue the armed struggle. Ravi Narayana Reddy writes that

> The party was in a state of disarray as a result of these large-scale arrests and many people were put in jails. Thousands

of Comrades were either arrested or they resigned from the party unable to withstand cruel torture. Those who resigned were all put behind the bars. With a membership of thousands the party strength dwindled to hundreds by the end of 1948. Fifty to hundred members were left in each taluk. They were not able to face the army in the plains and as such it became essential to move into forest areas for self-defence.[67]

Sundarayya presents a vivid picture of the atrocities committed by the military and the activities of the communist squads during the period.[68]

The communist leaders began to differ on the question of the continuation of the armed struggle, its nature, and the strategy to be adopted. Discussions were held for and against adopting the Chinese path and on the character of the struggle in Independent India.[69] A delegation of the Communist Party also met the Communist Party of the Soviet Union and Comrade Stalin. It was observed that as the support of the people became less and less, the armed struggle was getting transformed into acts of individual terrorism and, therefore, it was decided that the armed struggle be withdrawn.

It was clear that fighting the powerful Indian Union was not the same thing as fighting the crumbling regime of the Nizam, which was supported only by the minority religious community. Before making an open declaration of the termination of the struggle, the party tried to bargain with the government and obtain some concessions in favour of its leaders and the guerrilla volunteers. In the face of an uncompromising attitude on the part of the government, the party unilaterally declared, in October 1951, to withdraw the armed struggle unconditionally. The party also took a decision to take part in the general elections of 1951–1952. Since there was a ban on the party, the communists joined hand with other political elements and took part in the elections under the banner of People's Democratic Front. The Front won a big majority of seats in Nalgonda and Warangal districts. Thus, the Communist Party of India entered the era of parliamentary democracy in India.

After the police action, the Congress Party tried to spread the message of Gandhiji in different parts of the state of Hyderabad. As a part of this programme, Ashrams were set up in some villages. Outside the state, Acharya Vinoba Bhave was propagating the Sarvodaya philosophy. In April 1951, a Sarvodaya Sammelan was conducted in a village near Hyderabad to which the Acharya was invited. After the Sammelan was over, the Acharya decided to undertake a two-month *padayatra* and visited villages which had experienced the communist-led armed struggle. People in the countryside were surprised to see him and his followers walking through the villages across the hilly terrain without any fear of the army or the communists. He also took every opportunity to meet the communist leaders and wean them away from the path of armed struggle.

On 18 April, the Acharya camped at Pochampalli village where some local villagers had been killed by the communists. In a prayer meeting which was attended by the villagers, the local Harijans requested his assistance for obtaining some land for cultivation.[70] This request of the Harijans made Vinoba Bhave realize the importance of the problem of land in any effort to drive the peasants and labourers away from the path of violence. He immediately requested his audience to come forward with *bhoodan* to the Harijans. One rich farmer by the name of Ramachandra Reddy announced a donation of hundred acres of land.

Encouraged by this response, Vinoba Bhave took up the Bhoodan movement and spread it all over the country. U. Kesavarao, a long time worker in the Bhoodan movement, explained the significance of 18 April and the Bhoodan movement. According to him, the number eighteen is associated with a number of events in Hindu culture. The *Bhagavad Gita* has eighteen chapters, and the Kurukshetra war was fought for eighteen days with eighteen *akshownee* of troops. It is not our concern here to discuss the merits and demerits of the movement. What is, however, significant for us to note is the fact that a non-violent movement emerged out of the ashes of a violent revolution. The Bhoodan movement presupposes a change of heart on the part of the landlords. Even though Ravi Narayana Reddy did not agree with this ideology, he rightly claims that 'the peasant struggle for land was a prelude to the Bhoodan movement'.[71]

It is difficult to pass any judgement on the failure or success of the Telangana armed struggle. The judgement depends on the indices we adopt for measuring its success or failure. One thing is clear—the Congress government could not be blind to the movement if it were to gain legitimacy and public acceptance. The objective conditions were of exploitation and underdevelopment, and the misdistribution of land was the most important of all the problems. Accordingly, the governments which were formed after the 'liberation' of Hyderabad state took reformative measures one after the other.

The jagirdari system was abolished and progressive land reforms were enacted. Despite many loopholes in the implementation of the acts, the land reforms gave security to the tenant, and many became 'protected tenants' and subsequently became owners of the lands under their cultivation. The communist-led peasant movements, with its ideology of class struggle, definitely made the landlords feel that it would be difficult for them to continue to maintain large holdings and encouraged them to dispose of a major portion of their lands.

The above are some of the most important reasons that led to the call off of armed struggle in 1951, and there was no significant communist activity till 1967. Some consider this period (1951–1967) as a dormant period in the history of communist struggle, however there was high intellectual activity and introspection with the communist circles.

PERIOD OF INTELLECTUAL CHURNING: 1951–1967

The communist parties have played the important role of mobilizing the discontent or the rural masses in Telangana. The CPI played this important role during the Telangana peasant movement of the 1947–1949. In fact, as already discussed, this movement was the first major experiment of the CPI in insurrectionary revolutionary strategy.

The period of 1951–1967 was the most important chapter in the Indian revolutionary movement. We can call this period as churning ideology decade towards revolution. Here, interestingly Telangana provides a base to the formulation and formation of revolutionary communist parties such as CPI (M) and CPI (ML) which are splits of CPI.

The Telangana struggle, as Sundarayya says, brought to the fore 'almost all the questions concerning the strategy and tactics of the Indian people's democratic revolution for correct and scientific answers and realistic solutions'.[72] The origins of the

1962–1963 Indian communist split can be traced to the difference over the Telangana line during its last two years. Sundarayya rightly observes that these differences crystallized into two hostile trends and those who opposed the struggle are by and large with the present day CPI, while those favoured it went to the CPI (M). Though the CPI split synchronized with the international schism and was hastened by it, it did not represent a straight Moscow-Peking polarization. The real ideological split in the Indian communist movement came after Naxalbari, in 1968.

The 'national democracy' concept added a new dimension to the CPI's continuing struggle for a new programme to replace the 1951 document. As Nehru's domestic policies shifted to the right and tension grew on the Sino-Indian border, the attitude to the Indian bourgeoisie continued to be the central issue in the CPI debate which took a predictable form: national democracy versus people's democracy.

The Right-wing of the CPI, which had the Soviet backing, contended that India's bourgeois democracy could metamorphose into a national democracy. It placed heavy reliance on Soviet aid as the instrument to secure national democracy. The Left wing countered this by arguing that the bourgeoisie was compromising with domestic reaction and imperialism. Soviet aid, although necessary, was being used by the bourgeoisie to bargain for more aid from the West. Rival programme drafts were presented at the CPI's sixth Congress and the split was averted only by the intervention of Mikhail Suslov,[73] who headed the high level CPSU delegation to the CPI congress. Suslov, anxious to preserve CPI unity, managed to salvage the rightist line and to manoeuvre the congress into shelving the issue of a new CPI programme. The conflict continued behind the scenes until the CPI split in 1964, after which the CPI as well as what later came to be known as the CPI (M) adopted their own programmes.[74]

Thus, the factors underlying the 1962–1963 split date back to the Telangana armed struggle and the differences over it. The real significance of Telangana however lies elsewhere: it was the first application of the Maoist revolutionary model outside China even before the Chinese revolution had triumphed fully and China had proclaimed itself a people's republic. Over 20 years later, Naxalbari brought to the fore once again all the theoretical and ideological questions concerning the strategy and tactics of the

Indian revolution but in changed context: the international communist movement had split on issues of ideology and Moscow had ceased to be the sole centre of the International Communist Movement.[75]

Notes

1. Anwar Quereshi. *The Economic Development of Hyderabad*, Vol. 1. Bombay: Orient Longmans, 1947. p. 10.

   See also Barry Pavier. *The Telangana Movement 1944–51*. New Delhi: Vikas Publishing, 1981. p. vii.
2. Anwar Quereshi. *The Economic Development of Hyderabad*, Vol. 1. Bombay: Orient Longmans, 1947. p. 10.
3. Puchalapalli Sundarayya. *Telangana People's Struggle and Its Lessons*. New Delhi: Foundations Publications, 1972. pp. 4–5.

   See also Qureshi, Anwar Iqbal. *Economic Development of Hyderabad*, Vol. I. Bombay: Orient Longmans, 1947. pp. 110–111; Khusro, Ali Mohammad. *Economics and Social Effects of Jagirdari Abolition and Land Reform in Hyderabad*. Hyderabad: Osmania University Press, 1958. p. 5.
4. See "The Paigas" in AISPC File No. 65, 1938–1949 (Manuscript Section, NMML). pp. 6–7. This booklet studied three big Paigas in the state and came to the conclusion that these Paigas owners were a "typical feudal class," p. 17.
5. See for the conditions in these "Samsthanas", a research note by Nippani Ranga Rao "Misrule in Gadwal" in AISPC File No. 65 and 39, 1939. pp. 1–5.
6. Barry Pavier. *The Telangana Movement 1944–51*. New Delhi: Vikas Publishing, 1981. p. 8.
7. Quereshi, AI. "The Economic Development of Hyderabad", *The Rural Economy*, Vol. 1, Bombay: Orient Longmans, 1947. pp. 38–39.

   See also A.M. Khusro. *Economic and Social Effects of Jagirdari Abolition and Land Reforms in Hyderabad*. Hyderabad: Government of Andhra Pradesh, 1958. pp. 3–4.
8. Puchalapalli Sundarayya. *Telangana People's Struggle and Its Lessons*. New Delhi: Foundations Book Publications, 1972. p. 5.
9. Government of Hyderabad, *Report of the Administration of the H.E.H. the Nizam's Dominions for 1303 Fasli.* (1893–1894), pp. 14–15, for general summary and extent of land tenures (HAS).

10. See Inam Lands, File No. 29/13/50, Record No. 20 (HAS) and *The Imperial Gazetteer*, No. 2, p. 279.
11. Iyengar, S. Kesava. "General Survey", *Economic Enquires in Hyderabad State*. Vol. 1. Hyderabad: Government of Hyderabad, 1931, p. 12.
12. Puchalapalli Sundarayya. *Telangana People's Struggle and Its Lessons*. New Delhi: Foundations Books Publications, 1972. p. 6.
13. See Report of the Reforms Committee. 1938 (1347F.) (Hyderabad Deccan: Government Central Press, 1938), pp. 62–63.

    See also *Golconda Patrika*, 13 August 1936 for the big landholdings in various districts.
14. See also Syed Sirajul Hassan, *Castes and Tribes of HEH The Nizam's Dominions* (Bombay: 1920, and Census of India, 1941, Hyderabad), Vol. II, pp. 673–674.
15. Anwar Qureshi and Anwar Iqbal. *Economic Development of Hyderabad*, Vol. I. Bombay: Orient Longman, 1947. p. 28.
16. D.N. Dhanagare. "Social Origins of the Peasant Insurrection in Telangana", *Contributions to Indian Sociology*. New Delhi: Vikas Publishing, 1974. p. 113

    And also see Gray, Hugh. "The Landed Gentry of Telangana, Andhra Pradesh", Leach, Edmund, and Mukherjee, S. (Ed.). *Elites in South Asia*. London: Cambridge University Press, 1970. p. 129.
17. Iyengar, S. Kesava. *Rural Economic Inquiries & the Hyderabad State 1949–1951*. Hyderabad-Deccan: Government of Hyderabad, 1951. p. 333.
18. Ibid., p. 342.

19 In 1931, Population Census Report Muslims formed about 13 per cent of the state's population.

20 Anwar Qureshi Iqbal. *Economic Development of Hyderabad*, Vol. I. Bombay: Orient Longman, 1947. p. 30.

21. Smith W., Cantwell. "Hyderabad Muslims Tragedy", *Journal of Middle East*, Vol. IV, No. 1, 1953, 2–4.
22. Ravi Narayana Reddy. *Heroic Telangana: Reminiscences and Experiences*. New Delhi: Communist Party of India, 1973, p. 9.

    See also Pavier Barry. *The Telangana Movement 1944–51*. New Delhi: Vikas Publishing, 1981. p. 70.

    Nalla Narasimhulu, a contemporary of Ravi Narayana Reddy and P. Sundarayya also gives the details regarding in his autobiography titled *"Telangana Sayudaporatam: Naa Anubhavaalu, Gnanapakaalu."*

23. Ravi Narayana Reddy. *Heroic Telangana: Reminiscences and Experiences*. New Delhi: Communist Party of India, 1973. p. 9.

    See also Barry Pavier. *The Telangana Movement 1944–51*. New Delhi: Vikas Publishing, 1981. p. 69.
24. Reformist Hindu organization formed in Bombay in 1875.
25. Bahadur Yar Jung was a nobleman, perhaps that has something to do with the direction taken by the Ittehad.
26. Pavier (1981: 51) describe Ittehad specifically using this term.
27. Ravi Narayana Reddy, *Heroic Telangana: Reminiscences and Experiences*. New Delhi: Communist Party of India, 1973. p. 9.

    See also Barry Pavier. *The Telangana Movement 1944–51*. New Delhi: Vikas Publishing, 1981. pp. 69–112.
28. There are five languages. In descending order by number of speakers, they were Telugu, Marathi, Urdu, Kannada and Lambadi.
29. Ravi Narayana Reddy. *Heroic Telangana: Reminiscences and Experiences*. New Delhi: Communist Party of India, 1973. pp. 2–3.
30. In Urdu there is a saying-*telangi bedhangi*. Pejoratively used, it equated everything telangi with that which is deficient or inapt.
31. D.N. Dhanagare. "Social Origin of Telangana Insurrection (1946–51)", *Contribution to Indian Sociology*, Vol. 8, No. 8, 1974, 118.
32. Ravi Narayan Reddy. *Heroic Telangana: Reminiscences and Experiences*. New Delhi: Communist Party of India, 1973. pp. 1–12.

    See also Barry Pavier. *The Telangana Movement 1944–51*. New Delhi: Vikas Publishing, 1981. pp. 65–67.
33. Ravi Narayan Reddy. *Heroic Telangana: Reminiscences and Experiences*. New Delhi: Communist Party of India, 1973. p. 11.
34. Ibid., p. 14.
35. Barry Pavier. *The Telangana Movement 1944–51*. New Delhi: Vikas Publishing, 1981. p. 79.
36. Mohan Ram. *Indian Communism: Split within a Split*. New Delhi: Vikas Publishing, 1969. p. 5.
37. Ibid., p. 5.
38. M.R. Masani. *The Communist Party of India*. London: Verschoyle, 1954. p. 59.
39. Ibid., p. 59.
40. Barry Pavier. *The Telangana Movement 1944–51*. New Delhi: Vikas Publishing, 1981. p. 80.

41. Puchalapalli Sundarayya. *Telangana People's Struggle and Its Lessons.* Calcutta: Communist *Party* of India (M), 1972. p. 21.

    See also Barry Pavier. *The Telangana Movement 1944–51.* New Delhi: Vikas Publishing, 1981. pp. 80–85.
42. Ravi Narayan Reddy. *Heroic Telangana: Reminiscences and Experiences*. New Delhi: Communist Party of India, 1973. p. 19.

    See also Dhanagare, D.N. "Social Origins of the Peasant Insurrection in Telangana", *Contributions to Indian Sociology.* New Delhi: Vikas Publishing, 1974. pp. 116–117.

    Barry Pavier. *The Telangana Movement 1944–51*. New Delhi: Vikas Publishing, 1981. p. 83.
43. M.R. Masani. *The Communist Party of India*. London: Verschoyle, 1954. p. 79.
44. Ravi Narayana Reddy, *Heroic Telangana: Reminiscences and Experiences*. New Delhi: Communist Party of India, 1973. p. 34–35.
45. Ibid., p. 23.
46. Ibid., p 35.
47. There were 16 annas to a rupee.
48. See details Ravi Narayana Reddy. *Heroic Telangana: Reminiscences and Experiences*. New Delhi: Communist Party of India, 1973. pp. 20–22.
49. Palme Dutt was a member of the CPGB who was very influential in the politics of CPI.
50. Barry Pavier. *The Telangana Movement 1944–51*. New Delhi: Vikas Publishing, 1981, p. 88. Also see Dhanagare, D.N. "Social Origins of the Peasant Insurrection in Telangana", *Contributions to Indian Sociology*. New Delhi: Vikas Publishing, 1974. p. 118.
51. Ravi Narayana Reddy. *Heroic Telangana: Reminiscences and Experiences*. New Delhi: Communist Party of India, 1973, p. 42.
52. Barry Pavier. *The Telangana Movement 1944–51*. New Delhi: Vikas Publishing, 1981. p. 87.
53. Ibid., pp. 82–83.
54. Ravi Narayana Reddy. *Heroic Telangana: Reminiscences and Experiences*. New Delhi: Communist Party of India, 1973. p. 39.
55. Puchalapalli Sundarayya. *Telangana People's Struggle and Its Lessons.* Calcutta: Communist Party of India (M), 1972.

    See also Ravi Narayana Reddy. *Heroic Telangana: Reminiscences and Experiences*. New Delhi: Communist Party of India, 1973. pp. 28–32.

56. Nalla Narasimhulu. *Telangana Sayudha Poratam: Na Anubhavaalu*. Hyderabad: Vishalandhra Publishing House, 1989. p. 6.
57. *Mahojwala Telangana Rythanaga Sayudha Poratam-Viluvyna Anubhavalu*. Vijayawada: Janashakthi Prachuranalu, October, 1997. pp. 13–15.
58. M. Munshi Kanaiyalal. *The End of an Era: Hyderabad Memories*. Bombay: Bharatiya Vidya Bhavan, 1957. p. 154.
59. P. Sundarayya. *Telangana People's Struggle and Its Lessons*. Calcutta: Communist Party of India (M), 1972. p. 60.
60. M. Munshi Kanaiyalal. *The End of an Era: Hyderabad Memories*. Bombay: Bharatiya Vidya Bhavan, 1957. p. 76.
61. Ibid., p. 137.
62. P. Sundarayya. *Telangana People's Struggle and Its Lessons*. New Delhi: Foundation Books Publication, 1972. pp. 102–128.
63. Ibid., p. 128.
64. *Mahojwala Telangana Rythanga Sayudha Poratam-Viluvyna Anubhavaalu*. Vijayawada: Janashakthi Prachuranalu, 1997. pp. 18–20.
65. Ravi Narayana Reddy. *Veera Telangana–Na Anubhavaalu, Gnapakalu*. Vijayawada: Vishalandhra Publishing House, 1972. pp. 23–24.
66. Nalla Narasimhulu. *Telangana Sayudha Poratam: Na Anubhavaalu*. Hyderabad: Vishalandhra Publishing House, 1989. pp. 84–85.
67. Ravi Narayana Reddy. *Heroic Telangana: Reminiscences and Experiences*. New Delhi: Communist Party of India, 1973. pp. 60–61.
68. Sundarayya, P. *Telangana People's Struggle and Its Lessons*. New Delhi: Foundation Books Publications, 1972. pp. 95–99.
69. *Manaku Teliyani Mana Charithra: Telangana Rythanga Poratamlo Sthreelu*. Hyderabad: Stree Shakthi Sanghatana Prachuranalu, 1986, pp. XVII–XVIII.
70. Com. Devulapalli Venkateswara Rao. *Telangana Prajala Sayudha Poratam*. Hyderabad: Porunela Prachuranalu, 2014. pp. 37–41.
71. Ravi Narayana Reddy. *Heroic Telangana: Reminiscences and Experiences*. New Delhi: Communist Party of India, 1973. p. 78.
72. P. Sundarayya. *Telangana People's Struggle and Its Lessons*. New Delhi: Foundations Book Publications, 1972. pp. 392–393.
73. Shantha Sinha. *Maoist movement in Andhra Pradesh*. Unpublished PhD Thesis. New Delhi: JNU, p. 76.

74. Com. Devulapalli Venkateswara Rao. *Telangana Prajala Sayudha Poratam*. Hyderabad: Porunela Prachuranalu, 2014. pp. 493–518.
75. Mohan Ram. "The Telangana Peasant Armed Struggle, 1946–51". *Economic and Political Weekly,* Vol. 8, No. 23, June 9, 1973, 1025–1032.

III

Radical Left Movement in Telangana

The countryside in Telangana, the northern part of the Indian state of erstwhile Andhra Pradesh, has been witnessing an armed rebellion. Thousands of young men and women, inspired by revolutionary ideology, have taken up arms to put an end to what they call an exploitative socio-economic order and to overthrow the existing state power. The main objective of their struggle is to bring about a peasant revolution according to the Chinese model in India. These revolutionaries are organized and led by the most radical faction of the Indian Marxist-Leninist party CPI (ML). Historically, the roots of the contemporary CPI (ML)-led movement in Telangana lie in the Srikakulam Naxalite rebellion of the late 1960s. The Srikakulam rebellion, in turn, is considered to be a continuation of the Naxalbari peasant struggle.[1] Therefore, the current movement in Telangana is also regarded as a yet another expression of the Naxalite phenomenon.

Beginning in the early 1970s and continuing since, the Telangana Naxalite movement is perhaps the most long-drawn revolutionary people's struggle in Indian history. Over the years, the movement has grown in both intensity and magnitude and has become the most dominant aspect of the social and political life in northern Andhra Pradesh. The movement is perceived as a serious challenge to the law and order situation in the state. However, the larger significance of the movement lies in the fact that it is a socio-economic movement manifesting itself in a revolutionary political form. Although it is derivative of the Naxalbari movement and the Srikakulam struggles, the Telangana Naxalite struggle has nevertheless acquired a character and identity of its own. This chapter tries to map the trajectory of the Telangana Naxalite movement. It seeks to describe the nature of the movement and how it progressed over the years; and finally, to draw parallels and contrasts between the Telangana Naxalite movement and the Naxalite movements of the late 1960s.

THE GROWTH OF NAXALISM IN TELANGANA

The CPI (ML) and the Andhra Pradesh Revolutionary Communist Centre (APRCC) played an important role in leading the struggle in Telangana. It was the APRCC that initiated the struggle. The question as to how the Naxalite activity spread to the Telangana region has much to do with the APRCC's tactical line.[2] After its withdrawal from the scene in Srikakulam, their actions were based on a theory of uneven development. According to the APRCC, 'India with its size and sociocultural diversities presented not just one but different stages of development of revolutionary situation'. From this theoretical standpoint, the APRCC classified areas on the basis of regional variations into two groups: (a) areas with active struggles, (b) areas with party organization and inactivity as far as the movement was concerned, and areas with no organization and no activity. The leaders of the APRCC, T. Nagi Reddy (TN), D. Venkateshwara Rao (DV) and Chandra Pulla Reddy (CP), toured parts of Andhra Pradesh to propagate the line of 'graduated and protracted struggle'. Of the three regions of erstwhile Andhra Pradesh—Coastal Andhra, Rayalaseema, and Telangana, at first, the Coastal and Rayalaseema districts were tested for revolutionary potential.[3] However, the APRCC was unable to start any militant mass movements here. These areas were more useful in getting financial support for the party. The party's attempts at starting mass movements met with more success in the Telangana districts. As the APRCC began to organize movements in Telangana, differences in ideological and methodological position between its leaders started to plague the movement. While CP and his followers insisted on a more militant approach in leading struggles, very much akin to that of the CPI (ML), the other two leaders—TN and DV—continued to assert the APRCC's original tactical line of 'graduated and protracted struggle'. In 1970, the APRCC split into two distinct groups, one under the leadership of CP and the other led by TN and DV.[4]

Meanwhile, the CPI (ML) Andhra unit, after the complete withdrawal of struggle in Srikakulam, also started to concentrate its efforts on Telangana. The most significant development on this format of the Naxalite movement was the breaking up of the CPI (ML) at the national level. After the death of the party ideologue Charu Mazumdar in July 1972, the party disintegrated into myriad groups and factions. The major reason for the split in the party was the differences with the party's high command, Charu Mazumdar. The failure of the Naxalbari and Srikakulam movements proved the ineffectiveness and still more the disastrous nature of the 'adventurist line' propagated by Mazumdar. The rumbling of discontent with the tactical line of the party that began with the closing of the Srikakulam chapter finally resulted in the breaking up of the party immediately after his death. The party at the national level split into two camps, the pro-Charu and the anti-Charu factions. The anti-Charu faction was led by Asim Chaterjee and S.N. Singh and the pro-Charuite group was represented by Mahadev Mukherjee.

The implication of this split for the Naxalite groups in Andhra Pradesh led to the breaking up of the CPI (ML) Andhra committee as well. The group that had the largest following was the faction led by Kondapalli Seetharamaiah, which was pro-Charuite in its ideological and tactical position. This group joined the pro-Charu camp at the national level and together they formed the Central Organizing Committee (COC). The CP group united with the anti-Charu S.N. Singh group to form the Provisional Central Committee, while the TN group joined the anti-Charu group to form the Unity Centre of Communist Revolutionaries of India [UCCRI (ML)].

It is interesting to note that all three linkages with respective national level factions proved to be short-lived. By 1980, all three groups in Andhra resumed an independent existence. Many other tiny groups emerged through further splits and dissensions. But none of them could pose a serious challenge to the domination of the first three. Of the three, the group led by Kondapalli was the most powerful. Until 1980, this group functioned under the banner of the COC even though the alliance with the national level faction was long broken. In 1980, this group formally came to be known as the People's War Group (PWG) and since then it has represented the mainstream of the Naxalite movement in Andhra Pradesh.[5] Before an attempt is made to study the nature and different aspects of the Naxalite movement led by PWG in Telangana, it is important to analyse why the movement has occurred in this part of the state.

Therefore, the study will now examine the historical and political influence and other particularities in the Telangana region which have precipitated in the rise of a people's movement here.

The Roots of Naxalite Movement in Telangana

The Telangana Naxalite movement is primarily a socio-economic movement and therefore the roots of the movement are also essentially socio-economic in nature. A look at the conditions in Telangana even as late as the 1990s presents a grim picture.[6] Glaring economic inequalities, feudal social relations, an ever growing army of agricultural labourers, and overall economic underdevelopment of the region are striking.[7] The economic and social dimensions of exploitation in this region were summed up in the following words:

> While the Telangana region itself is known as a backward area, still more backward are the Karimnagar and Adilabad districts.[8] The striking factor in these districts is the extent of concentration of land in the hands of the top few which gives the landlord a political power which enables him to reign unchallenged. A cursory glance at the still prevailing social customs alone is sufficient to understand the degree of feudal exploitation. The social norms of behavior which the landlord imposes have to be scrupulously followed, whereby a peasant cannot wear white clothes, he cannot wear chappals (footwear) in the presence of the landlord and cannot send his children to school.[9]

Further, the proportion of agricultural labourers in Telangana is one of the highest in Andhra Pradesh. In the districts of Adilabad, Karimnagar, and Warangal, the number of agricultural labourers living below the poverty line was as high as 95.8 per cent, whereas in other parts of Andhra Pradesh it is recorded to be between 50 and 60 per cent.[10]

The living conditions of the poor peasants in the Telangana while no doubt oppressive and miserable are not too different from those experienced by people in other parts of rural India where revolutionary type movements have never occurred. Hence, socio-economic deprivation alone may not be an adequate reason to account for the manifestation of a revolutionary peasant struggle in Telangana. What then could adequately account for the occurrence of this prolonged revolutionary struggle? It can be argued here that three factors have played an important role in this regard: first, the social structure of the Telangana region; second, the role of the political system and the political elite; and third, the organizational capacity of the communist parties operation in Telangana. Each of these factors will be examined in greater detail in the next sections.

INFLUENCE OF POST-INDEPENDENCE DEVELOPMENTS ON SOCIAL STRUCTURE

This study now examines the impact of the developments in post-independence period on the social structure and relations between the various classes in rural Telangana. The most significant development on the agrarian front in this period was the introduction of technological innovations in agricultural production to increase food output. This strategy popularly referred to as the 'green revolution' laid emphasis on the use of high-yielding seed varieties, fertilizers, pesticides, and tractors in the agricultural production process. The general overall effect of green revolution on India was that it had led to a substantial increase in agricultural output. However, the impact of green revolution was not uniform in all areas. The implications of this strategy for the socio-economic profile of Telangana are crucial for our understanding of the Telangana movement.

The area that benefited most from the green revolution was 'wheat belt' of northern India which covers the states of Punjab, Haryana, and parts of Uttar Pradesh, which, even before the introduction of green revolution, were known to be agriculturally productive regions. Owning to the profitability of agriculture, the peasants in these areas, both rich and middle class, were seriously involved and were more willing to invest in agricultural production. Therefore, when the methods associated with the green revolution were introduced, the peasants in these areas took up agriculture on capitalist line and became a class of enterprising commercial farmers.

In erstwhile Andhra Pradesh, in contrast, large-scale mechanization of agricultural production did not occur.[11] The landlords and rich peasants in this region were not willing to invest much in agricultural production on their own, seeking only the inputs for irrigation which the state provided through its irrigation projects. The main effect of the green revolution, however, was that because of the introduction of modern irrigation projects by the state, larger tracts of land were brought under cultivation and new cash crops were introduced.[12] This had the effect of increasing the demand for agricultural labourers. With increased employment opportunities, the bargaining power of agricultural labour was greatly strengthened. The most important benefit of this increase in demand for agricultural labourers was that in addition to the opportunity of gainful employment it also gave the agricultural labour a sense of social and psychological freedom. This is well brought out by Frankel in her study of the effects of the green revolution on West Godavari district of Andhra Pradesh. She argues:

> With greater opportunities for work, casual labourers can now earn as much and more than permanent labourers. The landless no longer need to seek the protection of a permanent patron-client relationship in order to ensure their livelihood. On the contrary, they are in a position to choose their employer and even bargain over terms. This increase in concede the independence and dignity of agricultural labourers .... Landowners grumble at these trends, yet seem reconciled to the erosion of old status relationships and their replacement by new contractual agreements based on mutual satisfaction of both sides.[13]

Frankel, in her case study of West Godavari district, relates the social and psychological freedom earned by the agricultural labourers to their poor response to the efforts of the communist parties in organizing and leading peasant movements here.

It must be noted, however, that the social benefits of increase in demand of agricultural labourers did not have the same effect on all categories of landless labourers. It is the 'casual' labourer as against the 'permanent' and 'bonded' labourer that benefited most in this deal. The reason for this is obviously the absence of any previous agreement or any other sort of obligation of the casual labourer towards a particular employer, in contrast to the tied down situation of the bonded labourer. In Telangana, the social and psychological benefits of the green revolution were denied to the majority of landless labourers as bonded labourers were relatively larger in number in Telangana owing to the past feudal social structure.[14] Perhaps it is this denial of social freedom that has made the agricultural labour class in Telangana more susceptible to adopting more radical and violent means for fulfilling their demands.[15]

In sum, the social structure of the Telangana region is a representative of the semi-feudal and semi-capitalist order. As a result, the poor peasants of this region were subject to two forms of exploitation. First, under the impact of commercialization they suffered from the economic exploitation of the capitalist system. Second, due to the persistence of medieval feudal social institutions in the modern era they also suffered from the social exploitation of the feudal order.[16] Thus, the social structure of the region had resulted in sharpening class contradictions in this region.

AGRARIAN SCENARIO IN NORTH TELANGANA

The Naxalite movement was very active in the north Telangana during the 1970s, and it is necessary to understand the agrarian conditions of the region. Socio-economic conditions in the Telangana countryside, despite the state's agrarian reformist intervention, presented a country of oppressive landlordism. The ecology of this region presented extremely unequal landownership patterns, and the dominance of landed exploitative social relations showed the implementation of the tenancy and land ceiling legislations in poor light.

In the early 1970s, most of the villages in the district of north Telangana were still dominated by the landlords, as in Telangana of the 1940s. Dora usually dominated not only his village, but also a cluster of villages. Most of the doras belonged to the Velama,

Reddy, and in some cases Brahmin castes.[17] The variety of labour services extracted by doras from different castes in the Telangana countryside could be classified into two categories. The first form is the one related to the production process; the second is that which takes place outside the production process. *Vetti* (forced labour), which was a predominant form of labour exploitation and subjugation in the Telangana countryside until the 1940s, when the peasantry and agrarian poor rose in revolt against such a practice, continued in its form and spirit until the 1970s in certain pockets of northern Telangana, such as Karimnagar, Warangal, and Adilabad. This refers to all forms of 'extra-economic' exaction of labour and goods.

The *vetti* system can be defined as a deformed version of the *jajmani* relationship.[18] The violation of the principle of exchange and mutual cooperation is the quintessence of the *vetti* system, which prevailed in certain part of Telangana until the 1970s. The peasants were required to supply *vetti nagallu* (a free supply of ploughs) for a request number of days to the landlord; demands were also made upon the peasants to supply *penta* (organic manure), regardless of their own requirements. Shepherds, who usually charged a certain amount to farmers for resting their flock of sheep on their farms during the night, were to rest *vetti mandallu* (sheep herds) on the landlords land. Artisan such as blacksmiths (*Kammari*) and carpenters (*Vadla*) were required to repair the agricultural implements of the dora without any payment.[19]

In the case of agricultural labour castes such as the Madigas and Malas (*called vetti madigalu and vetti malollu*), *vetti* services were to be rendered to the landlord for requisite number of days on a priority basis during peak agricultural season, when there was a high demand for labour. Even when payment was made, it was less than what was paid by the rest of the farmers. *Vetti* is not limited to services and goods related to agricultural production alone but quite significantly extend to domains outside the production process.[20] Every caste had to supply its services and goods free of charge to the dora. Thus, the *Goudas* (toddy-tappers) had to reserve certain high yielding Palmyra trees for the dora, tap them, and supply the produce for free. The village *Kummari* (potter) supplied pots; *Chakalis* (washermen) and *Mangalis* (barbers), in addition to their caste occupation-related services, had to perform other household chores at the *gadi* (residence of dora).[21]

The Telangana also witnessed another change in the late 1960s. With the entry of industrial products into a rural markets, traditional, rural artisan communities experienced a gradual decline of their economic position and significance in rural society. Two numerically large communities that felt the impact of this competition on their livelihood patterns were the traditional handloom weavers and the Madiga leather workers. The former were affected by the entry of cheap powerloom products into the rural markets, which eroded their livelihood and caused their entitlements to decline. This forced the men to shift to work with the powerlooms and their women to beedi making. Technical change in agriculture led to a decline in demand for leather chappals, as preference was given to industrially produced *chappals* (footwear). This forced the Madigas to turn to agriculture as an alternative form of income. This only increased the pressure on agriculture and created surplus labour facilitating the 'landed classes' to hold onto the labour. This scenario formed the backdrop of the agrarian unrest for the class politics and mobilization in rural northern Telangana.[22]

Although the beginning of peasant unrest were visible in the early 1970s, it is only in the post-emergency period that an increased and expanded mobilization of the agrarian poor was witnessed in northern Telangana. The defeat of the Congress Party government at the centre, a sense of relief from long months of Emergency rule, during which even minimum democratic rights were denied, paved the way for popular assertion from below.[23]

POLITICAL FACTORS

Two political factors have played an important role in making the region ripe for revolutionary movement. The first is the politics of land reforms in the state and the second is the process of political accommodation in Andhra Pradesh.

The Politics of Land Reforms

Since independence, the Indian government has undertaken several land reform measures to reduce economic disparities on the agrarian scene. The land reforms initiated by the state can be classified into three types: (a) legislation for the abolition of intermediaries; (b) legislation for tenancy reforms; and (c) land ceiling legislation.

The abolition of intermediaries was the first major step of the state in the direction of land reforms. Under this piece of legislation, feudal systems of land tenure such as the zamindari and jagirdari systems were to be completely abolished. The Andhra Pradesh Estate Abolition and Ryotwari Tenure Amendment Act of 1948 led to the dissolution of the jagirdari system in Telangana and Ryotwari tenure was established throughout Hyderabad state.[24] The abolition of the jagirdari system undoubtedly put a formal end to an outright feudal setup. Illegal extraction of revenue by Jagirdars was completely stopped.[25] However, the jagirdari abolition had resulted in the dissolution of a class of wealthy landlords and the emergence of rural middle-level landlords.[26] It is in this context the rise of Reddy caste to political power occurred in Telangana. Under the rule of the Nizams, some of the Reddys merged with the medium landlords. In this manner, a broader and firmer base was acquired by the Reddy community to project its political power. This development coincided with the inauguration of electoral politics and the rise of the Congress Party to power for the first time in the erstwhile state of Hyderabad. The Reddy landlords of Telangana continued (and still continue) to dominate the Congress Party in the region ever since, that is, even after the merger of the Telangana region into the larger Andhra Pradesh state in 1956.

> (Under the Nizam) there were Reddi holders of jagirs ... but Reddis were not prominent in administration or in politics ... . The Reddis were always landlords—whether with large, medium or small holdings—but under the Nizam their power until the 1930s was localized and outside the capital. With the police action and the abolition of jagirs, the powerful Reddis to emerge were the medium landlords.[27]

Tenancy reforms were the second set of land reform measures undertaken by the state. These reforms were meant to protect tenant cultivators from unnotified evictions and exorbitant rents imposed by landlords and to ensure security of tenure to seek to ordinary tenants into a class of protected tenants. In erstwhile Andhra Pradesh, an act to this effect—Andhra Pradesh (Telangana area) Tenancy and Agricultural Lands Act—was passed in 1950.[28] Forty-five per cent of the tenants in Telangana became either owner-cultivators or protected tenants as a result of this act. But, it must be noted that this act was first implemented in the 1950s, soon after the Telangana peasant uprising, when the influence of the CPI was still strong in Telangana. But, when the Congress Party came to power in 1950, the power of the Communist Party got reduced and the rural elite began to exert their influence once again. Many landlords challenged the act in the law courts and this allowed many an unscrupulous landlord to escape the rigors of this law and to evict unprotected tenants.[29]

The third category of land reform legislation was related to land ceilings. Soon after independence, the Indian government recognized the need to redistribute land in rural India in order to break up concentrations of landownership and also to ensure employment and a reasonable standard of living to all. A model version of such laws was recommended by the central government and several state governments enacted legislation on such lines. In erstwhile Andhra Pradesh, the Andhra Pradesh (Telangana area) Tenancy and Agricultural Lands Act imposed limitations on the maximum area an 'individual' could own.

Of all the categories of land reforms, the land ceiling laws have always been the most controversial and difficult to implement. Litigation has been only one of the villains of the piece. Lack of political will compounded by the compulsions not to upset the interests of political support structures and vested interests is another significant factor. In erstwhile Andhra Pradesh, landlords have always been a very powerful pressure group. With quite a few of them in positions of political authority in the state, the landlord lobby has been slowing down legislation, and when the implementation of the ceiling laws began, a group of 800 landlords from the state met the Prime Minister Mrs Indira Gandhi and appealed for a re-examination of land ceiling laws. Although in this case the landlords' attempt failed, the influence exercised by this group was still considerable in contributing to delays and circumventions in the implementation of the act.[30]

The wide array of land reform measures initiated by the state brought about several notable changes in the agrarian structure in

Telangana even though the problem of rural poverty could not be efficiently handled. The jagirdari abolition reforms had only benefited the landlords and rural elite. The tenancy and land ceiling laws, which could have, if properly implemented, improved the conditions of the poor and landless peasants, remained only on paper. However, the major impact of these state policies was that of raising the expectations of the people. Also, the few minor changes that were brought about as a result of these reforms had the effect of emboldening the masses to demand further changes in their conditions of living. Given the magnitude of the agrarian problem on the one hand, and the absence of political will and administrative and judicial impediments on the other, the state was unable to meet the demands of the people. Thus, the Telangana Naxalite movement could in one sense be regarded as a revolution of rising expectations of people leading to a flood of frustration.

The Process of Political Accommodation

In 1969 Telangana Movement for separate statehood was predominantly led by students and youths. They formed Telangana Praja Samithi (TPS) to expose their statehood cause and elected Marrichenna Reddy as the party president. After Congress government repressed the movement by killing 369 students, Marrichenna Reddy in stead of fighting for the cause, merged his political party with Congress. This political betrayal by the leaders led to a huge unrest among students and youth, many of whom took revolutionary path in Telangana.

SRIKAKULAM MOVEMENT

Background

On 31 October 1967, at Levidi, in Parvathipuram agency area situated on the north-eastern tip of Andhra Pradesh, two tribal peasants were shot dead by agents of landlords. This confrontation was the culmination of an extensive history of struggles by the *jatapu* and the *Savara* tribals—and also constituted a turning point for the future course of history.[31]

Parvathipuram agency belonged to the Srikakulam district and was about 300 square mile in area. Adivasis or tribals who resided generally on the forest hills of the region were known as

Girijanulu. The forest played a vital role in their day-to-day living. They survived on 'podu' or what was well-known as shift farming, under which bits of forest were cut down and burnt. The land was then cleaned and used for harvesting the crops, mostly food grains. They depended on this kind of cultivation until the British people came to power.

In earlier times, the adivasis used to enjoy ample privileges and rights over the produce of the forests—fruits, roots, leaves, and wood. However, during later times, the regulations brought for the protection of forests banned their access to miniature forest products for household uses.[32]

As in the other parts of rural India, here also the hold of the moneylenders was strong over the poor tribals, several of whom were reduced to landless labourers, and they disposed of their rights on the forest and were forced to live in miserable conditions as wage labourers in their own lands. The local administration firmly implemented a set of laws for forest protection depriving the adivasis from a secured life and disrupting their social life. Meanwhile communist teachers began working among the tribals by the 1950s. It should be noted in this connection that the tribals of this region had a streak of militancy. From 1922 to 1924, in the Vishakhapatnam Agency nearby Srikakulam, tribals fought a war against the British, under the leadership of Alluri Sitarama Raju who used guerrilla strategies against the British rulers.[33]

The cluster of communist teachers who organized the Girijans for a movement against illegitimate extractions by the landlords and for better wages was led by Vempatapu Satyanarayana, who settled down among the tribals. He used to be addressed as 'Goppa Guru' or chief guru among the tribal population. His militancy struggles against the local landlords made them inconvenient and there were a number of efforts to kill him between 1960 and 1967. Under Satyanarayana's leadership, an organization called *Girijan Sangham* was set up to struggle for the betterment of the tribals. Its first meeting was held at Mondemkhal in January 1961.

The movement which began for enhanced wages and against persecution by forest officials rapidly developed into a rebellious struggle for the right to yield on wastelands. After the split in the Communist Party in 1964 and until the formation of CPI (ML), Satyanarayana and Adhibhatla Kailasam another teacher who was working among the tribal peasants in the Parvathipuram agency led the movement.[34]

The police were fast reacting. Thousands of Girijans were detained, and a number of cases were booked against the poor tribals. Verifying the conspiracy between the political parties behind the landlords and the police, a newspaper reporter commented 'they (the political parties) relied and continued to rely heavily on the police to keep the tribals in check'.[35]

Nevertheless, neither the high-handedness of the landlords, nor police pressure could break the wave of the Girijans' militancy. By 1967, the landlords were forced to raise the wages of the labourers and grant two-third share of crops to the share-croppers. These successes made the tribals' trust more in political associations.

The administration was, however, getting alarmed. After the Naxalbari rebellion in May–June 1967, the authorities, apparently apprehending similar troubles in the Parvathipuram agency, set up police patrol. The landlords under police security sought to reassert themselves and continued their violence on the Girijans. Following conflicts, Section 144 was declared in 200 villages from 24 July to 25 August 1967.[36]

It was against this background that the 31 October episode happened at Levidi. A Girijan convention was being held on that date at Mondemkhal. Some Girijans on their way to the convention were beaten by the landlords at Levidi. As a fight developed between the Girijans and the landlords' men, the latter brought out their guns and shot dead two peasants.[37]

During this period, the CPI (M) party supported the poor tribals and condemned police action and demanded the government to implement the laws, which were brought for the benefits of the tribals. They further demanded the state government to take necessary steps and vacate the *shavukars* and illegal landlords from tribal areas. However, their party did not support the revolutionary guerrilla struggles. Thus, the Communist revolutionaries working among the tribals, who were the members of the CPI (M), suspected the party because of the insensitive attitude of the Andhra Pradesh CPI (M) leadership towards the subjected tribals.[38]

By early 1968, police atrocities augmented. Special police camps were brought into the affected areas. By March, hundreds of villages were attacked and many small tribal peasants were arrested and put behind bars.

In Burajaguda village of Seetampet agency, peasants were assaulted by hired goons of the landlords. Police fired on tribals in Peddakaraja village which was under Sivinpet police station.

In September 1968, the judgement of the Levidi case was declared. Those charged of killing the tribals were not found guilty. This judgement, along with the police oppression, hardened the attitude of the tribals. The Marxist revolutionaries explained the peasants that in the established socio-economic setup the legal system was a sign of the welfare of the ruling feudal class.[39]

Therefore, the revolutionary party asked the tribals to free themselves, fight against the landlords and state machinery which had until then worked only for the benefit of the ruling classes. 'if we have to carry on our activity on any people's issue, our struggle should be higher inform aimed at seizing political power.[40]

For this purpose, the Srikakulam communist leaders took the initiative to accept the strategy of the communists of Naxalbari and contacted the All India Coordination Committee for Revolution (AICCR).

The Andhra Pradesh CPI (M) state committee mainly the dissident group rejected the central committee's official draft on the question of the 'big bourgeois', which ruled the country which was of a comprador-bureaucratic nature, a characterization which the CPI (M) was not ready to recognize.[41] For dissident Andhra communists, the 'comprador nature consists mainly in its trading character in addition to industrial aspect, bureaucratic character in its growth with the main assist of the State machine'.[42]

Thus, two branches of armed struggle developed in Andhra Pradesh, one in Srikakulam in the north-east and the other covering the Telangana region; the former led by Tarimala Nagi Reddy (TN), Devulapally Venkateshwara Rao (DV), Ramanarshaiah, Chandra Pulla Reddy, Baththula Venkateswara Rao, and Rayala Subhash Chandra Bhosu.[43] However, these two branches were originally divided into two groups due to ideological tactics and strategies regarding how to proceed with the revolutionary movement.

The Differences in Leading the Revolution

The differences were primarily concerning the strategies to be followed. Nagi Reddy and his faction—Andhra Pradesh Revolutionary Communist Committee (APRCC) which was formed in March 1968, were in favour of a mixture of legal and extra-legal resists, and assumed in a lengthened groundwork, essentially through economic struggles, prior to the initiation of a complete armed movement. The communist revolutionaries of Srikakulam, were motivated by the armed struggle especially by the strategy of annihilation of the enemy of Bengali Naxalbari or All India Coordination Committee of the Communist Revolutionaries (AICCCR), which was formed in May 1968 and their experience in their own district, were in favour of immediate way out to arms.[44]

The Srikakulam district organization of the communist revolutionaries was politically revitalized at this time by the active support offered by a group of young communist medical and engineering graduates. The majority of these young blood graduates who were in their early life realized the liberal Congress government's acts of interruption and were attracted to Marxism in mid-1960s. The Naxalbari revolution and the ideological disparities within the CPI (M) facilitated them to take a step forward in the political understanding, and they slowly amended to the politics of agrarian revolution.[45] Medical students in 1968 formed the Naxalbari Sangeebhaava Committee in Guntur. Youth leaders such as Bhaskara Rao, Mallikarjuna Rao, and other established relationship with revolutionary leaders such as Vempatapu Satyanarayana. The Guntur group actively involved themselves in recruiting the middle class youth into party activities and getting the arms ready.[46]

Differences between the Srikakulam communist and the State Coordination Committee got widened by 1969. The Srikakulam wing decided to declare the war on landlords and state with full support and alliance from the Bengali Naxalbari Committee, while the Nagi Reddy group maintained an autonomous strategy even though they accepted the Naxalite movement.[47]

The Srikakulam communist sent Tejeswara Rao Chowdhury to Calcutta in October 1968, for a dialogue with Charu Mazumdar. After Tejeswara Rao's discussions, the newly formed

Srikakulam district coordination committee arranged a secret meeting at Boddapadu where it was determined that an armed struggle should be initiated without delay.

Guerrilla 'dalams' (or squads) were formed in the plains as well as in the hills of Srikakulam, with the eventual objective of capturing power by conquering the existing government and launching a people's democratic dictatorship led by the proletariat.[48]

Guerrilla Struggle in Srikakulam

The guerrilla movement advanced on 24 November 1968, by the forceful cutting of crops from the land of a rich landlord at Garudahadra, near Boddapadu. Another important triumph was that on the following day in Pedagottli village of the Parvathipuram agency area, about 250 Girijans from different villages armed with bows, arrows, and spears, under the leadership of Vempatapu Satyanarayana, attacked the house of a notorious landlord-cum-moneylender, Teegala Narasimhlu and took possession of his saved paddy, rice, other food grains, and property worth about ₹ 20,000. They also detained documents, promissory notes, and other records that had bound the tribal peasant all these years to the landlord through loans.[49]

Several similar actions followed, and the communists were able to raise daily wages and *jeethagla or paleru's* (paid servants) remuneration, provide the right to have share in crops to peasants, and distributed 5,000 acres of cultivable land to tribals. More importantly, revolutionaries made efforts to free the tribals from ancestral debts.[50]

Setback

By 1970, the Srikakulam armed struggle received a setback as leaders Sathyam, Kailasam, and others were annihilated by the police. Police forces set 300 tribals on fire during the revolt.[51]

Apart from this, the revolutionary communists organized secret convention at Guthikonda Belam, Pedugurall mandal in Guntur district in Andhra Pradesh from 19 to 21 February 1969. Panchadi Krishna Murty, Tejeswara Rao Chowdhury, K.G. Satyamurthy, Y. Koteswar Rao and his wife Mani, Aruna, Mamidi Appalasuri, Shaik Buday, Mulpuri Venkata Rathnam, Kondapally Seetharamaiah, and his son Kondapally Chandra Shekar attended this convention and it was addressed by the Bengali Naxalbari leader Charu Mazumdar.[52]

Tejeswara Rao Chowdhury was elected as state committee secretary and Kondapally Seetharamaiah was included in the party after the expulsion from United CPI party in 1964. After this meet K.G. Satyamurthy and Kondapally Seetharamaiah were given the responsibility to organize the party in Telangana region and the remaining members concentrated on coastal Andhra.

While the movement was gaining pace and spreading in the north-eastern parts of Andhra Pradesh under the Srikakulam group, on 7 February 1969, the AICCCR disaffiliated the Andhra State Coordinating Committee, particularly the Nagi Reddy group from the coordinative activities. On 22 April 1969, the Bengal Naxalite rebel communist formed Communist Party of India (Marxist Leninist)—CPI (ML)—which was actively associated with Srikakulam revolutionary group. Simultaneously in the Telangana region, the political developments among the rebellious communists were taking a different form.[53]

Reorganization

The original CPI (ML) that led Srikakulam struggle almost disintegrated, both at national and state levels with heavy repression on one hand and internal divisions on the other, by 1972, and there were attempts to rebuild the party or at least to coordinate the struggles in various areas. It was Andhra Pradesh State Committee that took lead in this direction and by January 1974, the CPI (ML) COC was formed with remaining forces of the CPI (ML) from West Bengal, Bihar, Uttar Pradesh, Kashmir, Punjab, and Tamil Nadu to coordinate and unite the revolutionaries in different states.[54] As part of the unity and consolidation efforts, it was also decided to critically review the past experience and pave the way for future. Thus, by November 1974 the COC had developed a Self-Critical Report and Road to Revolution, a new strategy and tactics document. These two documents humbly accepted the Left sectarian mistakes of the past and suggested several corrections. The corrections included setting up mass organizations and adhering to mass line without leaving armed struggle and continuing boycotting parliamentary path, the two distinct features of Naxalbari-Srikakulam line.[55]

EMERGENCY

However, when the attempts of the COC to set up mass organizations and spread its influence both in Andhra Pradesh and elsewhere were beginning to take shape, there was a severe jolt on the movement in the form of proclamation of Emergency in the country on 25 June 1975. The party hardly began implementing its policy of establishing mass organizations with an experiment in forming Radical Students Union (RSU) and preparing to form Radical Youth League (RYL), and RCS. With the proclamation of Emergency and suspension of fundamental rights, it was not possible for any democratic activity and the RSU could not take up its work openly in educational institutions.[56]

Even as half of Virasam members (35 out of around 60) were arrested and any person with remote Naxalite leanings was under surveillance and threat of immanent arrest, the members of RSU chose to go to villages to evade arrest. Particularly, their work in Karimnagar and Adilabad districts in analysing rural agrarian social structures, forms of exploitation, and the need to wage struggles paved way for mobilizing and organizing agricultural labourers and small peasants in a big way.

The twenty-point programme announced by the government at that time came in handy for these students in their campaign of exposing the shallowness of ruling class policies. By making people demand the implementation of some 'welfare' measures of the programme, these students could easily demonstrate that the government was not sincere enough to translate its promises into practice. Based on this realization, the students could persuade people to take up militant struggle path and inculcated the idea of agrarian revolution as the only alternative.[57] The RSU provided a fertile recruiting ground for PWG cadres and significantly expanded the original nucleus of activists. In the late 1970s and early 1980s, the RSU active on high school, college, and university campuses in the Telangana region and everywhere in erstwhile Andhra Pradesh organized indoctrination trips for students styled as a 'Go to villages' campaign on the model of Mao's China.[58] These campaigns reaped fruitful results in hundreds of villages with thousands of poor agricultural labour and small peasant masses rallying behind radicals.

RAITU COOLIE PORATAM IN SIRICILLA AND JAGITYAL

The Sircilla and Jagityal taluqs of Karimnagar district were important centres to the peasant struggle in Telangana region after the emergency period. These two taluqs saw initial attempts at agrarian mobilization in the early 1970s, inspired by the Naxalbari and Srikakulam uprisings.[59] The beginning of peasant movement in this area is seen as a result of the spread of the message of revolution from the tribal areas to the plains. Huge repression and the declaration of a state of Emergency in 1975 imposed severe restrictions on people movements and forces. The lifting of the Emergency and the coming to power of the Janata Party at the centre tremendously changed the political conditions in the state and the country.[60] The promise of improved civil rights paved the way for the RCSs to come into the open and organize the rural poor for better social change.[61]

The issues highlighted upon and the demands put forward in these struggles can be broadly discussed into two types. The first was the refusal to perform *vetti*, pay *mamools*, and approach the landlord for arbitration of disputes. The second category consisted of demands for higher wages, which were below the minimum wage prescribed by law, repayment of huge sums of money collected from the villagers as *dandugalu* (fines) and bribes taken earlier, and the return of lands forcibly seized from peasants.[62]

Demonstrating the popular response, the Sangham forced landlords to yield to the former category of demands. The initial success in villages such as Nimmapally in Sircilla and Maddunur in Jagityal demonstrated the possibility of organized protest succeeding in making landlords concede without much resistance. The spread of these success stories encouraged people in other villages to follow suit. It is no exaggeration to suggest that in the initial phases of the struggle, a mere call of 'social boycott' worked wonders, as this meant that, apart from stopping agricultural operations on the landlords' farms, no washermen or barbers would be available to provide (even paid) services at the landlord's *gadi*. This social boycott of the landlords by service castes in particular caused great inconvenience to their normal everyday lives.[63]

Thus, in the early stages of the peasant movement, 'social boycott' was used as the main form of struggle to exercise considerable social pressure on landlords and to isolate them in villages. The people in these villages stopped rendering *vetti* services, carrying disputes to the landlord, and offering *mamools* and bribes.[64] It is interesting to note that attempts were made to settle the disputes through public hearings. The success in this regard enthused people to push further for the second category of demands. What is noteworthy is the fact that in a number of places the RCS conducted public hearings to enquire into illegal exactions such as *mamools* and *dandugalu,* land-grabbing—both private and public or common—and landlord atrocities.[65] The landlords in these places were made to pay back huge sums to the people.[66] Similarly, attempts were made to settle disputes among the poor people.[67] As said earlier, huge tracts of the *poramboku, shikam,* temple lands, forest lands, and lands illegally held by landlords were distributed to the landless. Further, the demand for an increase in the wages of agricultural labour, *palerus* (farm servants), and tendu leaf[68] collectors were articulated.

The main issues taken up in the villages during this phase of the struggle can thus be summed up as follows:

Here the study list out some of the unendurable methods of oppression and exploitation perpetrated by the landlords. These landlords actually deserve to be called as despots of middle ages. Their oppressive activities can be listed endlessly. Here we deal with some prominent practices only:

1. Money extortions variously called as gifts, *nazaranas*, fines, and compensations.
2. Tributes: Annual *mamools* for each caste are fixed. Besides that, a certain amount should be paid as tribute on the occasion of joy, sorrow, or dispute.
3. *Vetti:* Labour, ploughs, sheep herds and goat herds, milk, provisions, vegetables, and all kinds of services should be rendered to the landlord free of cost.
4. Bonded labour.
5. Expulsion from village.
6. Usury.
7. Appropriation of commons and government lands.
8. Encroaching *patta* lands of poor and middle peasants.

9. Commission on sale and purchase of land and other assets.
10. Brokerage.
11. Exploitation of forest produce.
12. Processing and appropriation of loans from Land Mortgage Banks and Cooperative Central Banks.
13. Charging both the parties huge sums of money in the name of settling disputes.
14. Threats and intimidation.
15. Atrocities on women.
16. Social oppression.
17. *Mamools* from traders and contractors of various works.
18. Maintaining private armies.
19. Keeping licensed and unlicensed lethal weapons.

Given the substantial material interests involved in this, landlords opposed the demand to raise wages and surrender lands forcibly occupied from the peasants and the illegally controlled common lands. To achieve these demands, various forms of mobilization and methods of protest such as demonstrations, *gheraos*, strikes, and, of course, social boycotts were adopted by the RCS. As the movement expanded and the organizational structure of the RCS spread out following the *Jaithra Yatra* held in Jagityal town, the injury not only to landlords' *pettandari* (domination) and pride but also to their material interests became substantial and expansive, and they sought to quell the unrest.[70]

Reaction to the movement evolved in two phases. In the first, the landlords' response was local. They tried to organize gangs and use them against the peasant activists and to break the RCS network. Thus, beating up workers, raiding their houses, and unleashing terror became a common feature of the landlords' reaction.[71] The landlords resorting to violent means forced the RCS to shift away from its initial strategy of peaceful protest. The peasants organized resistance which led to a further escalation of violence from the landlords.[72]

The second phase of reaction to the peasant movement developed with the direct involvement of the state in the agrarian conflicts. As the movement expanded and an organized resistance was built up against the landlords, state reaction assumed a new form. Thus, the entire area was declared a 'disturbed' area, under the Suppression of Disturbances Act, 1948.[73] This act was enforced to tackle the spillover effect of the Telangana peasant struggle on the region of coastal Andhra 'to make better provision for the suppression of disorder in the Madras Presidency' and defines a disturbed area as one 'for the time being declared to be disturbed area by a notification under Section 3'.[74] The section referred to conferred the powers to declare thus to the subjective satisfaction of the provincial government, which so decided must notify the same in the State Gazette.

This response is a clear instance of the state understanding rural tensions as 'law and order' problems and suppressing them through violent means, rather than going to the root of the problem, that is, the socio-economic basis of rural unrest. This understandably generated its own dynamics: violence leading to further violence, without any light at the other end of the tunnel.

The two taluqs of Sircilla and Jagityal were declared 'disturbed areas' in the month of October 1978 under the Suppression of Disturbances Act, 1948.[75] It facilitated the possibility of collaboration between the police and the landlords, thus making the life of peasant activists much more difficult as they had to face not only the landlords' force but also the organized might of the state.[76]

THE PEDDAPALLI STRUGGLE

With the declaration of Sircilla and Jagityal taluqs as 'disturbed areas', attempts were made to extend and expand the movement to the neighbouring areas by forming RCS units. The movement in Peddapalli taluq thus assumed importance as the next phase of the peasant struggle.

Peddapalli, the third largest taluq in Karimnagar district, is important due to the two major Telangana industrial centres of Ramagundam and Godavarikhani, known for the thermal power project, coal mines, fertilizer, and cement factories that are located there. It had a population of more than 3 lakh in the 1970s, half of whom were workers. Agricultural labourers comprised only 55 per cent of the workforce.[77]

This taluq also displayed iniquitous land relations. Making best use of the loopholes of land ceiling laws, the landlords, belonging predominantly to the Velama community followed by Reddy, Kshatriya, and Brahmin castes, continued to own and control hundreds of acres of land.[78] A study by the District Weaker

Sections Association of the Congress Party identified 94 landlords with a landownership of 70 to 400 acres and stated that around 16,000 acres of land 'was transferred to various fictitious names overnight' in the taluq.[79] In this taluq, two or more big landlords, often belonging to different castes, dominated many villages. Thus, many villages often presented a picture of 'rigid caste divisions'. This was reflected not only at the grassroots level in political competition for political power, positions in Panchayat Raj institutions, and for a share in the resources made available for agricultural and rural development, but also in the political factions at taluq and district levels.

What is paradoxical about this region is the fact that despite the concentration of modern industries providing substantial employment to the labouring classes of the neighbouring villages, feudal relations of production were prevalent in the countryside.[80] The following extract from a report on the peasant struggle captures the essence of social relations in agriculture in the countryside:

> The *taluka* president of the Radical Youth League could think of only four landlords in the whole *taluq* who had tractors (in contrast to Jagityal where many landlords have turned modern). None of the landlords shows any interest in crops other than paddy and millets, and even then they do not go in for fertiliser-hungry high-yielding varieties but stick to the traditional ones. This is in spite of the fact that Peddapally now gets water from the Pochampad project (on the Godavari river), as a consequence of which the price of land has appreciated from about ₹ 3,000 to ₹ 20,000 per (wet) acre. Further, the clue for the absence of the impact of new wealth on the agrarian relations and prevalence of pre-capitalist agriculture could be seen as a consequence of the practice among the members of the landed gentry here to 'either consume' or 'invest' the surplus in mercantile activities rather than 'to transform it into productive capital'.[81]

As the same report further observes:

> Unlike the rich *kulak*s of Green Revolution Andhra, the landlords of Peddapally do not even invest in rice mills. Husking is done domestically, though many of them use machines for the purpose. Most of the surplus goes into PWD contracts (including the Pochampad canal itself), shops (the favourite being the

'wine' shops), and real estate in Karimnagar town or Hyderabad city.[82]

In spite of advanced industrial activity in the towns and this taluq, as in the case of Sircilla, Jagityal, and most parts of Telangana, extra-economic forms of exploitation such as *vetti*, *dandugalu*, and social and cultural degradation of the vast masses by the landed gentry were witnessed. This scenario in Peddapalli created favourable conditions for the peasant struggle.[83] If the repression in the area of Sircilla and Jagityal necessitated an expansion of the area of struggle, then the emergence of a land market and a hike in land prices following the Pochampad project were also important factors in increasing the landless and poor peasantry's hunger for land.

Thus, the struggle in Peddapalli was initially organized around two issues. The issue of repayment of people's money, collected by landlords in the form of *dandugalu* and *mamools*, was a major demand in the earlier phase. The value of the exactions was estimated and the demand to repay that amount back to the people was made. In addition, substantial donations were also demanded from landlords as reparation for their unjust actions in the past.

The second important issue was that of the distribution of *porumboku* and *bancharai* (the village grazing and wasteland) to the landless. As discussed earlier, these lands were invariably in the hands of the local *pettandar*[84] after forcibly occupying these lands with the RCS's help, an important aspect of the struggle was that these lands either be *equally distributed* on an individual basis among the landless or used for *collective farming*.[85]

The movement's major achievement lies in the fact that within the period of six months it took to expand, the practice of *vetti* and the collection of *dandugalu* and *mamools* completely stopped. The wages of agricultural labourers increased from ₹ 3–4 to ₹ 6–7 per day, while the increase was from ₹ 800 to ₹ 1,200–2,000 per annum for a *paleru* or farm servant. In a number of villages, the *poramboku* lands were occupied. However, although around 600 acres were available to be occupied, the peasants were able only to cultivate 30 acres.[86]

As the movement expanded in the taluq, the reaction from the powers-that-be also increased. Police camps were set up in the villages that had seen hectic activity by the RCS. The methods of repression employed by the police for crushing the people:

> make a macabre reading. They destroyed crops by driving animals into fields ripe for harvesting or by stopping water supply and starving the crops (it is a general rule that water from the local tank has to pass by the landlords' field to reach other people's fields and so the police only have to enlist the help of the only-too-willing landlords to stop water supply to the peasants' crops); if a peasant has a motor to draw water from a well, they would smash the motor and throw it into the well; if a peasant went into hiding they would raid his house and throw clothes, utensils and bags of paddy into the well.[87]

TENDU STRUGGLES

The struggles in Manthani have a special place in the history of the Karimnagar peasant movement. Located on the easternmost part of the district, the taluq includes 57 per cent of all forests in the district.[88] While the western part of Manthani consists of plains, the eastern part bordering Sironcha and Bastar in Mahadevpur area is mostly forest area. It is this geographical specificity that gave rise to struggles around the tendu leaf issue.[89]

Tendu leaf is used in the making of beedis (country cigars). Karimnagar and Nizamabad are important northern Telangana districts with a large concentration of beedi manufacturing units owned by both outside manufacturers and local persons. Manthani's importance lies in the fact that its forest area is a major source of the tendu leaf and that it supplies the beedi factories in the district.[90]

Tendu leaf collection is a seasonal occupation, taking place during the months of April and May. As this is the period when hardly any work is available for agricultural labourers, tendu leaf collection is the major source of sustenance during this lean season. Both children and women are engaged in this occupation in a major way.[91]

Collected tendu leaves must be sold to a contractor at his *kallam*. The right to purchase the leaf is auctioned to contractors by the government. Although the unit of auction generally consists of four to five villages, contractors bid for more; in fact, a few major contractors dominate the whole exercise of auction.

Contractors collect the leaves from the people through a network of *kalladars* (those who manage *kallams*).[92]

The tendu is purchased in bundles of 100 leaves. The minimum rate for a bundle in 1975 was five paise. Even this was not paid properly and promptly. Contractors used to pay only four paise per bundle. The poor people involved in the strenuous collection of tendu leaves had to give a requisite number of bundles as *vetti*, 'the first bundles brought to the *kallam* each day and one bundle each in the name of deities like Pochamma, Maisamma, etc.'.[93] The people were made to suffer further on account of the mischief and corruption of the petty *kalladar* employed as a collection agent by the contractor. The *kalladars*, paid a miserably low salary, resorted to various devious methods to augment their income. Thus, in addition to the collection of their share of '*vetti* bundles', *kalladars* used the rejection of bundles as a device to deceive people. The *kalladars* would pick up the bundles rejected as spoiled and make money on these.

This scenario gave rise to the famous tendu leaf struggles of the late 1970s. The struggle was for putting an end to the system of extracting *vetti* bundles, for the unreasonable rejection of leaf bundles by the *kalladars*, and for the payment of five paise per bundle as per the government stipulation. Later, struggles were launched for an increase in the purchase rate from five to ten paise.

The struggle for higher piece rates and against the high-handedness of contractors and the petty corruption of the *kalladars* at the time of leaf collection was a regular feature of the CPI (ML)'s mobilization strategy in the forest areas of northern Telangana districts such as Karimnagar, Nizamabad, Warangal, and Adilabad.[94] These struggles, in addition to those of women beedi workers, played a crucial role in preparing the ground and building a broad mass base for the CPI (ML) groups in this region.[95]

STATE RESPONSE TO THE NAXALITE MOVEMENT

One cannot deny the fact that Naxalite movement, from any perspective, from its inception to the present day, is a social movement. Any social movement strives for social transformation for a better society. And Naxalite movement, if not now at least in its initial phases, worked for the social transformation. They strove for the upliftment of the downtrodden. How to understand the acts such as rising of minimum wages of the labour or abolition of *vetti* (forced labour) or distribution of land to the landless but to agree the pro-poor stand of the Naxalites and the violence that they unleash? Here Azad says (an official spokesperson of CPI [Maoist]) though a Naxalite, the logic and weightage of the argument cannot be denied.

> The question of violence is the single most important thread passing through all the articles. No real communist is for violence per se. Communists are for a peaceful social system built around equality and justice. But when they seek to work for such a system they are attacked most brutally. This has been the case ever since the birth of the communist movement. They have been massacred and exterminated right from the days of the Paris Commune. It would be naïve to think that the Indian ruling classes, who have a lengthy record of violence unleashed on the oppressed masses, are any better. Besides it is not just State violence that people face; in a class society, as in India, violence is endemic to the very system and the oppressed masses are exposed to it in the course of their daily lives—by the feudal authority and by factory managements, and also as a result of untouchability, patriarchy, etc.[96]

We can argue that the use of violence is from two sides, the state and the Naxalites. But the state has also tried other tactics to tackle the Naxalite movement while it is vague that the Naxalites have also tried any such strategies.

State's response can be classified into two types: non-coercive measures and coercive measures.

Non-Coercive Measures

When the Naxalite struggle broke out in the Telangana districts in the early 1970s, the state government, then ruled by the Congress (I) under Chief Minister J. Vengal Rao, introduced some socio-economic welfare measures in the affected areas. These reforms show that the state government did in fact recognize socio-economic deprivation as one of the causes behind the uprising. During this phase (1970–1983), the state adopted mainly a 'preventive approach' towards the spread of Naxalite *influence.* Just as in Naxalbari and Srikakulam, the state did not show any sympathy towards the Naxalites and continued to look upon them as a bunch of criminals indulging in unlawful activities and used force to put an end to the Naxalite movement. However, it also tried to draw the rural poor away from the Naxalite influence by offering them certain economic benefits.[97]

Providing Livelihood

Agricultural cooperative banks were opened in the affected Telangana districts to provide loans to agricultural labourers and tribals. Agricultural equipment including diesel engines and cattle—sheep and milch animals—were distributed among the poor. These were meant as immediate measures to relieve the masses from poverty and to provide, in the short term, a source of livelihood to the poor.

Land Reforms

Apart from these rather less substantive measures, the Congress (I) government in Andhra Pradesh also undertook an aggressive campaign for land reforms. Of the three categories of land reform laws which were discussed in the previous chapter—abolition of intermediaries, tenancy reforms, and land ceiling laws—the last category and the most important of these, the land ceiling laws, officially began to be implemented during this period. It was precisely during this period that the revenue department in the state began filing declarations of the size of landholding from all landowners in the state.[98]

The government's socio-economic reform programmes of the 1970s did not help in improving the lot of the poor and landless in Telangana. In the first place, the government's immediate welfare measures were not a major success as they were not proportionate to the magnitude of the problem of rural poverty. Even for the few who benefited from them, these measures proved very inadequate. Second, with regard to the more critical measure, land reforms, the government dragged its feet on implementation.[99] The government's attitude reflected not just a lack of seriousness, but also a complete absence of political will about the implementation of land reforms.

The government laid emphasis on more superficial and ad hoc welfare measures, which were also inadequate, in preference to substantial long-term socio-economic reforms. The government did not seem very serious about the question of rural poverty but only appeared to make it an issue for political purposes. Thus, much of the talk about socio-economic change in the countryside was of little significance.

The same can be said about the successive governments which came to power after Congress (I). When TDP, the first non-Congress Party in Andhra Pradesh, came to power in 1983, it came with huge promises. Once, during his (NTR) election campaign, NTR termed Naxalites as 'true patriots'.[100] After forming his government, he announced 30 days truce period and had urged the Naxalites to join the mainstream. He had extended the period twice. He had also announced ₹ 1,00,000 to the surrendered Naxalites to help them in rehabilitation.

Throughout its regime, the TDP government relied chiefly on such efforts at reconciliation through negotiation to tackle the Naxalite problem. Other welfare measures aimed at improving socio-economic conditions of the poor in rural areas and bringing about much-needed change in the agrarian structure were ignored.[101]

By the end of 1989, the Congress (I) returned to power in Andhra Pradesh. This time the Congress (I) government took a more conciliatory and accommodative stand on the Naxalite issue, much in contrast to its ruthless and uncompromising approach in the late 1970s. This was perhaps in response to the civil liberties movement in the state which had repeatedly put pressure on the government to soften its approach towards the Naxalites. Soon after coming to power, Chief Minister M. Chenna Reddy released all the Naxalite prisoners held without trial. He also announced a policy whereby all legal activities of the Naxalite groups would be allowed. More importantly, a socio-economic welfare package was delivered to the affected areas to wean people away from Naxalite influence.[102] Plans to accelerate development of the nine 'Naxalite districts' were drawn up and implementation of these plans was entrusted to the local people, especially tribals and youth who were regarded as vulnerable to Naxalite influence. Usual bureaucratic procedures such as government licensing for contracts were relaxed in order to eliminate corruption and red-tapism. After Chenna Reddy's exit, his successor N. Janardhana Reddy adopted the same approach.[103]

This time, the state government seemed a little more serious about socio-economic development in rural Telangana, although it once again remained silent on the question of land reforms. But again, the government's efforts were not adequate to meet the magnitude of the problem of rural poverty.[104] Meanwhile, in a less repressive atmosphere which permitted legal activities, the Naxalites were able to regroup, reorganize, and extend their mass base. Following this, there was an increase in Naxalite activities in the state. Eventually, the government abandoned its soft approach and relied more on coercive means to put down the Naxalite activities.

Coercive Measures

The Naxalite movement is considered a serious challenge to the maintenance of 'law and order' in the state, and governments have often responded in ways they considered appropriate to meet the challenge. As in Naxalbari and Srikakulam, in Telangana also repeated attempts were made to crush the movement. During the 1970s, the Congress (I) government in the state made several efforts to nip the movement in the bud. In this phase, the state government was outright anti-Naxalite both in ideology and in practice. Its attitude perhaps stemmed from the bloody story of Srikakulam which was then still very fresh in everyone's memory. This period represents the most outwardly repressive phase of state response.[105]

The attitude of the government was reflected even in rhetoric. J. Vengal Rao, who was the Chief Minister as the Telangana Naxalite struggle unfolded, took tough stand towards these rebels as he took towards the insurrectionists of the Srikakulam rebellion of the late 1960s.[106] As early as 1971, just when isolated incidents of Naxalite activity were reported from Telangana, the state launched a police force on a military scale to crush the movement. Nearly 100 police camps employing 15,000 policemen were set up in the Naxalite affected districts of Khammam and Warangal. In addition, Section 144 of the Criminal Procedure Code (CRPC), according to which citizens are prohibited from moving in groups of more than two persons, was frequently imposed in those rural areas. Night time curfew was also imposed in these villages. The tough stand of the state did not, however, help in bringing down the movement. Between

1971 and 1974, the Naxalite movement spread to almost all districts in Telangana. In 1974—the pre-Emergency period—when Naxalite violence reached its zenith and a series of attacks was launched against landlords in rural Telangana, the state government went a step further in seeking the cooperation of the central government in inducting one of the paramilitary forces, the CRPF (Central Reserve Police Force), to quell the movement.[107]

In the following year, the imposition of national Emergency struck a serious blow to the movement.[108] At a time when even democratic opposition was not tolerated, the state's attitudes towards open and violent opposition was all the more tough. As a result, in the Emergency period the movement suffered a serious setback. All Naxalite groups went further underground.[109] Even nonviolent popular mass movements could not be organized. The success of state repression was such that the Naxalites had to confine their activities to publishing radical literature secretly.[110]

When, in 1977, the national Emergency was lifted and the Janata Party came to power at the centre, the tense atmosphere of the Emergency period gave way to a relatively relaxed political climate. Support for restoration of liberal democratic principles of freedom of opposition got a boost. Everywhere in the country, the state governments had to be accountable to the public and press charges against atrocities that were committed by the state apparatus during the Emergency times. In Andhra Pradesh also a similar movement for the restoration of civil liberties got underway. While it was, no doubt, felt in some official quarters that the pressure against the movement ought not to be relaxed, such was the reaction to the Emergency that governments were frightened of continuing with repressive policies even against violent challenges such as the Naxalite challenge. Thus, immediately following the lifting of the Emergency there was no option but to abstain from using repressive means.

Making a virtue out of necessity, the Andhra Pradesh government put forward a conciliatory stance towards the Naxalites. Paradoxically, this enabled the Naxalites to regroup their forces and start a more aggressive campaign against the state. In the early 1980s when the Naxalite movement gained substantial momentum and when normality was restored in the political atmosphere, the state government once again reverted back to its coercive methods. In 1978, the two Naxalite strongholds—Sircilla and Jagityal taluks, both in Karimnagar district—were declared to be disturbed areas.[111]

Under the Andhra Pradesh Suppression of Disturbances Act,[112] the police were allowed to open fire on mere suspicion at anyone. The disturbed areas proclamation can be regarded as a sort of mini-Emergency declared by the state government vis-a-vis the Naxalites. It was virtually a legitimization of police rule. It was this measure that helped in liquidating the Karimnagar peasant struggle discussed in the previous chapter.

The change of ruling party in the state legislature and the coming to power of TDP in 1983 did not, however, change the overall state policy towards the Naxalites. As noted earlier, this phase was marked by simultaneous efforts at peaceful reconciliation and brutal suppression. On the one hand, the government appeared to have made a dramatic change in its attitude towards the Naxalites. Initially, it even praised the Naxalites as 'true patriots' and made pious appeals and rewards for the so-called surrender of Naxalites. On the other hand, the government did not abjure dependence on coercive methods to tackle the problem.

One of the most unpopular policies of the NTR government was the move to liberalize arms licenses to help people defend themselves against Naxalites. This step of the TDP government was severely criticized and opposed by the general public and bureaucracy alike. Many interpreted this move as a deliberate attempt of the state government to strengthen the position of the landlord class in the rural areas, for the new policy would benefit only the rich. Others thought the policy was an irresponsible move which would only result in an increase in crime. In view of the public criticism, the government could not go ahead with the new policy. Another major step taken during the TDP regime was the government's creation of an elite police force called the 'greyhounds' meant specifically to tackle Naxalism. This special police squad was to consist of 800 personnel provided with sophisticated arms and specially trained for guerrilla warfare.[113]

In 1989, when Congress (I) returned to power in the state legislature, the Chief Minister, M. Chenna Reddy, had for a while given a degree of freedom to the Naxalites. After a brief phase of attempts at peaceful coexistence with the Naxalites, the state, in response to a growth in Naxalite activities, once again became determined to 'wipe out the Naxalites'. A marked alteration of government policy from a softened and conciliatory stand to an outright repressive stance is once again visible in this phase. The Andhra Pradesh special police, some central paramilitary forces, and a special task force of plainclothesmen began patrolling in villages in rural Telangana.[114] Five battalions of CRPF were deployed in Adilabad district alone, which since the late 1980s had become the strongest Naxalite foothold. A landmark event of state repression was the official ban on the PWG on 20 May 1992, in response to the PWG's violence. The ban gave unlimited powers to police and paramilitary forces, which significantly deterred Naxalite activities in the following months.[115]

So far, specific policies pursued by the two state governments in Andhra Pradesh—the Congress (I) and the TDP—to meet the Naxalite challenge have been outlined. Apart from these, there are also other coercive measures commonly used by both the Congress and the TDP governments in response to the Naxalite movement in the state.[116] In fact, this package of coercive measures is common to other parts of the country as well, where violent confrontations against the state have become manifest. The common package, known as TADA (the Terrorist and Disruptive Activities [Prevention] Act), emerged in 1985 in response to the violent secessionist movements in Punjab and the north-eastern states. In time, this act also came to be widely used in Andhra Pradesh to meet the Naxalite challenge.

TADA permitted police to arrest persons suspected of being involved in criminal activities against the state and retain them for an unspecified period without trial. In Andhra Pradesh, thousands of arrests have been made under this act. Innocent villagers who were suspected of aiding the Naxalites, tribals, rural youth, journalists, and civil liberties activists were booked under TADA and retained in prison for months or even years without even being produced before a magistrate, much less given a proper trial. Under Constitution which in spirit incorporates the principle that every person is innocent until proven, otherwise this act represented a mockery and in fact an antithesis of the legal system. It is a threat to the fundamental rights of citizens guaranteed in the Constitution.

In Andhra Pradesh, the state governments, both TDP and Congress, have resorted to the use of TADA as a means to curb Naxalism. In practice, TADA did indeed have a deterring effect on the spread of the Naxalite influence. The fact that in recent years the movement has become isolated from the masses and has become confined only to a limited number of people who are known as hard-core Naxalites can be, to some extent, attributed to the effectiveness of this act. It could deter potentially sympathetic groups from joining the Naxalite cadres.[117]

Along with TADA, there is the Andhra Pradesh Suppression of Disturbances Act, which, as mentioned earlier, provided the state government with wide arbitrary powers of detention, search, and seizure in areas declared as disturbed. This act has been declared in the Naxalite affected districts in Telangana a number of times since 1978.[118] This is the only law which in effect allows the police to open fire on groups of people on mere suspicion of being engaged in violent activities. This law gives the executive wide powers to confront violence and has been widely misused by the state. While in theory, this law permits police to act only if the suspect is armed and poses a considerable challenge to life and liberty of other citizens; in practice, the police have used the law to indiscriminately kill innocent people.[119]

The so-called 'encounter killings' in recent years are a consequence of this act. Typically, an 'encounter' is an incident in which armed Naxalite confront the police somewhere in a thickly forested area and an exchange of fire takes place between the two. The accidental death of a Naxalite in such a confrontation is described as an encounter killing. While this is what an encounter is understood to be, the reality is quite different. In the majority of cases, it is neither true that the victim is an armed Naxalite activist nor that he/she died after making an attempt on the lives of the police, thereby creating a situation where the police had to fire back in self-defence. In most cases, the victim is an unarmed villager who is taken into custody by the police on mere suspicion and shot dead in cold blood in the forest areas.[120] According to one estimate, 1,066 encounter deaths have been reported in Andhra Pradesh in the period between 1968 and 1993.[121] Most are instances of terrorism producing legal sanction for state terrorism which soon gets out of control in the dialectic of insurgent terrorism versus state terrorism. It is particularly against such state-sponsored terrorism that the civil liberties movement got started in Andhra Pradesh.

THE ROLE OF CIVIL LIBERTIES MOVEMENT

The Indian Constitution is almost unique among the Third World constitutions and for that matter even among those belonging to the so-called Western democratic world in incorporating a chapter on fundamental rights enforceable through judicial review. Though certain provisions compromising the true spirit of democracy, such as preventive detention, are written into the Constitution, the courts have afforded protection against the rigors of this provision.

A vigilant public opinion buttressed by a free press has also been a watchdog. Various associations promoting civil liberties have monitored the record of the government in the preventive detention area. However, there have been several instances, especially in times of acute crisis, when the government has resorted to extra-legal methods in order to deal with dissident groups.[122] There have been equally strong reactions from civil liberties associations protesting and condemning government actions. So effective has been the pressure from such groups that the government has often been forced to respond by taking certain remedial measures.

It is in the context of the state response to the Naxalite movement that the civil liberties movement in Andhra Pradesh started. The civil liberties movement in Andhra Pradesh today is headed by an organization of mostly urban middle class intellectuals, academics, writers, and lawyers, known as the Andhra Pradesh Civil Liberties Committee (APCLC). Before the formation of the APCLC, there were other civil liberties groups such as the organization of Peoples Union Democratic Rights (PUDR) and Citizens for Democracy, an organization established by Jayaprakash Narayan.

The role of civil liberties groups has been mainly in protecting the rights and liberties of minority dissident and radically protesting groups such as the Naxalites.[123] The Andhra Pradesh government's use of outright repressive means in dealing with Naxalites has attracted the attention of these groups and they have since been putting pressure on the government to adopt democratic methods in dealing with the Naxalites. Since the post-Emergency period, the civil liberties groups have been constantly exposing the extra-legal and unlawful methods adopted by the police, such as encounter killings and illegal detentions.[124] Often these groups have forced the governments at the centre and the state levels to check their policies and at times take serious remedial measures to correct them.[125]

The civil liberties groups, particularly since the post-Emergency period, have been involved in conducting inquiries into alleged violations of the human rights code by the state. In 1977, in the period following the rise of the Janata Party to power at the centre, Jayaprakash Narayan, as president of Citizens for Democracy, set up a committee headed by V.M. Tarkunde to collect evidence about the use of extra-legal means by the state vis-à-vis the Naxalites. The Tarkunde Committee, after a thorough investigation, concluded in its report that there was sufficient evidence to warrant a judicial inquiry into all so-called 'encounters killings' in Andhra Pradesh.[126] Further, the committee also concluded that the Andhra Pradesh government was heavily involved in the 'crimes' against the Naxalites.[127] It recommended that the central government institute a judicial inquiry into the encounter deaths that took place during the Emergency period.[128]

The Bhargava Commission was formed as a consequence of the recommendations. But it was the state government, under the direction of the centre, which constituted this commission. In fact, Justice Bhargava's name was suggested by the central government. The main purpose of the Bhargava Commission was to collect facts about the allegations of murder, torture, and brutal treatment of Naxalite prisoners and to suggest alternative administrative measures to deal with this problem in the future. However, the commission was not told to pinpoint the responsibility for the crimes (if any were committed). In the first few months of the inquiry, various non-governmental civil liberties groups participated in the proceedings of the Bhargava Commission. But, as the inquiry gained momentum, the state government's interference in the procedures of the commission increased.[129] One significant method of manipulation was the insistence of the government that the commission hold some of its sittings in camera as the issues unfolding before it were highly sensitive. This insistence of the state government came in response to threats from police officials to resign if further evidence before the commission were not gathered in camera.[130] With this, private civil liberties groups withdrew from the proceedings of the Bhargava Commission. Some of them instituted their own fact-finding committees.

Meanwhile, the Bhargava Commission, even within the narrow scope of its operation was eliciting evidence and it became evident both from the nature of the evidence gathered and the comments and remarks that Justice Bhargava was making during the inquiry that state government officials, especially the police, were coming under heavy indictment.[131] Soon the commission itself was wound up and its report never saw the light of the day. The whole Bhargava Commission inquiry proved only to be a farce, a half-hearted measure by the state to pacify civil liberties groups. Its importance is limited to being a symbolic gesture of the state's concern for civil liberties.[132]

The next major step taken by the Indian state towards protection of civil liberties was the establishment of a human rights commission by the central government. In view of the pressure from prominent human rights bodies such as Amnesty International and civil liberties groups in various parts of the country, the central government formed a national human rights commission in 1993 under the chairmanship of Justice Ranganath Mishra. Within a year of the formation of the NHRC, the APCLC, which had been the most active civil liberties association in the state, submitted a complaint against the Andhra Pradesh state government concerning the incidents of encounter killings of Naxalites. The commission responded with alacrity and a fact-finding committee of the NHRC visited Andhra Pradesh in August 1994. The inquiry proceedings of the NHRC reveal the power exercised by the police in Andhra Pradesh. All potential witnesses before the commission, particularly one member of the APCLC, were repeatedly harassed and even beaten up by the police. In spite of such obstacles, the commission conducted its inquiry.[133] (National Human Rights Commission, New Delhi, India. Annual Report, 1994–95, Chapter–IV).

PEACE TALKS

A situation has emerged in Andhra Pradesh, particularly in the Telangana area, where the states and its agencies show little respect for law and life and the Naxalite parties too practice ruthless violence regardless of people's concerns and sufferings. While one death is as tragic and as a meaningless as another, over 2,500 persons have been killed by the state in police encounters during the past 35 years, and almost as many have lost their lives at the hands of Naxalites during the same period. In this discourse of violence that has been engaging the state and the Naxalites, the society is getting progressively brutalized and people becoming increasingly insensitive, often reduced to passive spectators.[134]

The idea of the 'Peace Talks' was put forth by Committee of Concerned Citizens (CCC) in 2000.[135] The CCC stated that its purpose was to bring down the violence levels from all sides as well as more responsive and law-abiding governance, and an end to the excessive use of force. Initially, Naxalite were not keen to participate in the talks and even the government did not respond enthusiastically.[136]

Despite these obstacles, the CCC continued to try and persuade both the government and the Naxalites to engage in a dialogue.[137] In May 2002, the Peoples War unilaterally declared a ceasefire and appointed two representatives, a revolutionary poet and a singer, to discuss the modalities for talks with the government. From 4 to 11 June, they met two state cabinet ministers appointed by the government for this purpose, but these ministers lacked power and a clear agenda.[138] The government was only interested in a unilateral surrender of the Naxalites. The 2002 talks were not taken seriously and consequently the CCC's initiative was not successful.

In the May 2004 elections, the Congress Party promised in its manifesto to hold talks with the Naxalites. And after the Congress Party came to power, the Chief Minister immediately announced the stopping of police encounters and combing operations for Naxalites and called for talks. The CPI (ML)-Peoples War (Politburo and State Committee) as well as CPI (ML-Janashakti) announced their readiness for talks and a ceasefire on their part, if a ceasefire was announced by the government. The government announced a 'ceasefire' for a period of three months commencing from 16 June 2004, at the initiative of the Home Minister of the State, a series of discussions took place on various aspects of modalities for talks with the emissaries of Peoples War/ Janashakti, the CCC, and others. The ban imposed by the state government on the CPI (MdavarthyL) Peoples War and its allied organizations which was in force for almost nine years was allowed to lapse on 21 July 2004. For the purpose of having a conducive atmosphere for talks, there was an exchange of letters between the government and the CPI (ML)-Peoples War, CPI (ML-Janashakti) parties laying down the ground rules, to be followed during the period of the talks (commonly known as ceasefire agreement). A set of seven ground rules was also agreed upon. A monitoring committee was also set up to oversee the adherence to the ground rules.[139]

After finalization of the modalities and the tentative agenda; the Peace Talks actually commenced on 15 October 2004. The government team was led by the Home Minister Jana Reddy and consisted of some other ministers as well as leaders of the Congress Party. The team of mediators included S.R. Sankaran, K.G. Kannabiran, and six others. The CPI (ML)-Peoples War (which has since become known as CPI (Maoist), after the merger with Maoist Communist Centre) and CPI (ML–Janashakti) were represented by their state leaders. The discussions were completed with regard to the first two items of the agenda (out of a total of 11). The first item was with regard to the democratic atmosphere including withdrawal of cases against people for agitations; release of political prisoners; removal of price on the heads of revolutionary leaders, and controlling of mafia and anti-social elements. The second item discussed in great detail was land distribution to the poor, including issues relating to lands of tribal people. The first round of talks ended on the night of 18 October 2004 in a cordial atmosphere with the hope of meeting again for the next round to discuss other items such as self-reliance.[140]

The government termed the talks cordial and productive but the Naxalites described them as unsatisfactory because the government had given no concrete assurance. The mediators described the talks as historic and appealed to both the parties to maintain their restraint on the ground and hoped that the next round of talks could be convened in a month or two.[141]

But the next round of talks almost became impossible. The government neither showed any signs of extending nor extended the period of ceasefire. The cabinet met on 16 December when the ceasefire was due to be extended but said nothing, thus smashing any possibility of second round of Peace Talks. And the statements of the then Chief Minister Y.S. Rajashekhara Reddy that there would be no talks with Naxalites about peoples' problems and there would be no toleration of armed men and women further reflected the government's intentions.[142] The absence of any concrete agenda from the government's side and not providing the suitable platform for second round of talks showed the government in poor light and raised serious questions about its commitment in resolving Naxalite problem peacefully.

On the other hand, Naxalite parties gained a fresh ideological ground and sympathy among common people. During the last decade, Naxalite became infamous for causing loss to public property and killing police and political leaders. These talks provided them a chance to show the public that they fight for the public issues such as land distribution to the poor, free access to education and healthcare, regional underdevelopment, and corruption by government officials, when Naxalite leaders included these issues in their agenda.[143] This was also evident when scores of people went to meet the Naxalite leaders when they were stationed at the government guest house with their problems asking the leaders to include them in their discussions with the government.[144]

However Radical Left movement suffered a huge loss in terms of their cadre and top leaders. Soon after Peace Talks, top leader Riyaz was killed in an encounter.[145]

> There was a huge conspiracy behind 'Peace Talks'. Covert operations was in full swing and through its intelligence wing the State Government traced out important locations and Maoist hideouts in Nallamala forest and began the process of extermination.[146]

There was a severe repression on the party activities. They were pushed back from their strong holds to Chhattisgarh and Madhya Pradesh.

Notes

1. N. Venugopal. *Understanding Maoists: Note on Participant observation in Andhra Pradesh*. Kolkata: Setu Prakashani, 2014. pp. 11–14.
2. Vasanthada Ramalingachari. *Srikakula Girjanodyamam: Anubhavalu-Avagahana (Telugu)*. Hyderabad: Vasanthada Ramalingachari Smaraka Committee, 2005. pp. 98–101.
3. C. Bhaskar Rao. "The Problem of Fragmentation in the Naxalite Movement". Ed. by Pradip, Basu, *Discourses on Naxalite Movement 1967–2009: Insights into Radical Left Politics*. Kolkata: Setu Prakashani, 2010. pp. 345–360.
4. Meganath. *Comrade Tharimela Nagi Reddy Jeevitha Sangraham*. Vijayawada: T.N. Memorial Trust Publications, 1986. pp. 1–24.
5. M. Kodandram, S. Sudhakar (Ed.), *Moodu Dhasabdhala Naxalbari: Gamyam-Gamanam (1967–1997)*; Kodandram, M., *Moodu Dasabdhala Naxalbari Vudyamam*. Hyderabad: Perspectives Prachuranalu, 1998. pp. 21–29.
6. G. Satyanarayana. *Changing Agrarian Structure and Labour Relations*. Jaipur: Rawat Publications, 1992. pp. 32–33.
7. K. Balagopal. "Maoist Movement in Andhra Pradesh", *Economic and Political Weekly*, July 22, 2006, 3181–3187.
8. K. Balagopal. "Drought and TADA in Adilabad", *Economic and Political Weekly*, Vol. 24, No. 47, November 25, 1989, 2587–2591.
9. C.V. Subba Rao. "Resurgence of Peasant movement in Telangana", *Economic and Political Weekly*, November 17, 1979, 1869.
10. N. Venugopal. *Understanding Maoism: Notes of a Participant Observer from Andhra Pradesh*, Kolkata: Setu Prakashani, January 2013. pp. 30–32.
11. Robinson S. Marguerite. *Local Politics: The Law of the Fishes*. The Law of the Fishes: Development through Political Change in Medak District, Andhra Pradesh (South India). New Delhi: Oxford University Press, July, 1989. pp. 44–48.
12. Vamsi Vakulabharanam. "Agricultural Growth and Irrigation in Telangana: A Review of Evidence", *Economic and Political Weekly*, March 27, 2004, 1421–1426.
13. Francine R. Frankel. *India's Green Revolution*. Princeton: Princeton University Press, 1971. pp. 73–74.
14. Ajay Gudavarthy. "Telangana Movement: Democratisation? Or Authoritarianism", *Economic and Political Weekly*, Vol. XLVII, No. 37, September 15, 2012, 22–25.

15. Purendra Prasad. "Agrarian Class and Caste Relations in 'United' Andhra Pradesh, 1956–2014", *Economic and Political Weekly*, Vol. 50, No. 16, April 18, 2015, 77–83.
16. Personal Interview with K. Srinivasulu on 23 January 2015.
17. Barry Pavier. *The Telangana Movement 1944–51*. New Delhi: Vikas Publishing, 1981, p. 13.
18. D.N. Dhanagare. "Social Origin of the Telangana Peasant Insurrection (1946–51)", *Contribution to Indian Sociology*, 1983, 185.
19. K. Srinivasulu. "Caste, Class and Social Articulation in Andhra Pradesh: Mapping Differential Regional Trajectories" (monograph). London: Overseas Development Institute, 2002. pp. 18–19.
20. P. Sundarayya. *Telangana People's Struggle and Its Lessons*. New Delhi: Foundations Book Publications, 1972. p. 7.
21. Ibid.
22. Personal Interview with Kurra Rajanna, on 16 August 2014.
23. The proceedings of Bhargava commission constituted to examine the question of the violation of the human rights and fake encounters the developed coastal region has in a substantive sense of confidence among the CPI (ML) groups.
24. P. Sundarayya. *Telangana People's Struggle and Its Lessons*. New Delhi: Foundation Books Publications, 1972. pp. 328–329.
25. Devulapalli Venkateswarrao. *Telangana Prajala Sayudha Poratam*. Hyderabad: Porunela Publications, 2014. pp. 474–475.
26. M.S. Robinson. *Local Politics: The Law of Fishes: Development through Political Change in Medak District, Andhra Pradesh (South India)*. New Delhi: Oxford University Press, 1988. p. 51.
27. Ibid., p. 55.
28. Barry Pavier. *The Telangana Movement 1944–1951*. New Delhi: Vikas Publishing, 1981. p. 148.
29. For details see P. Sundarayya. *Telangana People's Struggle and Its Lessons*. Calcutta: CPM Publications, 1972. pp. 120–136.
30. D.N. Dhanagare. "Social Origins of Peasant Insurrection in Telangana, 1946–51". Ed. by Ghanashyam Shah, *Reading in Indian Government and Politics: Social Movements and the State*. New Delhi: Sage Publications, 2002. pp. 91–124.
31. Vasanthada Ramalingachari. *Srikakula Girjanodyamam: Anubhavalu-Avagahana (Telugu)*. Hyderabad: Vasanthada Ramalingachari Smaraka Committee, 2005. p. 94.

32. Sivarami Reddy. *Mahaththara Srikakula Poratam: Charitrika Parisheela (Telugu)*. Hyderabad: Chaganti Bhaskar Rao Publications, 2006. pp. 4–30.
33. See Nagi Reddy, N.S. *Communism in Andhra Pradesh*. Hyderabad: Cauveri Publications, 1989. pp. 100–119.
34. For details see Sivarami Reddy. *Mahaththara Srikakula Poratam: Charitrika Parisheela (Telugu)*. Hyderabad: Chaganti Bhaskar Rao Publications, 2006. pp. 74–95.
35. Ghanashyam Shah. *Social Movements and the State*. New Delhi: Sage Publications, 2002. p. 141.
36. "Reports on Srikakulam Girijan Movement", *Liberation* (An English Monthly Journal), May 1969, 7.
37. Vasanthada Ramalinga Chari. *Srikakula Girjanodyamam: Anubhavalu-Avagahana (Telugu)*. Hyderabad: Vasanthada Ramalingachari Smaraka Committee, 2005. pp. 96–97.
38. Nagam Kumaraswamy. *Dalits and the Autonomy: Towards Construction of Dalit Movement in Andhra Pradesh*, Unpublished PhD Thesis, Hyderabad: Department of Political Science, OUP, 2011, pp. 152–153.
39. Vasanthada Ramalinga Chari. *Srikakula Girjanodyamam: Anubhavalu-Avagahana (Telugu)*. Hyderabad: Vasanthada Ramalingachari Smaraka Committee, 2005. pp. 96–97.
40. Shah, Ghanashyam (Ed.). *Social Movements and the State: Readings in Indian Government and Politics*. New Delhi: Sage Publications, 2002. pp. 140–142.
41. Alam, Javeed. "State and Making Communist Politics in India 1947–57", *Economic and Political Weekly,* November 9, 1991, 2573–2583.
42. Ibid.
43. Manoranjan Mohanty. "Naxalite Vudyamam: Moodu Dasabdhala Anubhavaalu", Ed. by Kodandaram, M., Sudhakar, S., *Moodu Dasabdhala Naxalbari: Gamyama-Gamanam*. Hyderabad: Perspectives Publications, 1998. pp. 123–139.
44. Mohan Ram. *Maoism in India Delhi*. New Delhi: Vikas Publishing, 1971. pp. 196–200.
45. Rabindra, Ray. *The Naxalites and Their Ideology*. New Delhi: Oxford University Press, 1988. pp. 100–105.
46. Shivarami Reddy. *Mahottara Srikakula Poratam: Oka Charithraka Pariseelana*. Hyderabad: Chaganti Bhaskar Rao Prachuranalu, November 2006. pp. 310–311.

47. Chunnu Prasad. "Naxalism Fighting for What: Question of Exclusion, Dignity and Livelihood". Ed. by Pradip Basu, *Discourses on Naxalite Movement 1967–2009: Insights into Radical Left Politics*. Kolkata: Setu Prakashani, 2010. pp. 239–251.
48. Vasanthada Ramalingachari. *Srikakula Girjanodyamam: Anubhavalu-Avagahana (Telugu)*. Hyderabad: Vasanthada Ramalingachari Smaraka Committee, 2005. p. 71.
49. Hiranya. Maromaru Vasantha Megaha Gharjana Viplavanni Varshinchena? *Vijayaviharam,* Maasa Patrika, Secunderabad, 2004. p. 64.
50. Shivarami Reddy. *Mahottara Srikakula Poratam: Charitraka Parisheelana*. Hyderabad: Chaganti Bhaskar Rao Prachuranalu, November 2006. pp. 26–27.
51. Ghanashyam Shah (Ed.). *Social Movements and the State: Readings in Indian Government and Politics*. New Delhi: Sage Publications, 2002. p. 148.
52. C. Bhaskar Rao. "The Problem of Fragmentation in the Naxalite Movement". Ed. By Pradip Basu, *Discourses on Naxalite Movement 1967–2009: Insights into Radical Left Politics*. Kolkata: Setu Prakashani, 2010. pp. 345–360.
53. Sumanta Banerjee. "Naxalbari and the Left Movement". Ed. by Shah, Ganashyam, *Social Movements and the State: Readings in Indian Government and Politics*. New Delhi: Sage Publications, 2002. pp. 125–192.
54. N. Venugopal. *Understanding Maoism: Notes on Participant Observations in Andhra Pradesh*. Kolkata: Setu Prakashani, 2013. pp. 30–31.
55. Ibid.
56. C. Bhaskar Rao. "The Problem of Fragmentation in the Naxalite Movement". Ed. by Pradip Basu, *Discourses on Naxalite Movement 1967–2009: Insights into Radical Left Politics*. Kolkata: Setu Prakashani, 2010. pp. 345–360.
57. *Jagithya Jungalmahal (Telugu)*. Hyderabad: Kranthi Prachuranalu, 2011. pp. 11–16.
58. Sumantra Bose. *Transforming India: Challenges to the World's Largest Democracy*. London: Harvard University Press, 2008. p. 183.
59. T. Papi Reddy. *Agrarian Unrest, Peasant Struggles and Social Change: A Study of Telangana*. Warangal: Sony Publications, 1990. pp. 180–187.

60. K. Balagopal, M. Kodandaram Reddy. "Andhra Pradesh For Ever Disturbed: Peasant Struggle of Sircilla–Vemulawada", *Economic and Political Weekly,* Vol. 17, No. 48, November 27, 1982, 1897–1901.
61. *Jagithya Jungalmahal (Telugu)*. Hyderabad: Kranthi Prachuranalu, 2012. pp. 6–8.
62. T. Papi Reddy. *Agrarian Unrest, Peasant Struggles and Social Change: A Study of Telangana*. Warangal: Sony Publications, 1990. pp. 178–180.
63. N. Venugopal. *Understanding Maoism: A Participant Observations in Andhra Pradesh.* Kolkata: Setu Prakashani, 2013. pp. 22–23.
64. "Sircilla Rythanga Poratam-Purvaparalu", Hyderabad: CPI (ML)-Janashakti Prachuranalu, Andhra Pradesh State Committee, 1994. pp. 5–15.
65. Ibid.
66. T. Papi Reddy. *Agrarian Unrest, Peasant Struggles and Social Change: A Study in Telangana*. Warangal: Sony Publications, 1990. pp. 196–197.
67. C.V. Subba Rao. "Peasant Movement in Peddapalli", *Economic and Political Weekly,* Vol. 14, No. 46, November 17, 1979, 1869–1871.
68. Tendu leaf is used in beedi-making. The beedi industry is a major employer of women in Telangana district.
69. N. Venugopal. *Understanding Maoism: Participants Observations in Andhra Pradesh*. Kolkata: Setu Prakashani, 2013. pp. 38–40.
70. M. Shatrugna. "Suppressing Rural Unrest", *Economic and Political Weekly,* Vol. 19, No. 3, January 21, 1984, 109–111.
71. C.V. Subba Rao. "Peasant Movement in Peddapalli", *Economic and Political Weekly,* Vol. 14, No. 46, November 17, 1979, 1869–1871.
72. "Thupaki Rajyam: Peruguthunna Nirbhandam Midha Nivedhika", Vijayawada: Andhra Pradesh Poura Hakkula Sangam (APCLC) Prachuranalu, April 1991. pp. 63–64.
73. M. Kodandaram Reddy. "Terrorising Civil Rights Movement", *Economic and Political Weekly,* Vol. 20, No. 20, May 18, 1985, 861.
74. Mohan Ram. "Mini Emergencies to Suppression the poor", *Economic and Political Weekly,* Vol. 13, No. 46, November 18, 1978, 1880.
75. T. Papi Reddy. *Agrarian Unrest, Peasant Struggles and Social Change: A Study of Telangana*. Warangal: Sony Publications, 1990. 70–73.

76. Sircilla Rythanga Poratam-PurvaParalu, Vijayawada: CPI (ML)-Janashakthi Prachuranalu, February 1994, p. 50.
77. K. Balagopal. “Peasant Struggle and Repression in Peddapally”, *Economic and Political Weekly*, Vol. 17, No. 20, May 15, 1982, 814–816.
78. Ibid.
79. K. Balagopal. “Peasant Struggle and Repression in Peddapally”, *Economic and Political Weekly*, Vol. 17, No. 20, May 15, 1982, 814–816.
80. “Jagityal Jangil Mahal”, Vol. 1, Hyderabad: Virasam Prachuranalu, 2012. pp. 120–128.
81. K. Balagopal. “Peasant Struggle and Repression in Peddapally”, *Economic and Political Weekly*, Vol. 17, No. 20, May 15, 1982, 814–816.
82. Ibid., p. 815.
83. Hussain Khan, P., Bilal Ahmed, P. “Naxalite Movement in Andhra Pradesh”. Ed. by Basu, Pradip, *Discourses on Naxalite Movement 1967–2009: Insights into Radical left Politics*. Kolkata: Setu Prakashani, 2010. pp. 503–519.
84. C.V. Subba Rao. “Peasant Movement in Peddapalli”, *Economic and Political Weekly*, Vol. 14, No. 46, November 17, 1979, 1869–1871.
85. T. Papi Reddy. *Agrarian Unrest, Peasant Struggles and Social Change: A Study in Telangana*. Warangal: Sony Publications, 1990. pp. 99–102.
86. “Jagityala Jangal Mahal”, Hyderabad: Viplava Rachaitha Sangam (VIRASAM) Publications, 2012, pp. 28–30.
87. K. Balagopal. “Peasant Struggle and Repression in Peddapally”, *Economic and Political Weekly*, Vol. 17, No. 20, May 15, 1982, 815.
88. Jaya. “Tunikakau poratam lo Mahilalu”. Ed. by Tarakam, Bojja, *Nalupu*. Hyderabad: Hyderabad Book Trust, 1989. pp. 15–16.
89. N. Venugopal. *Understanding Maoism: A Participant Observations in Andhra Pradesh*. Kolkata: Setu Prakashani, 2013. pp. 43–44.
90. Giri Nagabushanam. “Beedila Kaaluthunna Bhatukulu”. Ed. by Tarakam, Bojja, *Nalupu*. Hyderabad: Hyderabad Book Trust Publications, March 15, 1990. pp. 30–32.
91. K. Srinivasulu. “Impact of Liberalisation on Beedi Workers”, *Economic and Political Weekly*, Vol. 32, No. 11, March 15–21, 1997. pp. 515–517.

92. V.G. "Tendu Leaf Labourers in Telangana: Working Conditions and Struggles", *Economic and Political Weekly,* Vol. 19, No. 46, November 17, 1984, 1941–1943.
93. T. Papi Reddy. *Agrarian Unrest, Peasant Struggles and Social Change: A Study in Telangana*. Warangal: Sony Publications, 1990. p. 180.
94. "Thunukaku Poratam-Oka Pariseelana", CPI (ML)-New Democracy. Hyderabad: Prajapandha Prachuranalu, 2001. pp. 16–20.
95. K. Balagopal, M. Kodandaram Reddy. "Forever 'Disturbed': Peasant Struggle of Sircilla-Vemulawada", *Economic and Political Weekly,* Vol. 17, No. 48, November 27, 1982, p. 1897–1901.
96. Azad. "Maoists in India: A Rejoinder." *Economic and Political Weekly,* Vol. 41, No. 41, October 14–20, 2006, 4379–4383.
97. Ajay Gudavarthy. *Politics of Post Civil Society: Contemporary History of Political Movements in India*. New Delhi: Sage Publications, 2013. pp. 42–43.
98. K. Balagopal. "Land Unrest in Andhra Pradesh-1: Ceiling Surpluses and Public Lands", *Economic and Political Weekly,* Vol. 42, No. 38, 2007, 3829–3833.
99. T. Papi Reddy. *Agrarian Unrest, Peasant Struggles and Social Change: A Study in Telangana*. Warangal: Sony Publications, 336–337.
100. M. Laxmaiah. "Vuththara Telanganalo Thupaki Rajyam", *Suprabhaatham* (Telugu), January–February 1996, 1–9.
101. K. Balagopal. "The Man and the Times", *Economic and Political Weekly*, Vol. 34, No. 26, June 26–July 2, 1999, 1654–1658.
102. K. Vijay Kumar. "Telangana! O Telangana!". Ed. by Tarakam, Bojja, *Nalupu*, July 1–31, 1992. pp. 30–31.
103. M. Kodandaram Reddy. "Marosari Marry Chenna Reddy". Ed. by Tarakam, Bojja, *Nalupu*. Hyderabad: Hyderabad Book Trust Publications, May 16–31, 1989. p. 10.
104. Sumanta Banerjee. "Reflections of a one-time Maoist activist", *Dialectical Anthropology,* Vol. 33, No. 3/4, December 2009, 253–269.
105. K. Balagopal. "Murder of a Veteran Democrat", *Economic and Political Weekly*, Vol. 21, No. 50, December 13, 1986, 2168–2169.
106. *Thupaki Rajyam: Peruguthunna Nirbhandam Meedha Nivedhika*. Vijayawada: Andhra Pradesh Poura Hakkula Sangam (APCLC), Prachuranalu, April 1991. pp. 1–16.

107. K. Balagopal. "Two 'Missing' Women of Karimnagar", *Economic and Political Weekly*, Vol. 26, No. 5, February 2, 1991, 201–205.
108. Azad. "Maoists in India: A Rejoinder", *Economic and Political Weekly*, Vol. 41, No. 41, October 14–20, 2006, 4379–4383.
109. K. Balagopal. "Chenna Reddy's Spring", *Economic and Political Weekly*, Vol. 25, No. 12, March 24, 1990, 591–595.
110. Mallepalli Laxmaiah. "Vuththara Telanganalo Thupaki Rajyam", *Suprabhaatham* (Telugu), January–February 1996, 1–9.
111. K. Balagopal. "Chenna Reddy's Spring", *Economic and Political Weekly*, Vol. 25, No. 12, 1990, pp. 591–595.
112. It was in M. Chenna Reddy's government that brought in this act in 1978.
113. Mallepalli Laxmaiah. *Dalita Paksham Part-1*. Hyderabad: Centre for Dalit Studies Publications, November 2010. pp. 35–38.
114. *Thupaki Rajyam: Peruguthunna Nirbhandam Meeda Nivedhika*. Vijayawada: Andhra Pradesh Poura Hakkula Sangam Prachuranalu, April 1991. pp. 10–11.
115. For details see Venugopal, N. "Fake Encounters: Story of Andhra Pradesh", *Economic and Political Weekly*, 2007, 4109–4111.
116. Deva Krishna Rao. "Encounter Killings in Andhra Pradesh", *Economic and Political Weekly*, Vol. 30, No. 44, November 4, 1995, 2787–2788.
117. K. Balagopal. "Chenna Reddy's Spring", *Economic and Political Weekly*, Vol. 25, No. 12, 1990, 591–595.
118. K. Balagopal. "Drought and TADA in Adilabad", *Economic and Political Weekly*, Vol. 24, No. 47, November 25, 1989, 2587–2591.
119. "Karim Nagr Zillalo Dalitula pai, Shtrila Pai Dhaadulu", Ed. by Sabha Shiva Rao, *Dalita Rana Ninadam*, Hyderabad: Edureetha Publications, 2005. pp. 152–154.
120. Bojja, Tarakam (Ed.), "Lalasalam Nundi Longi pommanadam Varaku", *Nalupu*. Hyderabad: Hyderabad Book Trust, August 1–15, 1989. pp. 7–8.
121. "Mystery Killings by the Police," Andhra Pradesh Civil Liberties Committee Report, June 6, 1987.
122. Ajay Gudavarthy. *Politics of Post-Civil Society: Contemporary History of Political Movements in India*. New Delhi: Sage Publications, 2013. pp. 44–58.
123. K.G. Kannabiran. "A One in a Century Rights Activist", *Economic and Political Weekly*, Vol. 44, No. 46, November 14–20, 2009, 8–11.
124. "Balagopal Kidnap". Ed. by Tarakam, Bojja, *Nalupu*. Hyderabad: Hyderabad Book Trust Publications, September 15–30, 1989, p. 9.

125. Bernett R. Rubin. "Then Civil Liberties Movement in India: New Approaches to the State and Social Change", *Journal of University of California Press*, Vol. 27, No. 3, 1987, 371–392.
126. Munmun Jha. "Ideology, Violence and the Human Rights Movement", *The Indian Journal of Political Science*, Vol. 67, No. 4, October–December 2006, 679–694.
127. Upadyaya. "Prabutvam-Naxalism Oka Pariseelana". Ed. by Tarakam, Bojja, *Nalupu*. Hyderabad: Hyderabad Book Trust Publications, September 1–15, 1989. pp. 9–11.
128. Ibid.
129. *Human Rights in India: Police Killings and Rural Violence in Andhra Pradesh*. New York: Human Rights Watch Publications, Asia, 1992. pp. 9–10.
130. Mohan Ram. "Getting Away with Murder", *Economic and Political Weekly*, September 3, 1979, 1209.
131. EPW Editorial. "People's Protest against Police Brutality", *Economic and Political Weekly*, Vol. 13, No. 17, April 29, 1978, 719–720.
132. K. Balagopal. "Murder of a Veteran Democrat", *Economic and Political Weekly*, Vol. 21, No. 50 December 13, 1986, 2168–2169.
133. K.G. Kannabiran. "A One in a Century Rights Activist", *Economic and Political Weekly*, Vol. 44, No. 46, November 14–20, 2009, 8–11.
134. Azad, "Maoists in India: A Rejoinder", *Economic and Political Weekly*, Vol. 41, No. 41, October 14–20, 2006, 4379–4383.
135. Kannabiran, K.G. "A One in a Century Rights Activist", *Economic and Political Weekly*, Vol. 44, No. 46, November 14–20, 2009, 8–11.
136. Committee of Concerned Citizens (CCC), *Negotiating Peace: Peace Talks between Government of Andhra Pradesh and Naxalite Parties*. Hyderabad: Committee of Concerned Citizens, 2006, p. 96.
137. Ajay Gudavarthy. *Politics of Post-Civil Society: Contemporary History of Political Movements in India*. New Delhi: Sage Publications, 2013. pp. 52–55.
138. K. Balagopal. "People's War and the Government: Did the Police Have the Last Laugh?", *Economic and Political Weekly*, Vol. 38, No. 6, February 8–14, 2003, 513–519.
139. K. Balagopal. "Naxalite in Andhra Pradesh: Have We Heard the Last of the Peace Talks?" *Economic and Political Weekly*, Vol. 40, No. 13, March 26, 2005, 1323–1327.
140. Kannabiran, K.G. "A One in a Century Rights Activist", *Economic and Political Weekly*, Vol. 44, No. 46, November 14–20, 2009, 8–11.

141. Committee for Concern Citizens (CCC). *Report on Peace Talks*. Hyderabad: CCC Published, 2006. p. 78.
142. K. Balagopal. "Naxalites in Andhra Pradesh: Have We Heard the Last of the Peace Talks?", *Economic and Political Weekly,* Vol. 40, No. 12, March 12, 2005, 1323–1328.
143. Committee for Concern Citizen (CCC). *Letter to the People's War Party*. Hyderabad: CCC Report, 2006, p. 48.
144. "Conflict Resolution: Learning Lessons from Dialogue Processes in India", New Delhi: Centre for Human Dialogue and Delhi Policy Group Publications, July, 2011. pp. 8–19.
145. Personal Interview with Varavara Rao dated on 21 July 2014.
146. *Maoists in India: Writings & Interviews* by Azad. Hyderabad: Friends of Azad, Published, 2010. pp. 74–78.

IV

Mapping Caste–Class Debate

This chapter begins with the brief description of caste and class by different scholars. And it moves on to map the class and caste debate to understand how these two concepts are understood in relation to one another in trying to understand the society. The different perspectives on class and caste debate are considered by broadly classifying them into four categories. Though debates and discussions on caste and class are never ending, they definitely increase the scope of better understanding of the concept.

The relationship between caste and class has been perceived by various intellectuals and activists in diverse viewpoints. The bulk of the poor in India are not only is landless poor peasants and unorganized workers but are also from the SCs, backward castes, and STs. The distinction among castes was also related to division of labour and its justification in ideological and cultural terms.[1]

In the post-independent India, the liberal democratic politics and the mixed economic structure has created many complexities and pressures and the then politics created autonomous realms of struggle and competition.[2] The emergence of Dalits as the special agents of the new democratic revolutionary force is itself evidence of an aggravation of the age-old caste–class contradictions in contemporary Indian social reality.[3]

Before mapping the debate on the class and caste in Indian perspective, it is relevant to understand the basic concepts of class and caste respectively as follows.

CASTE

Caste is a social group placed in a hierarchical order derived from certain Hindu cultural prescriptions originated as *Varna*. Caste system is a distinctive institution of India and is said to be the fundamental characteristic of its social organization. The influence of caste system on the life of most of the people in India is such that it is caste which guides the march of human life cradle to grave. This system has resulted in a diverse cleavages in the society, the end result of which is the most cruel and inhuman traits. These inherent traits of inequality evoked subjugation of one section of society by the other.

Conceptually, the idea of caste has been understood by various people in different perspectives. The scholars such as Anthony Giddens relate caste only to 'a form of stratification in which an individual's social position is fixed at birth and thus cannot be changed. There is virtually no inter-marriage of the members of different caste groups'. But, this definition of caste fails to provide the modern contexts in which caste emerged as the dreadful denomination of socio-political mobilization in post-colonial Indian society.

While many Indian scholars have tried to study and define caste as the significant factor in conceptualizing Indian social order, the ideas of M.N. Srinivas are worth mentioning in this regard. Defining caste by way of identifying its fundamental characteristics, Srinivas succinctly points out caste as a 'hereditary, endogamous, usually localized group, having an association with a hereditary occupation, and a particular position in the local hierarchy of castes'.[4] So, this definition tries to bring out the basic traits which continue to strengthen the caste system in India.

Caste system has been a dictatorial factor in the Indian society and that no section of the society remained immune from the forbidden implications of the same. As is said earlier, caste system distinguishes Indian society amongst various social formations, the two poles of which happen to be the upper castes in the form of the Brahmins and the Kshatriyas occupying the top position and the Dalits, lying at the bottom of the caste hierarchy.

While the former enjoys the undue advantages of the caste system, the latter becomes the most significant section bearing the brunt of prejudices and exploitations borne out of the caste system.

Drawing their sense of superiority, the upper caste people continue to command a very high sociocultural status in the society, thereby putting them up with a false sense of superior social status. Second, the impact of caste system has been horribly denying a dignified life for Dalits in Indian society. Just by being born in a particular caste, the Dalits are placed in a far inferior and degrading position in the social order.[5]

Moreover, the Indian social setup permitted the recognition and acceptance of untouchability, which is probably the greatest crime against the humanity. Dalits live a life of perpetual subjugation and humiliation in society and are not allowed to any sort of social upward mobility.

Finally, the position and status of women have been influenced in a complex way by the caste system in India. The caste system has been a weakening factor for the status and position of women in the Indian society for at least two reasons. First, sociocultural taboos put on women of upper castes in the name of safeguarding them and second, in case of the Dalit women being allowed to move out to earn the livelihood which was a model of women empowerment is more in the nature of demeaning the life and personality of such women.

CLASS

The idea lying at the core of modern capitalist societies is the class. The concept of class is based on the application of the Marxist method of dialectical materialism to the understanding of history. Class relations are basically the relations between groups of production which may be different from social groups.[6] On the basis of the idea of Marx about class, the theory of class struggle had been evolved and lies at the core of the Marxian critique of the capitalist mode of production and the ultimate demise of the capitalist societies. However, the other sociologists have tried to understand the idea of class more as a sociological concept aimed at understanding the stratification in society rather than mere economic notion as in the case of the Marxian discourse.

In the strict, Marxian parlance, class is understood as a group of people standing in a common relationship to the means of production. Ordinarily, the ownership of wealth along with the particular type of occupation seem to be the two major components on which the various classes in the society are differentiated.

Applying this notion of class in the historical perspective, Lenin defines classes

> as large groups of people which differ from each other (i) by the place they occupy in a historically determined system of social production; (ii) by their relation to the means of production; (iii) by their role in the social organization of labour, and consequently, (iv) by the dimensions and mode of acquiring the share of social wealth.[7]

In Marxian perspective, class is defined absolutely in terms of its relation to the economic parameters prevailing in the society, to the total exclusion of the social dimensions of the concept. Marx identified class as a group of people who stand in a common relationship to the means of production or the means through which one gains one's livelihood. Max Weber conceptualized class as a product of the economic relations in society being conditioned by the factors such as 'status' and 'party' in society.[8]

This class configuration underwent a subtle transformation in the modern industrial societies with the change in the means of production. With the setting up of factories, industries, offices, and the use of machinery, the previous landowning classes got themselves transformed into the industrial class, owing the establishments critical in carrying out the function of mass production in society. Similarly, the formerly serfs, landless, or the tenant class changed their nature to become the working class, earning their livelihood by working in the establishments set up by the capitalists.

The interconnectedness of class with other such categories of social organization remains weak without having any powerful impact on other categories of people. For instance, if one is not able to understand the notion of caste and its implications for various sections of Indian society, it would be almost impossible for that person to grasp the complexities that surround the proper understanding of the idea of India.[9]

Anand Teltumbde forcibly argues that caste is the central issue for any social change in India. While dealing with the caste–class debate, he says that the understanding of caste in the Indian context has wide effects and caste is very much part of class. The interrogation of the Marxists' position by him continues on the caste and the class.[10]

Despite the centrality of caste in Indian sociology, few studies have empirically analysed the relationship between caste and class or the influence of modernization processes on this relationship, particularly at the national level.

DEBATE ON CLASS AND CASTE

The debates on caste–class relationships and social versus political changes which were initiated in the Ambedkar era are being carried forward even today. The literature on the interpretations of caste–class projects and the relationship between the two and also between anti-imperialists and anti-caste struggles have been scanty.[11]

The debate about the association between caste and class is discussed in the context of historical and contemporary perspectives in India, maintaining that what exists in India is caste in class, not caste per se or caste and class.[12]

The New Leftists widened the political role of the working class in relation to the new social movements, which are based not only on class but on other categories of caste, gender, culture, and ecology.[13] Influenced by this broadened New Left thought, there emerged the phenomenon of subaltern historiography, popularly known as the Cambridge School of Indian scholars. However, the problem with this New Left or Subaltern studies, as Kancha Ilaiah points out, is that they have not given due importance to caste subordination and exploitation. In order to understand the specific caste–class position of subordinated Dalit-bahujans, Ilaiah characterized them as sub-subalterns.[14]

In observance of the Indian social reality, attempts have been made to blend the ideas of Ambedkar and Marx to explain the caste–class phenomenon. As part of this trend, an Indian version of Marxism is proposed by fusing the comforts in annihilation caste with class annihilation.

MARXIST PERSPECTIVE ON CASTE AND CLASS

According to Marxist theory, class struggle is the main principle for the liberation of working classes in any country where antagonistic classes prevail and problems specific to a particular country can only be solved, governed by that main principle, by altering the fundamental conditions in that country.[15]

The Marxists demystified 'caste' as a category of social and historical analysis and, like the nationalists, debunked the Orientalist construction of caste as India's essence.[16] At the same time, Marxist historians in India also castigated nationalist histories for positing India as an undivided, autonomous, glorious agent of its own history and for ignoring the heterogeneous, contesting materialities that underpinned its evolution.

The Marxists generally relegated caste to the domain of the superstructure, situating Indian history within a transition, mode-of-production narrative. Thus, its 'existence and efficacy are [were] to be understood as the ideological products of the specific pre-capitalist social formations that ... made their appearance in Indian history'.[17]

There is endless discussion on caste and class in Marxist circles, but here this study dwells on select Marxists for analysis, beginning with Marx himself.

As is evident from the above paragraphs, there is a lack of appreciation on the part of Marxists of the caste system, its origin, and contents. Marx in his letter addressed to P.V. Annenkov in Paris wrote about caste as, 'the series of economic evolutions of the eternal reasons begins with division of labour'. To M. Proudhon, division of labour is perfectly simple thing. But was not the caste regime also a particular division of labour? And is it not the division of labour under the system of manufacture, which in England begins in the middle of seventeenth century and come to an end in the last part of the eighteenth, also totally different from the division of labour in large-scale modern industry?

In the same book, he described about the village system and said as:

> We must not forget these little communities were contaminated by distinction of caste and by slavery, that they subjugate men to eternal circumstances instead of elevating man to be the sovereign of circumstances, that they transformed a

> self-developing social state into never changing natural destiny, and thus brought about a brutalizing worship of nature, exhibiting its degradation in the fact that man, the sovereign of nature, fell down on his knees in adoration of *Hanuman,* the monkey, and *sabbala*, the cow.[18]

In future results of British Rule in India, Marx said, 'Modern industry, resulting from the railway system, will dissolve the hereditary divisions of labour, upon which rest the Indian caste, those decisive impediments to Indian progress and Indian power'.[19]

Caste assumed a centrality in D.D. Kosambi's relentless quest for the origin of Indian society, since for him it was a category to understand socio-economic difference. Caste was undoubtedly one of the most significant categories in Kosambi's understanding of early Indian history. At one level, he equated the institution, often explicitly, with class. In his classic formulation, for instance, he stated: Caste is an important reflection of the actual relations of production, particularly at the time of its formation.[20]

Kosambi expressed three critical, somewhat conflicting ideas. One is an equation of caste with class, second was the religio-ritual dimension of caste, and its implications for understanding of historical change. The third idea pertains to an association between caste and social stagnation, typified by the Asiatic mode of production.

Kosambi was of the opinion that the supposed unshakeability and inherent strength of the caste system vanish as soon as new forms of production come in. The modern Indian city implies productive relations not based upon caste, often in conflict with caste, when the system is least effective in our cities, in contrast to the villages.

One of the ways in which Kosambi developed the equation between caste and class was through his analysis of the category of the shudra as he visualized the shudra as constituting a class of more or less dependent labourers with virtually no independent access to productive resources.[21]

As is evident, even as Kosambi argued that caste is class, the equation was, for him, rarely simplistic, or even simple. Kosambi attempted to work with the equation between caste and class, defining both with a somewhat narrow precision.[22]

Caste system in India is thoroughly connected with relations of labour. The majority of people does not possess means of production and are divided into SC, ST, and OBC categories. These castes are not merely classes, but are a set of knotted relations of labour. The reason for their economic and social difficulty is the kind of role that they play in the relations of labour.

One ought to take the aspect of 'annihilation of caste' from Ambedkar's theory, but such annihilation is possible only by means of class struggle which is aimed at a radical transformation of relations of labour.[23] According to Ranganayakamma, annihilation of caste will not take place before the economic conditions of lower castes are changed.

On the whole, according to Marxists of the orthodox school, the political revolution led by the proletariat or working class to capture state power would ultimately emancipate all other forms of oppression. Going by this doctrine, it followed that the emergence of Dalit consciousness and identity as a separate social movement was non-progressive and sectarian.

Neo-Marxism or New Left, which challenged this orthodox historical materialism, brought about a general renaissance of Marxist thought, led by Georg Lukacs and Antonio Gramsci. The other luminaries of the new structuralist Marxism were Louis Althusser, the Frankfurt school of critical theory led by Herbert Marcuse, Theodor Adorno, and Max Horkheimer, all of whom sought to give relevant answers to many acute problems of society and politics. They widened the political role of the working class in relation to the new social movements, which are based not only on class but also on other categories of caste, gender, culture, and ecology.[24]

Influenced by this broadened New Left thought, there emerged the phenomenon of subaltern historiography, popularly known as the Cambridge School of Indian scholars, with Ranajit Guha in the forefront.[25] Their mode of historiography is distinctly different from the mainstream history. They write 'history from below'. According to the subaltern historiographers, all forms of social consciousness are an outcome of spontaneous impulse to resist imperial dominance. These historiographers focussed on popular social movements in colonial India, keeping in view the dyadic relationship between imperialism or colonial dominance and people's resistance.[26]

However, the problem with this New Left or Subaltern studies, as Kancha Ilaiah points out, is that they have not given due importance to caste subordination and exploitation. Moreover, they did not differentiate between Gandhi and Ambedkar or Nehru and Periyar. It is Ilaiah's view that Gandhi and Nehru represented the interests of the upper caste, feudal, and bourgeois forces, whereas Ambedkar and Periyar represented the poor, the oppressed, and the suppressed. In order to understand the specific caste–class position of subordinated Dalit-bahujans, Ilaiah characterized them as sub-subalterns.[27]

This study considered these select Marxist reading of caste to point at the way the communist movement manifested itself in the Indian political domain. And also to suggest that it did not have the wherewithal to rethink the question of class struggle from the point of view of the Dalit movement. The latter's engagement with the millennia—long pain of caste oppression could not be accommodated within the Indian communist movement's dogmatic acceptance of the primacy of class struggle. The untouchables were welcome into its fold but first as members of the working class.

AMBEDKARITE PERSPECTIVE ON CASTE AND CLASS

Dr B.R. Ambedkar while talking about caste said:

> The caste problem is a vast one, both theoretically and practically. Practically, it is an institution that portends tremendous consequences. It is a local problem, but one capable of much wider mischief, for as long as caste in India does exist, Hindus will hardly intermarry or have any social intercourse with the outsiders: and if Hindus migrate to other regions on earth, Indian caste would become a world problem.[28]

The problem of caste and its consequences that Dr B.R. Ambedkar talked about is what we see in Marxist and Radical Marxists circles now. And he went on to say:

> It may be an exaggeration to assert the theory of class-conflict, but the existence of definite classes in a society is a fact. Their basis may differ. They may be economic, or intellectual, or social, but an individual in a society is always a member of a class. This is a universal fact and early Hindu society could not

> be an exception to this rule, and, as a matter of fact, we know it was not. If we bear this generalization in mind, our study of the genesis of caste would be very much facilitated, for we have only to determine what was the class that first made itself into a caste, for class and caste, so to say, are next door neighbours, and it is only a span that separates the two. *A Caste is an Enclosed Class*.[29]

Ambedkar accepted most of the economic analysis of Marxism, during much of his social and political life, roughly from the late 1920s through the 1940s, and even attempted to organize along these lines, creating a radical movement of Mahar and Kunbi peasant against landlords, allying with communists in the working class struggle.[30]

These were years in which the pages of *Janata*, Ambedkar's weekly, were filled with reports of the struggles of workers and peasants against 'capitalists and landlords' as well as the fight of the Dalits against atrocities. Ambedkar did not have much time for theoretical writing in this period of tumultuous organizing, but his programmes and speeches indicate that he accepted broadly the Marxist analysis of class struggle so far as economic issues were concerned. What this led to, though, was a kind of dual system theory which saw capitalism and Brahmanism (casteism) as separate systems of exploitation, one to be fought by class struggle, the other by caste struggle. As he put it in his famous address to the Mahar railway workers at Mahad:

> There are in my view two enemies which the workers of the country have to deal with. The enemies are Brahamanism and Capitalism. I do not mean the power, privileges and interests of Brahamins as a community. By Brahamanism I mean the negation of the spirit of liberty, Equality and Fraternity. In that sense it is rampant in all classes and is not confined to the Brahamins alone though they have been the originators of it.[31]

Ambedkar took as his basic goals the ending of exploitation and oppression, and the achievement of equality, liberty, and community.[32] He was flexible about what he called it, insisting that it represented all that Marx had wanted to achieve with 'communism' but frequently describing it as 'social democracy'.

He had a vision of development that emphasized the creation of a modern society of abundance; though by the end of his life he rejected the economics of Marx, his positive approach to economic growth, his insistence on creating a society free from suffering, and his readiness to take the best of the global heritage were radically different from a Gandhian orientation to the traditional village and limitation of needs.[33]

The path to achieving this was backed up by an understanding of the nature of human society and an interpretation of human history. Human society, as he saw it, was characterized not only by conflict and contradiction but also by reason and will. Not simply 'economic factors' were motivating force in history, but also efforts to achieve power and efforts at liberation.[34] Similarly, along with class and caste (and by implication patriarchy) were stratification defined sections of society which represented decisive factors in contradiction and processes of social change.

Within India, Brahmanism/Hinduism was the historical basis of the stratification system, of the social inequality which was constituted in the caste system. Hinduism meant the lack of liberty, the negation of inequality for all groups but especially for women and untouchables, and the destruction of the community. Historically speaking, where a Buddhist upsurge had been revolutionary, Hinduism was the 'counter-revolution of ancient India'.

Dalits of ex-untouchables had a crucial role to play in defeating Brahmanic Hinduism and opening the road to a society of equality and liberation. Whereas, originally, Ambedkar had emphasized on the destruction of caste as a prerequisite to economic quality (socialism), now he began to argue that untouchables were the carriers of Buddhism, the liberatory message of Indian tradition.[35]

The process of change involved internal (spiritual) change, the 'slave's rejection of slavery', and also a social struggle and political dialogue and political organizing. Ambedkar rejection of violence was not a principle of absolute principle, like the Gandhians, but simply because he saw it as ineffective as a main method of change.

Ambedkar philosophy was an Enlightening philosophy that could be described as of 'social liberation' combined with an emphasis on caste as a social reality; and it distinguished Ambedkar from both Marxists who saw the proletariat as revolutionary and neglected cultural and social factors, and from both the dominant and Congress trends (not to mention the Hindu Right wing), which refused to see elements of exploitation and oppression in Indian tradition.[36]

Another Marxist scholar of Dalit political and social history who took this stand is Gail Omvedt. She, while differing from the classical Marxists in crucial respects, emphasizes that the resolution of the caste issue must precede all other revolutionary movements in India.

Omvedt differs from the classical Marxist historians in that she rejects the superstructure theory of caste. Following Godelier, who formulated a trenchant Marxist critique of Louis Dumont, Omvedt situates caste firmly in the domain of the base and sees it functioning at the level of the relations of production. She draws on Godelier's infrastructural argument that 'each structure—social, kinship, political, etc. has its own content not reducible to any other and its own mode and time-scale of evolution'.[37] She demonstrates that in a fundamentally agrarian society such as India, caste, and material/economic factors have always been deeply intertwined. Thus, relegating the question of caste to the domain of the 'social' or of pure 'form' renders any traditional Marxist account of Indian history and society which locates 'reality' in the class struggle not only historically inaccurate but also ideologically questionable:

> Traditional Marxist analyses are ... showing themselves as inadequate. The view that though there are class differences among the peasantry (rich, poor, landless, etc.), these are non-antagonistic and that the main contradiction is between 'peasants' as a group and landlords, has left the major communist parties tailing after the rural rich rather than building an independent political movement based on the rural toilers.[38]

In her major work on the Dalit movement, *Dalits and the Democratic Revolution* (1994), Omvedt notes that most Marxist analyses of caste have been based on a narrow reading of economic exploitation in the sense that they have drawn on the foundational category of class as it has been conceptualized within the capitalist mode of production. Class in such conceptualization is defined in terms of ownership of the means of production and class struggle, those who do not toil but live and thrive on the expropriation of the surplus produced by the labour of the toiling masses. In such a reading, where classes come into existence only in the capitalist 'core' areas of factory production, there is no theoretical space to account for caste-based and other forms of economic exploitation that do not necessarily follow from the concept of ownership of the means of production. As Omvedt says:

> Some owners are exploited (e.g. small peasants); some non-owners exploit (e.g. controllers of state property in societies described as 'socialist'; lords and upper castes in certain feudal societies). Proletarian husbands may benefit from the exploitation of their wives' unpaid labour. Moreover, many ecologists would argue that nature itself can be 'exploited' in the double sense that resources from nature incorporated into the accumulation cycle increase the accumulation of capital, and that this has a destructive effect on the ecologies of regions that provide such resources.[39]

Omvedt is also against theoretical attempts that extend the analytical reach of class to include every other form of economic exploitation. This, for instance, is the stance of activist scholars such as Sharad Patil who argue that caste is class in a South Asian form. In such readings, caste is read non-ideologically, and caste struggle or jaati sangharsh is seen as a form of class struggle.[40] Such attempts, Omvedt maintains, continue to assert the hegemony of the analytic of class. Omvedt would rather maintain the narrowness of the classical Marxist theorizing of class and argue that as an analytic category it cannot begin to encompass all forms of economic exploitation, such as those based on patriarchy or caste hierarchy, for instance. The latter are not merely superstructural or ideological, but have a pronounced economic dimension as well. The forms of exploitation they assume contribute to the accumulation of capital, but they are not determined at every instance by the sphere of surplus value and capitalist production in the narrow sense: that is, by manufacturing and processes of wage labour. One could argue from here that together they constitute the outside that inheres in the categories of class and capital. Omvedt, of course, does not argue for such a deconstructive reading of capital and class. Rather, she puts forward a historicist reading of caste-based forms of economic exploitation as those that had a prior existence outside the spheres of capitalist production and which was subsequently brought into the domain of capital. Her caste as infrastructure thesis is based squarely on the historicism of 'then' and 'now'. From this position, she formulates her theory of liberation of caste–class oppression by arguing that in the South Asian context one could not talk of class struggle in additive terms—that is, in terms of adding the issues of caste, gender, and ecology to the primacy of class but only in terms that recognized the fact that the very term 'class struggle' had no meaning unless it took the form of community-based struggles, whether such struggles were based on caste, gender, or religion.[41]

It is not a coincidence that of the many theories offered to account for the genealogy of caste, Omvedt endorses the materialist account put forward by Morton Klass in his book *Caste: The Emergence of the South Asian Social System*. Klass places the origin of caste at the very beginning of Indian class society. According to Klass, the pre-Aryan tribal societies were inherently egalitarian. Gradually, with the improvement in the means of production, such societies started generating economic surplus; such surplus led to inequality in economic status among the various tribal groups. This economic inequality then evolved into a very specific form of social stratification that we now know as caste. Caste has since coexisted with 'several different modes of production, from the very earliest ones which we would define essentially as tributary modes through the feudal period up to the present when capitalism has come to dominate'.[42]

Omvedt's argument that caste and class in India have always meshed together derives its strength from her invocation of Marx's thesis that the 'economic' began to be seen as a separate phenomenon, distinct from the political and the social, only with the advent of the capitalist mode of production. In pre-capitalist Indian society, as she says,

> unpaid surplus labour was pumped out of direct producers via a system that was itself defined and organized in terms of caste. While the sub-castes were a basic unit of the kinship system, the *jati* itself was a class phenomenon and was a basic unit of the division of labour ... caste structured the very nature and existence of the exploiting and exploited sections ... it was

> impossible to speak of a 'caste system' and a 'class structure' as separate concrete phenomenon.[43]

Another scholar and activist, Sharad Patil, the leader of the Satyashodhak Communist Party, has initiated theoretical debate based on this perspective (an Indian version of Marxism). According to his party formulation, 'the class system was manifested only through the *Varna* and *Jati* system'.[44] Taking jaati as the basic unit, Patil tried to explain the caste system within the frame of historical materialism. In Patil's view, only in colonial times jaati disintegrated and gave rise to the class system.[45]

CASTE AND CLASS PERSPECTIVE

The other scholars who adopted the caste-and-class approach are Gail Omvedt, Manoranjan Mohanty, Sharad Patil, D.L. Sheth, Madhusudan Subedi, Louis Dumont, Anand Teltumbde, Kancha Ilaiah, and other scholars who looked into this perspective.

Meillassoux, a scholar, underscored the material significance of caste by showing its role in organizing 'relations of production and reproduction'. In fact he conceptualized caste in terms of class. From his standpoint, the dominant caste, as the peripheral landowning group, occupies an important position; its control over the means of production confers on it the capacity to exploit a 'labouring class' recruited from among low, usually, Dalit castes.[46]

According to Madhusudan Subedi, the discourse of caste has been shifted from ritual hierarchy and social discrimination to an instrument to mobilize people for economic and political gain. In the caste-based society, high caste groups promoted their own advancement and initiated various economic changes at the community and regional levels that effectively marginalized the people in several important ways. The ability of dominant groups to bring more and more labour under its control resulted rather quickly in exaggerated wealth inequities and higher social positions for some. Higher caste groups gained considerably more power, wealth, and influence than the lower caste groups, thus bringing them higher economic status.[47]

The nexus between caste and occupation can be broken but yet the overlap of caste and class can be very strong. A rigorous social and economic investigation into the caste composition of the occupational structure can help drive an objective, larger picture of the nature, and degree of change.[48]

A basic shift took place in caste: from ritual hierarchy to identity politics, from ascribed and designated status to negotiated positions of power, from ritual definitions of roles and positions to civic and political definitions of the same. The caste system eroded at the ritual level, but emerged at the political and economic levels.[49]

Caste, as a sociological construct, appears to be relevant only in deconstructing the underlying features of Indian society, as the phenomenon of caste does not exist as a powerful component of the social structure of other civilizations. A comprehensive understanding of the major sociological constructs such as caste and class seem to be incomplete without having a deep analysis of the mutual interactions and interconnectedness between these two concepts.

According to Manoranjan Mohanty, 'the capitalist class in the new phase of Indian politics was not the typical anti-feudal, secular, modern universalist social force that text books on European capitalism depict but it played politics of religion, caste and ethnicity from region to region to secure leverage in its operations'.[50]

The local non-Brahmin movements and backward class political groupings were also patronized by industrialists, who simultaneously patronized upper caste organizations. The emerging ideology of Indian capitalist class was partly shaped by the social dynamics within the country and partly by the global ideology of capitalism. Thus, the class politics of capitalist globalization got seriously entangled with politics of caste, ethnicity, gender, and such other categories. So it is extremely important to see the interface of caste, class, and gender in politics and understand the specific form that they take in the particular context.[51]

However, we observe that when caste and class are studied together, the influence of caste is much weaker than that of class origins where access to certain class destinations is concerned. Thus, we conclude that the importance of class origins on class destinations has so far been under-emphasized in the Indian literature.[52]

The neo-Marxists who adopted the synthetic caste–class approach within the broad new historical materialism provide a rich insight into the Indian social reality, notwithstanding their limitations. The view that the radicalization of Dalit theory and praxis through the synthesization of Ambedkarism and Marxism for the guidance of true revolutionary transformation of caste–class society is at present in its embryonic form and needs much greater and comprehensive understanding.[53]

Omvedt maintains that notwithstanding the many inadequacies of existing Marxist theories, the Marxist methodology is fully adequate to throw light on the structure and role of caste in South Asian society.[54]

Omvedt argues that the orthodox Marxists have invalidated the pre-capitalist sociological categories such as caste, gender, family, kinship, and the state, which, in her view, are as much exploitative as class. In these categories, the fight against exploitation takes place through communities, tribes, castes, and kinship groups. In order to understand the linkage between ideological superstructure and economic base, she has constructed 'a revised historical materialism'. She argues that class defined solely in terms of the ownership of private property and the ownership or control of the means of production does not explain major aspects of exploitation and capital accumulation. Hence, she begins her revised historical materialism with defining the caste system and its exploitative features of endogamous principles and practices, purity and pollution, and hierarchy, which shaped Indian society and the Indian economic system.[55]

Kancha Ilaiah, in his study of the Dalit-bahujan consciousness in Andhra Pradesh, has adopted the caste–class approach. He finds limitations, both subjective and objective, in the writing of both Western and Indian upper caste scholars in their approach to Dalit-bahujan history. In his view, caste constructed consciousness in ways that were fundamentally different from the consciousness created by class in European societies.[56]

The most substantive challenges to earlier understandings of caste have emerged from Marxist feminist and Dalit feminist perspectives. The former is exemplified in the Indian context in the writings of Uma Chakravarti. Uma draws attention to the need to reconceptualize both caste and class in terms of gender.[57]

One of the most significant contributors to the study of caste, Srinivas (2003) argued that the subsistence economy of rural

India, dependent on jaati-based division of labour, is the 'essence of caste'. As this is rapidly breaking down, it 'augurs the end of social order which has continued for 2000 years or more'. He suggested that production will become freed from jaati-based division of labour, economic relation will become autonomous, and payments in goods will be replaced by cash. Indian rural society will move, or is moving, from status to contract.[58]

Deshpande (2011) argued that the breakdown of the caste hierarchy has broken the traditional links between caste and profession, and released enormous entrepreneurial energies in the south. It is true that over time, occupational structure itself has undergone a profound change, while caste division has been relatively static. It is also true that any kind of skill acquisition (e.g. admission to a management or a computer course, or to a dental school) is not contingent upon one's caste status. Indeed, none of the modern occupations are determined by birth, and most are not caste-based.[59]

In an exploratory study, D.L. Sheth[60] overviews and examines the significant changes that have occurred in the caste system in modern times, which have resulted in the ideological and structural transformation of the caste system. The most important among the changes include the formation of a new, trans-local identity among the lower castes.

The nexus between hereditary ritual status and occupations which constituted one of the caste system's defining features is progressively breaking down. Today, members of a single caste are becoming increasingly differentiated among themselves in terms of their occupations, educational, and income levels and lifestyles.

When social and religious aspects of economic relationships are insisted upon by any caste, such as traditional obligations of one status group to another, it often leads to inter-caste conflicts and violence in the villages. The nomenclature that has stuck to these formations is the one that was devised by the state in the course of implementing its social and cultural policies—especially of affirmative action (reservations). As such, the new formations are identified as: the forward or the upper castes, the OBCs, the Dalits or SCs, and the tribals or the STs. Over the years, these categories have acquired a strong social and political content, each category providing a collective self-identification to its members.[61]

Regardless of the national focus of caste in Indian sociology, very few studies have observed the relationship between caste and class and/or the powerful influence of transformation and modernization processes on this relationship.[62] The resemblance of caste and class in contemporary India was studied by using the method of log linear analysis.

Divya Vaid empirically explores the relation between caste and class in contemporary India. The existence of a caste system places India in a unique position where the study of class mobility is concerned. Certain castes have been historically associated with particular occupations with modernization and resultant urbanization. While the relation between caste and class is not completely straightforward, a tentative picture of congruence between the two does appear; high castes are seen to be concentrated in the higher social classes such as the professional, large business, and farming classes. Also, the association between caste and class origins is not seen to weaken over time or at least not by very much. Furthermore, lower castes such as the SCs seem to be experiencing difficulty in gaining upward class mobility, though conversely high castes are not cushioned from the forces of downward class mobility.[63]

Divya also adds that in India, modernization has not had the expected effect as the association between caste and class has neither disappeared nor declined appreciably. The author used binary logistic regression to find out whether caste becomes a less important influence on destination. By applying the model of Constant Social Fluidity, it is also concluded that the relation between caste and class destinations has not changed appreciably over the birth cohorts. Thus, even though the class distribution in the country has changed subsequently with modernization, the 'underlying association' between community and class destination has not changed much.[64]

As castes have been historically associated with particular caste occupations, recent research argues that modernization may bring about changes in the relation between caste and class.

Panini summarizes these changes when he states that economic liberalization in the long run is likely to weaken the hold of caste over the economy. The quote[65] from Panini highlights a variant of the modernization theory specific to India. Panini concludes that 'evidence suggests accelerated occupational mobility which has broken down the caste based division of labour'.[66]

But at present, Panini and Srinivas' analysis of the transformations with liberalization and modernization that would bring to the caste system do not meet universal reality. The continued association of castes in particular occupations despite liberalization has been much debated. According to Jayaram[67] the 'conjugation of caste and class is no longer a sociological axiom', and Kumar[68] shows considerable occupational variation within castes.

Finally, Kancha Ilaiah comprehends that the Indian nationalist historiography of the liberal, the Marxist, or the subaltern did not differentiate between Gandhi and Ambedkar or Nehru and Periyar. He pronounces that though all these leaders must have made attempts to lead the people of the same constituency, due to the difference in their ideological moorings, they did not represent the same masses.[69]

Ilaiah states that the historic Telangana armed struggle and the subsequent Naxalite revolt have failed in transforming the caste–class relations in post-independent, the resultant of which were the signs of development of regional capital along with restructured class relations. In the course of this development, the caste structures began to rigidify within the sphere of subordination and domination.[70]

Analysing the communist and Naxalite movements and their role in class struggles, Kancha Ilaiah gets on that the communist parties articulated only economic questions and took all care to see that the SCs did not develop an independent identity by transmigrating Ambedkarism into Marxism.[71] But it appears to him that the future discourse would be that of caste and class but not of one dimensional class or one dimensional caste. It would be a sort of synthesization of Marxism and Ambedkarism.

LIBERAL PERSPECTIVE

The people who advocated this perspective based their arguments on comparative social theory. They claimed that social differentiation and stratification is common to most of the societies elsewhere in the world. While accepting the *Varna vyavastha* they argued for change on the periphery such as untouchability and temple entry. They believe that caste system is just a division of labour and the caste-based discrimination that we see today is an aberration of a well-defined social system. They also went on to say that caste system contributes to the society's self-sufficiency and stability.[72]

Comparative social theorists have generally placed caste systems not as a unique religious ideological or structural category but as a matter of social differentiation and social stratification. They argue that every system of social stratification allocates power and privilege in the society in which it occurs, and most, if not all, such systems are associated with some ranked division of labour that promotes interdependence.

Gandhi, while supporting *varnashrama dharma,* argued for reform and protection from above.[73] When Ambedkar stressed the need for political power for Dalits, Gandhi said, 'what these people need more than elections to the legislatures are protection from social and religious persecutions'.[74] And I quote again. 'Those who speak of the political rights of the Untouchables do not know their India; do not know how Indian society is today constructed'.

It appeared that only the anti-imperialist, secular nationalist movement, represented by Indian National Congress, constituted the heart of India's democratic revolution, and that the various workers and peasants' mobilization allied with it in complex but antagonistic ways; however, mobilizations on the basis of caste or religion were seen as retrogressive, diversionary, and even pro-British.

We can guess the reason why Gandhi and his Indian National Congress and other Hindu politicians took this liberal stand when it came to address the issues of caste, which is expressed by an anonymous letter written to the *Times of India* in January 1933:

> Hindu politicians now embrace the depressed classes partly because of the latter's meteoric emergence into the political life of the country, and partly because of the apprehension of their own position in the future. They would now be ready to include the untouchables among Brahmans, not merely among Hindus, if Dr. Ambedkar wants it. This is the real condition today.[75]

The above are the four different perspectives on caste and class debate. Caste, as a sociological construct, appears to be relevant in deconstructing the underlying features of Indian society, as the phenomenon of caste does not exist as a powerful component of the social structure of other civilizations. The nexus between caste and occupation can be broken but yet the overlap of caste and class can be very strong. A comprehensive understanding of the major sociological constructs such as caste and class seem to be incomplete without having a deep analysis of the mutual interactions and interconnectedness between these two concepts. It can possibly be analysed through the concrete practices in the interconnectedness of Radical Left movement and Dalit movement in Telangana.

Notes

1. Manoranjan Mohanty (Ed.). "Introduction: Dimensions of Power and Social Transformation", *Class, Caste, Gender.* New Delhi: Sage Publications, 2004. pp. 20–21.
2. Anand Teltumbde, Shoma Sen. *Scripting the Change: Selected Writings of Anuradha Gandy.* New Delhi: Anuradha Gandy Memorial Committee Publications, 2011. pp. 72–73.
3. T.S. Madan. "An Understanding of Caste", *Economic and Political Weekly,* Vol. 6, No. 34, August 21, 1971, 1805–1808.
4. M.N. Srinivas (Ed.). *Caste in Modern India and Other Essays.* Bombay: Media Promoters and Publishers, 1962. p. 3.
5. Frank F. Conlon. "The Birth of Jati". Ed. by Ishita Banerjee-Dube, *Caste in History.* New Delhi: Oxford University Press, 2008. pp. 79–92.
6. Ashok Rudra. 'Class Relations in Indian Agriculture', *Economic and Political Weekly,* Vol. XIII. No. 24, June 17, 1978, 916.
7. N.D. Arora, S.S. Awasthi. *Political Theory and Political Thought.* New Delhi: Har Anand Publications, 2007. p. 49.
8. Marx Weber. "Class, Status, Party". Ed. by Gerth H.H., Mills, Wright C., *From Marx Weber Essays in Sociology.* London: Routledge & Kegan Paul, 1970. pp. 180–185.
9. K.L. Sharma. *Social Stratification and Mobility.* Jaipur: Rawat Publications, 1994. pp. 58–59.

10. Anand Teltumbde. *Anti-Imperialism and Annihilation of Caste*. Thane: Ramai Prakashan, 2005.
11. Ibid.
12. Ramkrishna Mukherjee. "Caste in Itself, Caste and Class, or Caste in Class", *Economic and Political Weekly*, Vol. 34, No. 27, July 3–9, 1999, 1759–1761.
13. W. Outhwaite, T. Bottomore (Ed.). *The Blackwell Dictionary of Twentieth Century Social Thought*. Oxford: Basil Blackwell, 1993. pp. 421–422.
14. Kancha Ilaiah. *Caste or Class or Caste-Class: In Dalit Bahujan Consciousness and Struggles in Andhra Pradesh in 1980s*. New Delhi: Nehru Memorial Museum and Library. Teen Murti House, 1995.
15. Ranganayakamma. *For the Solution of the "Caste" Question, Buddha Is Not Enough, Ambedkar Is Not Enough Either, Marx Is a Must*. Hyderabad: Sweet Home Publications, 2001. pp. 33–40.
16. H.H. Risley. "Caste and Nationality". Ed. by Ishita Banerjee-Dube, *Caste in History*. New Delhi: Oxford University Press, 2008. pp. 70–75.
17. Madhusudan Subedi. "Some Theoretical Considerations on Caste", *Dhaulagiri Journal of Sociology and Anthropology*, Vol. 7, 2013, 51–86.
18. Karl Marx, Engels. *Selected Works of Marx and Engels*. Vol. I. Moscow: Moscow Edition, 1969. p. 43,
19. Ibid., p. 494.
20. Kumkum Roy. "Kosambi and Questions of Caste", *Economic and Political Weekly*, Vol. 43, No. 30, July 26–August 1, 2008, 78–84.
21. "The Emergence of National Characteristics among Three Indo-European Peoples" appeared in 1939.
22. Kumkum Roy. "Kosambi and Questions of Caste", *Economic and Political Weekly*, Vol. 43, No. 30, July 26–August 1, 2008, 78–84.
23. Ibid.
24. W. Outhwaite, T. Bottomore (Ed.). *The Blackwell Dictionary of Twentieth Century Social Thought*. Oxford: Basil Blackwell, 1993. pp. 328–330.
25. Ranajit Guha (Ed.). *Subaltern Studies: Writings on South Asian History and Society*, Vol-I. New Delhi: Oxford University Press, 1982.
26. Ranajit Guha. *Dominance without Hegemony: History and Power in Colonial India*. USA: Harvard University Press, 1997. pp. 3–11.

27. Kancha Ilaiah. *Caste or Class or Caste-Class: A Study in Dalit Bahujan Consciousness and Struggles in Andhra Pradesh in 1980s*. Nehru Memorial Museum and Library (NMML), New Delhi: Teen Murti House, 1995.
28. B.R. Ambedkar. "Caste in India: Their Mechanism, Genesis and Development". Ed. by Manoranjan Mohanty, *Readings in Indian Government and Politics: Class, Caste, Gender.* New Delhi: Sage Publications, 2004. pp. 131–153.
29. Ibid.
30. Gail Omvedt. "Ambedkar and After: The Dalit Movement in India". Ed. By Ghanshyam Shah. *Readings in Indian Government and Politics: Social Movements and the* State. New Delhi: Sage Publications, 2002. pp. 293–309.
31. Ibid.
32. Hirendranath Mukherjee. *Gandhi, Ambedkar and the Extirpation of Untouchability*. New Delhi: People's Publishing House, 1982. pp. 12–23.
33. Ibid., p. 26.
34. B.R. Ambedkar. "Caste in India: Mechanism, Genesis and Development". Ed. by Mohanty, Manoranjan, *Class, Caste, Gender: Reading in Indian Government and Politics*. New Delhi: Sage Publications, 2004. pp. 131–152.
35. Eleanor Zelliot. "Gandhi and Ambedkar: A Study in Leadership". Ed. by Dube, Ishita Banerjee, *Caste in India*. Jaipur: Oxford University Press, 2008. pp. 197–209.
36. B.R. Ambedkar. "Buddha or Karl Marx", *Dr. B.R. Ambedkar Writings and Speeches, Vol. III.* Educational Department, Government of Maharashtra, 1987. pp. 26–27.
37. Vijay Prashad. "Untouchable Freedom: A Critique of the Landlord Indian State". Ed. by Gautham Bhadra et al. *Subaltern Studies X*. New Delhi: OUP, 1999. p. 180.
38. Gail Omvedt. "Class, Caste and Land in India: An Introductory Essay". Ed. by Gail Omvedt, *Land, Caste and Politics in Indian State*. New Delhi: Authors' Guild Publications, 1982. p. 10.
39. Gail Omvedt. *Dalits and Democratic Revolution: Dr. B.R. Ambedkar and the Dalit Movement in Colonial India.* New Delhi: Sage Publications, 1994. p. 55.
40. Sharad Patil. Liberalism vs Left and Right, *Economic and Political Weekly*, Vol. XXXVII, No. 6, February 9, 2002, 12–16.

41. Ajay Gudavarthy. *Maoism, Democracy and Globalisation: Cross-Currents in Indian Politics*. New Delhi: Sage Publications, 2014. pp. 57–61.
42. Gail Omvedt (Ed.). "Class, Caste and Land in India: An Introductory Essay". *Land, Caste and Politics in Indian State*. New Delhi: Authors' Guild Publications, 1982. pp. 9–50.
43. Ibid., p. 14.
44. Sharad Patil. "Caste and Class", *Frontier*, June 9, 1979.
45. Ibid. For a deeper understanding of his argument see Sharad Patil. "Dialectics of Caste and Class Conflicts". *EPW*, Annual Number, 1979. His thoroughly researched work. *Das-Shudra Slavery*. Vol. 1. (New Delhi: Allied Publishers, 1980) and *Das-Shudra Slavery*. Vol. 2. Poona: Sugawa Publications, 1990.
46. As quoted in Anand Chakravarti. "Caste and Agrarian Class: A View from Bihar", *Economic and Political Weekly*, Vol. 36, No. 17, April 28, 2001, 1449–1462.
47. Madhusudan Subedi. "Some Theoretical Considerations on Caste", *Dhaulagiri Journal of Sociology and Anthropology*, Vol. 7, 2013, 51–86.
48. Ibid.
49. Rajni Kothari. "Rise of the Dalits and the Renewed Debate on Caste", *Economic and Political Weekly*, Vol. XXIX, No. 26, June 25, 1994, 1589–1594.
50. Manoranjan Mohanty (Ed.). "Introduction: Dimensions of Power and Social Transformation", *Class, Caste, Gender: Readings in Indian Government and Politics*. New Delhi: Sage Publications, 2004. pp. 20–21.
51. Ibid.
52. Divya Vaid. *An Empirical Exploration of the Relationship between Caste, Class and Mobility in India*. Department of Sociology, USA: Yale University Press, 2007. pp. 11–18.
53. T.S. Madan. "An Understanding of Caste", *Economic and Political Weekly*, Vol. 6, No. 34, August 21, 1971, 1805–1808.
54. Gail Omvedt. *Dalits and the Democratic Revolution: Dr Ambedkar and the Dalit Movement in Colonial India*. New Delhi: Sage Publications, 1994. p. 28.
55. Ibid., p. 30.
56. K. Ilaiah. "Caste or Class or Caste-Class: A Study in Dalit bahujan Consciousness in Andhra Pradesh in 1980's". Ed. by Manoranjan

Mohanty, *Readings in Indian Government and Politics: Class, Caste and Gender*. New Delhi: Sage Publications, 2004. pp. 216–254.

57. Uma Chakravarti. Conceptualizing *Gendering Caste: Through a Feminist Lens*. Calcutta: Stree Publications, 2003. pp. 37–65.
58. M.N. Srinivas. "An Obituary on Caste as a System". *Economic and Political Weekly*, Vol. XXXVIII, No. 5, February 1, 2003, 455–460.
59. Ashwini Deshpande. *The Grammar of Caste: Economic Discrimination in Contemporary India*. New Delhi: Oxford University Press, 2011. pp. 3–4.
60. D.L. Sheth. "*Caste and Class: Social Reality and Political Representations, Caste and Democratic Politics in India*", Ed. by Ghanshyam Shah. New Delhi: Permanent Black, 2002. pp. 209–233.
61. Ibid.
62. A. McMillan. *Standing at the Margins: Representation and Electoral Reservation in India*. Oxford: OUP, 2005.
63. Divya Vaid. *An Empirical Exploration of the Relationship between Caste, Class and Mobility in India*. USA: Yale University Press, 2007. pp. 11–18.
64. S. Kumar, A. Heath, O. Heath. "Determinants of Social Mobility in India", *Economic and Political Weekly*, Vol. XXXVII, No. 29, July 20, 2002, 2983–2987.
65. M.N. Srinivas (Ed.). *The Political Economy of Caste: Its Twentieth Century Avatar.* New Delhi: Penguin Publications, 1996. pp. 28–68.
66. Ibid., p. 29.
67. N. Jayaram. "Caste and Hinduism: Changing Protean Relationship". Ed. by Srinivas, M.N., *Caste: Its Twentieth Century Avatar.* New Delhi: Penguin Publications, 1996. pp. 69–86.
68. S. Kumar, A. Heath, O. Heath. "Determinants of Social mobility in India", *Economic and Political Weekly*, Vol. XXXVII, No. 29, July 20, 2002, 2983–2987; Sanjay Kumar, Anthony Heath, Oliver Heath. "Changing Patterns of Social Mobility: Some Trends Over Time", *Economic and Political Weekly*, Vol. 37, No. 40, October 5–11, 2002, 4091–4096.
69. Kancha Ilaiah. "Caste or Class or Caste-Class: A Study in Dalit bahujan Consciousness and Struggles in Andhra Pradesh in 1980s", Ed. by Manoranjan Mohanty, *Class, Caste, Gender.* New Delhi: Sage Publications, 2004. pp. 227–255.
70. Ibid.
71. In such way he feels that the communists have hijacked the Dalit movement but they have certainly played a significant role in

increasing the wages of Dalits as the communist movement is more 'economic determinist'.

72. Ishita Banerjee-Dube (Ed.), "Introduction Question of Caste", *Caste in History*. Jaipur: Oxford University Press, 2008, pp. xxii–xxiiii.
73. Gopal Guru. "The language of Dalit Bahujan Political Discourse". Ed. by Mohanty, Manoranjan, *Class, Caste, Gender: Readings in Indian Government and Politics*. New Delhi: Sage Publications, 2004. pp. 256–267.
74. Babasaheb Ambedkar. *Writings and Speeches,* Vol. II. Ed. Vasant Moon. Bombay: Government of Maharashtra, 1982. p. 661.
75. As quoted in Gail Omvedt. *Dalits and Democratic Revolution: Dr. B.R. Ambedkar and the Dalit Movement in Colonial India.* New Delhi: Sage Publications, 1994. p. 173.

V

The Interface Between Dalit Movement and Left Practice in Telangana

This chapter deals with, as the title propose, interface between Dalit movement and Left practice in Telangana. This chapter begins with assumption that given the Indian specificity, the caste question has to be central and integral to any Marxist understanding. In this sense, caste question is not different from or opposite to class, but intricately related to it. As stated by Ambedkar, in India it's not just division of labour but also division of labourers. Therefore, in Indian context, one cannot completely disassociate caste from class. Thus, Dalit movement and Marxist movement are not two exclusive practices but signify a mutually influencing historical continuation. This study thus attempts to analyse sources, events, and practices and comment on, if necessary, the actual and real tensions between Dalit movement and Marxist practice.

The Telangana peasant movement and Naxalite movement were organized and led by Communist Party and its leadership. These two movements were ideologically radical in nature. They directly challenged existing institutional arrangements of the society and sponsored non-institutional mass mobilization which challenged the oppression of the landlords, Razakars, and Nizam's state police. The major issues that the movement addressed were low daily wages for labourers, *vetti*, illegal extraction, and eviction from the agricultural land. The leadership of these movements came mostly from urban intellectuals and upper caste groups but the poor peasantry and labourers from SCs and STs were the driving force of the movement.

This study intends to analyse the dynamics of caste–class interface in four phases. Phase I deals with interface between Dalit movement and Telangana Peasant Insurrection. It looks at the limitations of the peasant movement in addressing the Dalit issues, which were invariably linked to their class in the society, and how did Dalits engage with the peasant movement with all their apprehensions regarding the issues taken up by the movement. Phase II discusses the interface between Dalit movement and Radical Left practices in the Naxalite movement from 1970s. Phase III deals with the interface between Dandora movement and Left practices in the state. And lastly, Phase IV deals with caste–class interface in the Telangana agitation.

PHASE I: CASTE AND CLASS INTERFACE IN TELANGANA PEASANT INSURRECTION

Land was the central issue on which the socio-economic and political conditions in the state depended. This aspect is elaborately discussed in Chapter 2. The exploitation of people also centred on land and agriculture since agricultural farming was the main occupation of about 60–70 per cent of the people in the state. As it has been already discussed, in the previous chapter the social and political conditions which had shaped up the movement, now this study will explore the interaction between Dalits and communists.

The growing influence of the communists in delta region slowly spread to adjacent Telangana region. A few young radical members such as Ravi Narayana Reddy within the Andhra Conference turned to communism and converted the cultural forum (AMS started as a cultural forum) into a mass militant organization. Through Andhra Conference, young communists voiced the peasants' grievances and paid more and more attention to agrarian problems in Telangana. The agrarian slogans and demands of the communists included abolition of *vetti*, prevention of rack-renting and eviction of tenants, reduction in taxes, revenues and rents confirmation of occupancy (*patta*) rights of cultivating tenants, and so on, which naturally attracted the poor peasants, tenants, and labourers to the Andhra Conference. This strategy also held different strata of the peasantry together. The agrarian social structure was conducive to an insurrectionary movement and the post-war political developments and economic crisis provided an impetus to a sustained peasant revolt that lasted nearly five years.

Mainly the demands such as abolition of *vetti*, increase in the daily wages of labourers, and call to establish *coolodi rajyam* by demolishing dora *rajyam* brought Dalits closer to the communists.[1] Communist Party never addressed Dalits as Dalits because cultural specificity of Dalit's participation in the movement was not integral to the Left revolutionary strategy. They considered these people as agricultural labourers in the fields and household labourers at landlords' forts (*gadi*) trapped in social practice called *vetti*. Therefore, excluding some of the communist leaders such as Ram Reddy,[2] one has to think that communists addressed Dalits as part of party strategy and communist ideology of working class.

The role of Dalits in the movement was not well documented and author such as Gail Omvedt doubts the magnitude of their participation in the movement. I quote:

> actual role of Dalits in the struggle appears to have been a subordinate one. Claims that 'most of the recruits in the *dalams* came from the untouchable castes (Malas and Madigas) and from among the tribals' are unsubstantiated, except for the obvious fact that once the communists were driven into the forests the tribals were the main group they worked among.[3]

Here, the question should not be whether the Dalits had played an active role or whether their participation is substantiated or not. Given the social stigma associated with untouchable castes, were they allowed to play significant role and considering the fact that the communist leadership belonged to upper caste and class, what if their participation never got the recognition it deserved? Dialectically Dalits were the most exploited people in terms of caste and class, hence if there is any resentment or resistance that should have come from the most exploited lot. Therefore, we can argue that Dalits were the principal and most active participants in the movement.[4]

In his article D.N. Danagare writes 'Most of the recruits to the *dalams* came from the untouchable castes (Malas and Madigas) and from among the tribes'. The caste-Hindus treated them as socially inferior. The deprived and peripheral groups had also lost all their rights in land owing to the fact that for the past several decades the power and instruments of justice were in the hands of the landlords and *deshmukhs*. Lack of alternative work had rendered them weak in bargaining for their rights. They were doubly exploited, culturally and economically. It was they on whom the burden of *vetti* labour, illegal extractions, and evictions fell more directly. By joining the communist *dalams* and revolting against the oppressive system they had nothing to lose and everything to gain.[5]

In spite of Dalits active participation in the movement, it seems that the communists never tried to address issues related to caste. It is obvious from the writing of Danagare, Omvedt, and Thirumali that the Telangana peasant movement did not address any caste issues. But for the organizational strength and ideological stance of the communists, it is very doubtful that they ever would have included untouchables in the movement. The communists aimed at 'unity' (which they thought could be achieved with the acceptance of the social constraints of the old order) and within the framework sought to deal only with some of the economic problems of the poorest sections of the society.[6]

While talking about the exploiters and the exploited, the communists considered them as the haves and the have-nots which is a class perspective to the whole issue of exploitation. What they comfortably ignored or hesitated to recognize is the strong relation of caste to the class in Indian society. In India, class is impossibility without caste. Telangana peasant movement was led and dominated by relatively upper caste section of the society; they were relatively prosperous section of the community. The leading communists in Telangana were, by and large, wealthy landholders, *pattadars* of substantial holdings, and men of some hereditary standing in their villages and talukas. Both Ravi Narayana Reddy and B. Yella Reddy (who were elected as the president and general secretary respectively at Bhongir session of the AMS) were prominent landlords. D. Venkateshwar Rao, leader of the Suryapet taluka, could be cited as yet another example. Some Telangana communists such as Raj Bahadur Gaur and Makhdoom Mohiuddin, came from the urban intelligentsia.[7] Considering the castiest nature of the then society, it was natural that they overlooked issues related to caste. In fact it seems that the communists very rarely took up the social issues of untouchability. D.V. Rao's statement, 'When we were working in the villages caste tensions did not arise. Caste differences were limited to the house, except for untouchable' is typical.[8] Here, one needs to differentiate between ideology and practice, particularly when it comes to village committees. I quote Inukonda Thirumali: 'the *asamis* and *kapus* within the party seized power and largely dominated the village committees and converted them mostly to protect their interests in many places and grossly violated the state committee circulars'.[9]

The demands for upliftments of the labouring class were not met. Land was not distributed to the rural poor; even if they did Dalits have many apprehensions regarding the occupation of dora's land.[10] The party itself accepted that 'all agricultural labourers and poor peasants could not get enough lands. Much discontent has grown among these revolutionary sections of the people'.[11] It seems that the party has realized by now that the fruits of the revolution has not reached the poor labourers. Whether the party tried to address these short comings during or after the movement was unclear but we can see that issues were considered seriously in the next phase of movement (Naxalite movement) which was more radical in its mode of fighting.

With all its shortcomings and failure to address the caste issues as promised or as expected, one has to acknowledge the fact that no other movement in Telangana has brought a change such as this movement in rural Dalits perception of the society. It helped them to break the shackles of upper caste hegemony. The people who lived on the outskirts of the village were made members of the village committees. In a time when Dalit were not even treated as human beings, the Communist Party recognized their strength and brought them into village and some of them even rose to become prominent members of the committees.

The movement, for the first time in history, questioned the normative arrangements and values that legitimized oppression and marginalization of poor peasants and labourers in the social, economic, and political systems of villages. This movement provided Dalits an alternative world view and life options which equipped them ideologically to question the legitimacy of existing oppressive and exploitative socio-economic and political system of the rural society. It also united the lower castes, Dalits, and tribals people; broke their isolation; and empowered them politically to fight against oppression and exploitation. The movement provided Dalits a space to articulate their issues and express their discontent against the existing forms and organization and values of the rural society. On the whole, this movement brought in the message and promise of an egalitarian society that aimed to radically change the old values, institutions, and norms of the existing society.

In spite of all the hope and promise the movement has given, caste system is not such an easy custom to be destroyed. However, the movement has diluted/liberalized caste dominance and subordination relations wherever the movement was strong.[12] With all their reservations the caste-Hindus worked with the Dalits in the committees. But once the movement was called off, when these people returned to their villages, again they became the part of the caste system and practiced the same old caste-related discrimination.

Before going into the next phase, it would be appropriate to discuss the political conditions to that created space for the emergence of Naxalite movement in 1970s. This is the brief outline of the political development that had taken place in 1950s to 1970s.

The AMS has been at the forefront of democratic struggles since the early decades of the twentieth century. In the beginning, it was dominated by pro-Congress Party elements, but by the 1930s it came under the control of communists who conducted a radical turnaround, by taking up issues such as the abolition of *vetti*, protection to tenants, and the demands of 'land-to-the tiller'. The anti-Nizam and anti-feudal peasant struggle, led by the communists through the AMS in the 1940s, was an important political development crucial to an understanding of political articulation in the subsequent period. The redistribution of the land of the

Brahmin-Karanam, Reddy, and Velama doras during the struggle was significantly influenced by the caste composition of the village committees assigned with this task. As mentioned above, the beneficiaries of these transfers were tenants and *ryots* predominantly belonging to the Kapu-Reddy cultivators' community.[13] The Dalits, who comprised the majority of *vetti* agrestic labour on dora's lands, remained landless even after the struggle.

And there were differences regarding withdrawal of the movement. Ravi Narayana Reddy, B. Yella Reddy, and C. Rajeswara Rao argued for the abandonment of the struggle, while P. Sundarayya and M. Basavapunnaiah advocated for continuation of the struggle as a peasant partisan struggle. Though the split is argued upon ideological differences between two groups which are not discussed here but caste interests cannot be ruled out.[14]

These developments were all within the Communist Party circles. On the other side, the developments within the Congress Party which in a way prompted the next radical phase of peasant struggle needs to be mentioned here.

The Congress Party adopted two-pronged political strategy in the early years of its rule. First, it sought to co-opt the radical slogans of the Left. Second, by creating new institutional structures and expanding and strengthening certain social classes, it sought to win over the support base of the Left-wing opposition.

The reformist agenda of the Congress Party consisted of the abolition of the *zamindari* and *jagirdari* systems. Immediately after independence, the post-colonial Indian state sought to address peasant grievances by abolishing intermediaries and enacting tenancy laws. With these legal reforms, two of the significant issues in the radical agenda that was shaped in the pre-independence period were co-opted by the Congress Party regime.

The beneficiaries of legislation implemented to remove oppressive landlordism and bestow rights of tenancy were members of the peasantry, the vast majority of whom also constituted the tenantry. They belonged to the Reddy, Kamma, and Kapu peasant castes, while the Dalit and OBCs predominantly comprised the agricultural labour. In effect, this created a new class of landlords.[15]

Not only this, even the areas of Telangana unaffected by the struggle of the 1940s continued to experience that period's feudal oppression until the 1970s. It is curious to note that even the new class of landlords that emerged in the post-independence period resorted to old feudal modes of exploitation and oppression, as was evident in certain areas of Karimnagar, Nizamabad, and Warangal districts.

PHASE II: INTERFACE BETWEEN DALIT MOVEMENT AND RADICAL LEFT PRACTICE IN TELANGANA

It was the above scenario that formed the backdrop of the peasant struggles waged by the CPI (ML) groups during the 1970s and 1980s in Telangana region. In this phase, an attempt is made to draw the dynamics of interplay of caste with class in the Radical Left mobilization in Telangana during the 1970s and 1980s.[16] It acquires importance in view of the fact that it could mix the question of anti-feudal struggle with subaltern caste mobilization by facilitating unity among them. Further, this movement also threw up an organic leadership subaltern society, for which reason it stands out an important political experiment.

With the first three Panchayat Raj elections conducted in 1959, 1964, and 1970, the Congress Party has consolidated its grass-roots leadership base in the state, by accommodating a large section of rich peasant elite in positions of power. This class, with their power of landownership and caste dominance, exploited the opportunities opened up by the democratic institutions and development channels. Congress Party's agrarian reforms had strengthened the hold of a new and aggressive landlord class in the countryside, and even these people resorted to old feudal modes of exploitation and oppression. Not only that, even the areas of Telangana unaffected by the struggle of the 1940s continued to experience that period's feudal oppression until the 1970s.[17]

The purpose of the Telangana peasant movement got defeated completely during the course of time. The fruits of the struggle were confiscated by few upper class and caste sections of the society.[18] All the forms of oppression such as *vetti* and low agricultural wages and caste-based discrimination and exploitation continued. In fact, in some of these areas, extreme forms of feudal exploitation and practices continued to exist until the Naxalite movement addressed them.[19]

Naxalite movement, one can argue, is the result of state's failure to bring about any substantial change in agrarian social relations and social life in the rural areas in spite of its progressive agrarian legislations. It may also be noted that the CPI (ML) groups established their support bases in the areas which were on the periphery of the earlier peasant struggle. In a sense, the CPI (ML) agrarian movement tried to finish the process that had remained unfinished since the 1940s.

CPI (ML) People's War began its work on a full scale when the ban on the party was removed after Emergency, that is, from 1977.[20] The RSU, which is a student wing of People's War Party (PWP), started *Garamalaku Tharalandi* (Go to villages) campaign in 1978 to reach agricultural labourers and poorest of the poor in the villages. Several cultural youth groups comprising educated youth and cultural activists moved to each and every village and campaigned for a revolutionary path. In fact, it attracted Dalit and other weaker sections into the revolutionary struggle. They spread this message through song, dance, and speech, which the Jana Natya Mandali (JNM) activists adapted from the rural folk forms from the common man.

By the end of 1978, the RCS (the peasant-landless poor organization) were established in most parts of Karimnagar district, Sircilla, Jagityal, and Peddapalli taluqs, which became the key centres. The RCS became a major force in mobilizing the rural poor, especially Dalits against the dora and village-based exploitations.[21] The significance of this period of agrarian mobilization has been illustrated as *Jaithra Yatra* (victory March).[22] On 7 September 1978, more than 35,000 people from 150 villages, comprising farm servants, agricultural labourers, and toiling peasants, were mobilized in a march to Jagityal town, which culminated in a huge public meeting. The participants' mobilization was unimaginable even to the organizers of this programme.

It demonstrated the people's hope in the party and their trust in the struggle. This gave strength to the party and courage to the landless poor to fight against the feudal landlords and state repression. With this inspiration in Nimmapalli of Sircilla and Maddunur in Jagityal and Peddapalli taluqs mass mobilization took place under RCS banner and struggled against economic and social exploitations.[23]

THE ISSUES TAKEN UP BY RCS RELATED TO CASTE

So far we have seen how successfully, effectively CPI (ML) party through its RSU and RCS organized people against the landlords and state oppression. The issues taken up in those struggles showed sensitivity to caste, though the party mobilized people using class-oriented language. We see two important changes in the CPI (ML) politics in general and the PWG in particular. One is the shift to popular mobilization by strengthening mass front organizations such as RSU, RYL, and JNM in the cultural front. Second is the clear direction to bring the subaltern social groups into the movement not in terms of class but in specific caste terms as SCs, artisans, and occupational communities.[24]

Here, I will list out some of the issues that the CPI (ML) party has taken up, which are sometimes directly and sometimes indirectly linked to caste. Since the origin and practice of Left parties is class oriented, this study is not going to lay stress on class-related practices of the party.

1. Against *Vetti Chakiri*

Vetti, in its most general sense, is bonded labour but it extends well beyond that definition.[25] It is caste specific. And it is this specificity to caste that makes Dalits most vulnerable and most effected people by this inhuman practice. In India, occupation of person depends more on caste in which he is born into and less on his talent or skill or passion for the profession. And each caste has to render its caste-specific services to the landlord without charging anything for the service rendered. All the toiling castes of the village had to supply free of charge to the landlord whatever products or services they produced. Thus, every caste in the village, including Brahmins, had to supply its services free of cost to the landlord. The peasants were required to supply *vetti nagallu* (free supply of ploughs) for a requisite number of days to the landlord; artisans such as blacksmiths (*Kammari*) and carpenters (*Vadla*) were required to repair the agricultural implements of the dora without any payment. The toddy-tappers (*Goudas*) were to reserve certain high yielding and good quality palm trees for the dora and supply the produce for free; potters (*Kummari*), the pots and other earthenware they produce; washermen (*Chakalis*) have to wash the clothes for free; barbers

(*Mangalis*) were to do hair cut to dora and his family for free, likewise the list extends with the number of castes in the village.[26]

When it comes to agricultural labourers and household servants, it was Dalits (mainly Madigas and Malas). They were called *vetti madigalu* and *vetti malollu*. They have to work for the dora for free as and like the dora wishes and any number of days he wants. They were called *vetti jeethagallu*. Their duties are not generally specified. It is mostly agricultural, household, and personal works of the landlords such as preparing beds, arranging baths, and cleaning the house. They were paid in kind just to let them survive. The landlord would lend some money for interest for these servants to perform customary duties such as death rituals and marriages. And to pay back this loan, he would take another loan and the burden increased year after year till he becomes bonded for life, and the worst part is that bondage would extend to their children as well. Like this, Dalits were born into bonded labour.

In this way, *vetti* affected Dalits more than any other caste in the society. CPI (ML) through RCS and RSU made people stop rendering *vetti* services to the landlord.

2. Distributing Land to Landless

Land was the primary issues around which struggles of Left parties were centred. Through the slogan 'land to the tiller', Naxalite parties have distributed the land to the poor peasants. They also have given land to some Dalits. Their publications clearly mentioned the names of the Dalits calling them as Harijans.[27] This shows their sensitivity to caste.

3. Against the Domination of *Gadi*

Gadi is the manifestation of social domination and oppression. It was a huge fort-like house with tall gates in which the village dora lived with his family.[28] *Gadi* is just not a dwelling place, it's an office and it's also a centre of perpetuation of dominance and oppression. This is the place where caste hierarchy is strictly followed. This is where fines were collected and punishments given. This is where dora's authority was unchallenged. The very thought of the *gadi* (dora's residence and his court) evoked terror in the hearts of the rural masses.[29] All village disputes and settlements from disputes between wife and husband to disputes over land distribution were done here. It is this 'right' to enforce law and deliver judgement which kept their dominance intact. For resolving disputes, money was collected from both the parties and was never returned to either party. They intentionally created disputes and makes lakhs out of fines. Naxalite hit the very base of their power; they conducted people's court and resolved disputes. This has affected dora's social dominance.

4. Against Sexual Exploitation of Dalit Women in Telangana

In a feudal setup such as in Telangana, sexual exploitation of women was very common. There are scores of stories which explains the deplorable state of women in Telangana's feudalistic society. Landlords' atrocities on women were outrageous. Women were paraded naked, raped, and killed by doras.[30] They made sexual exploitation of women in the name of *jogini*, *basavi*, and *manthangi* became a social custom.[31] This evil practice was, quite obviously, forced on Dalit women whose social standing is inferior to any other women in the society.

5. Against 'Two Glass System'

Emergence of new political parties and inception of democratic politics did not alter society's perception of untouchables. In fact untouchability penetrated into emerging new social institutions such as hotels. In most of the hotels, Dalits were not allowed, even if they were allowed they were made to wash the plates and glasses in which they ate and drank.[32] There were two sets of glasses and plates, one set for Dalits and the other for caste-Hindus. Political parties did not dare to stop this practice, but Naxalites seriously objected to this practice and at times cautioned the hotel owners who practiced this system.[33]

6. Against Untouchability in Public Spheres

The practice of untouchability in public sphere has hindered the growth of Dalits in the society. There was no access to common drinking water sources in the villages. Dalit children were not allowed into the schools. Landlords strongly objected to education for the Dalits. Naxalites had strongly advocated education for Dalits as they had advocated for land to the landless. In some villages, Naxalites started peoples' school for Dalit children and education was given to them free of cost.[34]

Not only the above-mentioned caste-specific issues they have addressed, but also Naxalites established *sangams* in the name of caste in some parts of Telangana. In Nizamabad and some parts of Medak district, it (sangam) was organized under the banner called *Chillara Kulhala Sangam or Ambedkar Yuvajana Sangam*.[35] Therefore, we can say that they have recognized caste as base of different forms of exploitation in Telangana and started to work towards addressing the issue. This is where one has to disagree with K. Sreenivasulu when he says:

> Although caste has been central to semi-feudal forms of exploitation in Telangana (such as vetti, for instance), it has not received any explicit attention in the CPI (ML)'s agrarian politics. If this is because of the theoretical understanding of the communist parties, it is also because the issue of caste has been subsumed into the category of class.

The class-oriented struggles of the communists did help Dalits. Their daily wage was increased. Some of them even got land for themselves. They got education and a social space in the society to articulate their grievances. Dalits were definitely more close to Naxalite party than any other political party. Naxalite party on the other hand, within its theoretical limitations, has recognized certain sections of poor as Harijans and worked to eradicate the practice of untouchability in the villages. Therefore, there were never tensions between Naxalites and Dalits.[36] There always existed a kind of solidarity between Left parties and Dalits in Telangana by 1980s. The powerful presence of Radical Left parties and anti-feudal struggles throughout the 1970s and 1980s could be cited as the main reasons for the absence of an autonomous Dalit movement; and yet it would not be an exaggeration if we say that the roots of autonomous Dalit movement in Telangana lie in the Left movement.

KARAMCHEDU AND CHUNDURU MASSACRES: IMPACT ON DALIT AND RADICAL LEFT POLITICS

In the history of erstwhile Andhra Pradesh, the massacres of Karamchedu in 1985 and Chunduru in 1991 are the most shameful events.[37] There were many incidents before and after Karamchedu and Chunduru in which many innocent helpless Dalits were killed, but I have chosen these two events. The reasons for choosing these two are: first, no other incidents had generated so much debate and discussion about Dalit and Radical Left politics as these two incidents; two, due to constraints of time and space and to stay focussed on my study of the interface, but not to undermine the severity of other incidents. Though the incident took place in Andhra region of erstwhile Andhra Pradesh state, Karamchedu massacre becomes indispensable in the study of dynamics of caste–class interface. With this incident both Radical Left movement and Dalit movement went through a remarkable transformation. The independent Dalit movement that emerged after Karamchedu had forced Radical Left parties to reconsider their ideological stance.

Karamchedu Massacre

On 16 July 1985, a Kamma boy bathed a buffalo at the steps of the water tank of the Dalits and directed the dirty water into the tank which was meant for their drinking water. A lame Dalit youth and a young Dalit woman protested against this. The Kamma community retaliated against this protest by massacring several Dalits in the early hours of 17 July. Six Dalit men were killed and more than twenty-five others, including several women, were injured. The incident has severe repercussions in terms of the physical and mental health of the Dalit community of the village.[38]

Immediately after the incident, the Dalits fled to the nearby Chirala town and set up a *shibiram* (camp). It is around this *shibiram* that the Dalit struggle with demands and issues 'specific' to the community emerged. Initially, leaders began to mobilize their community all over the state around the issue of cultural assertion against the dominance of upper castes.[39] This assertion for an autonomous movement is remarkable because it demanded autonomy from both the state institutions and the mainstream parties and also the Radical Left movement led by the various Radical Left party groups.[40] Dalit leaders protested and rejected the CPI (ML) PWP's depiction of the incident as 'landlords attack against labourers' in their pamphlet. Instead, they represented it as an attack by 'Kamma landlords on Madiga coolies'.[41] Along with demanding autonomy from the ML groups, Dalit leaders rejected state institutions and even the Dalit leaders, both political representatives and bureaucrats, within them. Dalit bureaucrats were characterized as *Dalit dalaries* (Dalit compradors). As a symbolic representation of an autonomous struggle, Dalit leaders decided that only Dalits would occupy the dais and address others on the issue of Karamchedu. It was decided that no upper caste, however radical and sympathetic to the Dalit cause, would be allowed to share this space. This demand of 'only Dalits' was one of the earliest forms in which autonomy was articulated in Andhra Pradesh (erstwhile). All those Dalits who were part of the communist movement were now *discursively* re-articulated as 'Dalit communists'. Ambedkarism emerged as the guiding philosophy for an independent Dalit 'social revolution', which was later referred to as a 'New Dalit Democratic Revolution' both as a continuation and to counter the ML group's struggle for 'New Democratic Revolution'. Such alternate articulations created conditions for movements to rethink their position vis-à-vis each other.

In course of two months struggle after the incident, Dalit leaders also argued that there is need for 'Dalit organic intellectuals', who could alone conceptualize the aspirations of Dalits along with 'political power for Dalits' as the essential demand of an independent Dalit movement.

Establishment of Dalit Mahasabha (DMS)

Struggle to both rehabilitate the Dalits who left Karamchedu and punish the culprits began soon after.[42] 15 August was observed as a black day, followed by dharnas and indefinite hunger strikes. However, none of this could pressurize the government to take proactive measures. On 1 September 1985, a public meeting was organized where Dalits from all over the state were mobilized, rallying under the slogan 'Chalo Chirala'. JNM, PWG's cultural wing, took an active part and its lead singer Gaddar (a Dalit) inaugurated the meeting. This signified both the proximity an independent Dalit movement wished to have with the ML groups such as the PWG and its firm resolve to maintain autonomy by projecting Dalit leaders, writers, singers, and conceptualizing a *discourse* specific to the caste problem.[43]

At the end of this historic meeting, the formation of a state-level autonomous Dalit organization—DMS was formally announced. Two prominent Dalit leaders Bojja Tarakam, a civil libertarian, and advocate Kathi Padma Rao, a rationalist, were elected unanimously as its president and general secretary respectively.[44] Later, in February 1986, DMS held its first state level conference at Tenali and released its manifesto. It created interest among various sections of the society in general and the ML groups in particular as it were the first attempt to articulate and conceptualize the idea of an autonomous Dalit movement.[45]

Chunduru Massacre

Chunduru incident, which happened six years after Karamchedu, has to be seen with respect to the changes that occurred due to the raise in Dalit consciousness, advancement in education, hence the betterment in the socio-economic conditions of the Dalits in the village.[46] What differentiated Chunduru from Karamchedu was the relatively high level of literacy[47] and fairly large-scale employment among the Dalits. Due to modern education, public sector employment and easy mobility due to the railway connections, the Dalits of Chunduru demonstrated a great sense of awareness of their rights and, accordingly, assertion. Employment in the public sector gave the Dalits of this village a high sense of security and confidence. The Dalits also displayed a significant presence in the political arena.

The socio-economic specificity of Chunduru made the Dalits relatively less dependent on the Reddys and, therefore, less vulnerable to Reddy domination and manipulation. Upper caste Reddys, quite naturally, did not like this change in the lives of Dalits which fairly reduced their domination and hold on the village.

On 7 July 1991, a trivial argument that took place in a cinema hall triggered a series of events. A Dalit youth, Ravi, a PG college student in Nagpur, went to a cinema theatre in Chunduru. He 'rested' his foot on a seat in front which was occupied by an upper caste boy Kurri Srinivas Reddy. A minor altercation ensued between Ravi and Srinivas Reddy when the latter abused the Dalit youth in the name of his caste.[48]

On the following day, Ravi's father, who was a schoolteacher in a neighbouring village, was subjected to torture by the Reddy youth as a measure of retaliation. Fearing further assaults from the upper castes, the family decided to leave the village. Neither

Ravi nor his father lodged any complaint with the police. The decision of the family was not accepted by the Dalit community, describing it as an act of surrender to the upper castes. So they lodged a complaint against Reddys. This obviously attracted a severe response from the Reddys and their supporters in the village and even from those of neighbouring villages. They have decided to put an end to the mounting assertion of the Dalits.[49]

On 9 July, Reddys and Telagas held a meeting under the leadership of Sarpanch Sambi Reddy and decided to enforce a *social* boycott of the Dalits (Malas). Since then, the Dalits were not allowed to work in the fields of upper castes nor were they permitted to enter the upper caste locality. Land tenancies of the Dalits were cancelled, in many cases the upper castes did not return the money which was paid as rent in advance for the land they had rented. The upper castes even messaged Reddys of neighbouring villages to not employ Dalits of Chunduru in their fields. This forced and enforced social boycott of the Dalits led to tensions. At this stage, the police imposed Section 144 in the village. While the upper castes engaged outside labour to work in their fields, the Dalits left to places such as Tenali and Ponnur in search of work. A 50 strong police picket headed by Tenali Rural Circle Inspector (CI) was posted in the village since then. The presence of the police deterred them from a head-on collision and the next few days remained incident free. The prohibitory orders were lifted on 29 July, and two incidents that occurred on 4 and 5 August in which two Dalits were attacked and injured and on the same night additional forces were rushed to Chunduru even as prohibitory orders were re-imposed in village.[50]

The final attack on the Dalits came on the morning of 6 August. From the report of APCLC, it seems that this brutal incident was pre-planned and well-executed by the upper castes with the alleged connivance of the police officials present in the village.[51]

> One version is that a few Dalit youth attacked and inflicted minor injuries on some Reddys … . However, this was blown out of proportions by the upper castes who spread the falsity that three Reddy men were hacked to death by the *Dalits* … . The upper caste men of nearby Valiveru, Manchala Munangivaripalam and Vellaturu villages were also mobilised

> for an assault on *dalits*. Around 11 a.m. Saibabu [the CI of police] and Vemuru Sub-Inspector Sheik Madarvali came to the *dalit* quarters and asked them to flee as CRPF men from Mangalagiri might raid the village to pick them up following a complaint lodged by the upper castes. *When the dalits were hesitant to leave the village the police virtually chased them away.* However all the *dalit* women stayed back.[52]

The police terrified and hunted all the Dalit men towards the Tungabhadra canal. As all the Dalit men in the *Dalithawada* started fleeing, they found the Reddys and Telagas belonging to Chunduru and other neighbouring villages. They were all armed with deadly weapons. When they ran towards the railway track, they found another group of armed upper caste people waiting there as well.

What followed was a systematic and brutal assault on Dalits. The marauders, who came in tractors and scooters and were well armed, first caught the fleeing Dalits, beat them with iron rods, and killed them with daggers and axes. They then leisurely packed some of the bodies in gunny bags and dumped them in the Tungabhadra drain and irrigation canal. Though the final tally of deaths could not be clearly ascertained immediately as most of the bodies were thrown in the canal, but at least eight Dalits are murdered in the heinous manner and many more injured in what could be described as an unparallel case of brutality.[53]

As mentioned earlier, these two incidents have brought in a set of radical changes in both Dalit and Radical Left practices. There was serious discussion between and among Dalit leaders and Naxalites on how to address the issue of caste and how to construct their future course of action. In this regard, it is necessary to mention and analyse the role of two magazines *Nalupu* and *Edureetha.*

The Role of Nalupu

It is against this backdrop of an emerging politics of solidarity that the DMS officially launched its journal called *Nalupu* (Black) in April 1989. Its focus and purpose clearly reflected this need to evolve a broader strategy for the Dalit movement. It also reflected the need to forge solidarity with ML parties such as the PWG and yet fight for the benefits the existing socio-legal system offered.

Nalupu emerged as an important platform reflecting the nature of the Dalit movement and the possible directions it would take in times to come. Though it was published for a short span of four years (1989–1993), when it was discontinued, 'every educated Dalit and the whole Dalit community felt that their potent leader had vanished'.[54] In fact, in most of the issues of *Nalupu* it was repeatedly propagated that it is not just a journal but in fact a 'movement' by itself.

The president of DMS edited *Nalupu*. However, it is interesting to note that the editorial board had leading civil rights activists, academics, and journalists from the upper castes along with Dalit writers. The structure and issues in focus in the journal are also symptomatic of the 'broader cause' Dalit movement stood for in Andhra Pradesh. It carried detailed discussions on social movements such as NBP and anti-arrack movement; on issues such as problem of housing, health policies of the government leading to 'brain drain' in the medical field, privatization of education; struggles in Kashmir, and other international issues. Most of these issues were analysed with an ideological proximity with the Left politics.

Another significant feature of *Nalupu* was the various debates it carried on regarding issues pertinent to the ML movement. It repeatedly argued through its editorials that the ML movement was a political struggle for demands affecting the lives of lakhs of adivasis and Dalits. It also argued that the violence indulged in by the Naxalite groups was only 'counter violence' to the violence unleashed by the state. *Nalupu* protested against the ban on the PWG and the series of fake encounters against them and focussed throughout on the issue of land and various militant land struggles taking place in remote villages of Andhra Pradesh and that 'revolution' is a plausible means of transforming the society.[55] This however does not mean that *Nalupu* did not carry many ideological debates with the ML groups. Most important of them was the debate on using the available legal and constitutional means. *Nalupu* carried a series of articles on various institutions and part of the state structure. For instance, it constantly argued that Panchayat Raj institutions should be used for the empowerment of the weaker social groups, along with the various legal provisions in favour of land reforms.[56] It also projected the caste bias among some of the ML groups, for instance it carried a detailed coverage of an incident on 7 March 1993, where activists of the CPI (ML) Praja Pantha attacked and killed a Dalit boy, due to organizational differences between them and AYS. They criticized 'sectarian tendencies' in the ML groups that made any meaningful alliance difficult.

Nalupu also attempted to expand the contours of the Dalit movement by addressing the emerging 'internal' dynamics around the issue of larger unity with the 'bahujans'. For instance, it reported incidents of attacks by the OBCs on the Dalits, reflecting the caste–class complexities. It highlighted the necessity to agree with Ambedkar's interpretation that caste is both base and superstructure,[57] in order to overcome the bifurcated nature of the movements. The Dalit movement under the leadership of the DMS and its ideological propaganda through *Nalupu*—on the need for (a) pursuing both militant and legal methods; (b) articulating a broader identity of Dalit around caste–class dimensions; (c) emphasizing ideological unity between Ambedkarism and Marxism for innovative combinatory discursive articulations; (d) realizing the need for proximity with Radical Left struggles around social, cultural, and economic issues—provided conditions for a fuller articulation on politics of solidarity. However, it is pertinent to ask whether the Naxalite movement was in a position to grapple and coordinate with the changing *material*, *discursive*, and *strategic* dimensions, initiated by the Dalit movement.

To begin with, the ML movement was reluctant to accept an ideological combination of Marxism with Ambedkarism; autonomy (or giving equal significance) to cultural and identity-related issues with economic (land) struggles and combining armed-militant struggles with the use of legal-institutional means. This was seen as diluting of revolution and gravitating towards reformism. More immediately, reflection of this was the refusal to recognize Dalit movement as an independent political struggle. The Naxalite movement also strongly believed in the centrality of the armed wing and a hierarchized relation with various mass organizations.[58] The Dalit movement therefore could not fit into their scheme of political organization and modes of protest and mobilization. In fact, building mass organizations was considered for a very long time as compromising with revolutionary politics. By the end of 1970s and early 1980s, due to various historical reasons, most of the ML groups did begin to experiment with alternative forms of mobilization. Revising their earlier aversion, they began to organize 'open' mass organizations. Thus, the People's War's Central Committee wrote in early 1980s that 'today almost no revolutionary group in our country clearly holds it as in the 70s that either building "mass organizations itself is revisionism" or "carrying out partial struggles itself in revisionism" '.[59] However, they continued to enjoy very little autonomy and were considered 'secondary' in forging a revolution. Mass organizations were characterized as mere 'propaganda agencies' or 'recruitment centres'.[60]

They were divided into three broad types on the basis of the nature of work they carried out. First, there were the 'secret mass organizations' that propagated revolutionary (read armed) politics and recruited members for the party. Second, there were the 'open mass organizations', which used the available legal-democratic and constitutional means to build 'pressure, expose the state and contribute to further revolutionary politics'. Third, there were the 'cover organizations', which aligned with non-party organizations and carried the agenda of anti-feudal and anti-imperialist struggles into these organizations.[61] Such 'tactics' were necessary in conditions of extreme repression.[62] Most of these categories of mass organizations reflected the necessity of propagating the agenda of 'new democratic revolution' into various sections of the society rather than trying to develop independent methods of integrating diversified sections and their demands into the overall goal of forging a socialist revolution. It is with this backdrop that the Naxalite movement dealt with the independent Dalit movement as one of 'its' mass organizations and looked to 'co-opt' it both by entering the leadership positions and by characterizing it is a 'partial' struggle (the metaphor used was a 'stream that needs to flow back into the ocean'). The first phase of independent and autonomous struggles thus remained bifurcated and dichotomized and the issue of solidarity ambiguous and under problematized.[63]

The Role of Edureetha

It was to explore further possibilities of solidarity with the Naxalite movement that the Dalit writers started yet another journal called *Edureetha* (Swimming against the Tide), in May

1990. Two important Dalit leaders who were previously part of the Naxalite movement (while the editor of the journal came from the UCCRI (ML) group, another important member of the editorial board was previously a COC member of the PWG) started it. They together also started the Marxist-Leninist Centre. It is interesting to note that while the journal declared its perspective as 'Marxist-Leninist' and as a 'journal for revolutionary politics', none of the ML parties owned it but it was the Dalit organizations and writers who identified with it. A more explicit articulation of an ideological basis for solidarity in a synthesis of Ambedkarism and Marxism was acceptable to most of the Dalit groups, not so for many of the ML parties.

Edureetha's editorial declared that the purpose of the journal is to:

1. Critique the anti-democratic, authoritarian tendencies within the various revolutionary groups vis-à-vis the newly emerging caste and gender perspectives.
2. Invite discussions on caste by both revolutionary groups and autonomous Dalit organizations. It was supposed to be a platform for all progressive groups to negotiate their theoretical and ideological differences so as to make unity between them possible.

Edureetha was autonomous of both the Dalit movement led by the DMS and the various revolutionary groups. It strongly believed that critical intervention into the politics of both the Dalit and the Naxalite movement alone would make a meaningful dialogue between them possible and purposeful. As for the Dalit movement, (a) it was critical of DMS for appealing to the same upper caste state, which was perpetuating caste discrimination in the state; (b) it analysed the shifts in the programme of DMS and cautioned it against its politics of mobilizing just SCs and STs and not addressing issues concerning the bahujans and other poorer communities; (c) it also criticized DMS for neglecting its original agenda to struggle for land and other economic issues and instead restricting to demanding compensation and reservations from the government. It argued that Dalit movement in course of time has restricted itself to the 'sociocultural' domain and fought as if Dalits could be emancipated without addressing the issue of economic equality and redistribution. *Edureetha* was definitely in search of a new framework that could radicalize the Dalit movement against its possibilities of getting ghettoized.

On the other hand, it raised series of critical issues on the practice of the ML groups in the state. Among various others criticisms, it highlighted that while the ML groups though express outward support for autonomous women's and Dalit movement by being active within them, they also always attempted to either merge these movements with the Naxalite movement or actively participate in them to take over the leadership positions so that they could be subsumed under class struggle. Similarly, it was also pointed out that ML groups hegemonized the discourse over autonomy by branding all those seeking autonomy as 'revisionists', 'careerists', 'opportunists', 'stooges of ruling class', and 'agents of imperialism'. *Edureetha* argued that this was so primarily because the ML movement believed in recognizing autonomy only as a 'tactic' to accommodate these independent struggles, which enjoyed mass support. It was also argued that constituting most of the separate women's and caste wings by the ML parties was again only a 'tactical' move and these mass organizations do not enjoy any organizational or ideological autonomy.[65] In the political discourse on autonomy, *Edureetha* pointed towards a significant dichotomy between 'tactical' notions of autonomy as against 'substantive'. The debate on the moral, political, and ideological legitimacy of a 'tactical' approach as a *strategy* of transformation opened new dimensions in the dialogue on solidarity.

The dichotomy of 'tactical' versus 'substantive' notion of autonomy leading to 'fragmentation' between the movements subsumed a more important (hidden) dimension within the ML parties. *Edureetha* traced it to the lack of representation in leadership of members from more organic social groups such as the Dalits and women. They argued that most of the leaders of the ML groups came from the 'upper' caste and petty bourgeois strata that joined the movement during the student days from elite/urban institutions. Their petty bourgeois' and 'upper caste' tendencies get reflected later on in their functioning and the decisions they took. They also suggested that the Naxalite leaders such as T. Nagi Reddy and C. Pulla Reddy were all perceived, in spite of their radical credentials, as upper caste leaders belonging to the landed community.[66] The movement therefore failed to get organically integrated at the grassroots where Dalits constitute the struggling majority. As a possible solution, *Edureetha* suggested that it should be made mandatory to have only members coming from SC, ST, and OBC communities of the society to assume leadership positions. Most of the Dalit organizations fiercely agreed and propagated this idea in Andhra Pradesh. They felt that it was only by mutually adopting and incorporating the principles evolved in each movement that they could forge solidarity. In other words, while the Dalit movement was taking up the land issue and recognized armed method as valid and a legitimate political method, the ML groups should have incorporated the principle of distributing land in accordance with caste, so as making it mandatory to have 'only Dalits' as their leaders.[67]

The various ML groups rejected 'Dalits in leadership positions' as a means to overcome the problem of 'tactical approach' and 'fragmentation'. They countered by arguing that communists are those who have genuinely overcome caste, class, and gender prejudices and therefore to fix them in these categories (acquired by birth) was a reductionism; and they also argued that the underlying assumption of *Edureetha's* experiment was to either combine or equate Marxism with Ambedkarism, which would always remain an aborted attempt, as Ambedkar at worst was a 'petty bourgeois reformer' and at best a 'radical reformer'. They cited instances of atrocities on SCs and STs as part of the repression on the armed movements in Tebhaga and Telangana that Ambedkar did not condemn. He therefore had a narrow and constitutionally constrained notion of transformation.[68]

With the intervention of *Edureetha* in the on-going dialogue between the Dalit groups and the ML organizations, the debate got concretized in terms of (a) distribution of land on the basis of caste, (b) making it mandatory to have Dalits (and women) as leaders in all the ML groups, and (c) to theoretically accept the combined philosophy of Ambedkarism-Marxism as the only alternative for the Indian situation. These alternatives got further legitimized at the beginning of the decade of 1990s with the Chunduru massacre. It was again, on the lines of Karamchedu, retaliation by the upper caste communities, not against demands for higher wages or land, but about identity assertion by the Dalits for self-respect and dignity.[69] Immediately after the Chunduru incident, in spite of the fierce ideological differences, the ML and the Dalit groups formed 'Joint Action Committee', with the DMS, CPI, (ML) Vimochana, UCCRI (ML), Socialist Revolutionary Forum, and Ambedkar Youth Association.

MAROJU VEERANNA: CLASS AND CASTE DEBATE

The discussions carried in *Nalupu* and *Edureetha* have led to intellectual churning in Dalit and ML parties. These discussions stressed the need for a strong ideological base, especially among CPI (ML) parties, to include and address Dalit issues. This period of ideological conflict and uncertainty led to the rise of another dynamic leader, Maroju Veeranna, from Left parties.

Maroju Veeranna was an active student leader for PDSU (Vijrumbana) which was affiliated to CPI (ML) Janasakthi. It is under his leadership that PDSU, for the first time, supported reservations. It had also demanded to include Ambedkar's writing in school curriculum. With the same spirit he had taken up the issue of caste within the CPI (ML) Janasakthi Party.[70] He felt that the present communist ideology is insufficient and does not suit to Indian society. He strongly argued for the adoption of Ambedkar's ideology into Marxist ideology.[71] Veeranna proposed that without social transformation class transformation is not possible. He proposed a new revolutionary path for India which includes Phule-Ambedkar's thoughts and prepared a document towards this end which is called May 17th Comrades Document. In 1998 Veeranna's group[72] submitted their document titled *Indialo Emcheyyali* (What is to be done in India?) to the party for discussion on the new revolutionary path to be adopted by the party. But, the CPI (ML) not only did not accept this document but also expelled Veeranna's group from the party.

Veeranna's group came out and formed a new party called Communist Party of United States of India (CPUSI)-Dalita Bahujana Sramika Vimukthi (DBSV) on 25 December 1998.[73] The document became their manifesto. They aimed at establishment of casteless, classless India.

DANDORA MOVEMENT: CASTE VERSUS CLASS

Radical Left politics in Telangana has made Dalits more aware of their status and rights in the society. The awareness in terms of caste and class among Dalits has helped them to perceive the discrimination not only from outside their community but also from within their community. By 1990s, the constitutional safe guards such as reservations have improved the economic status of certain sections of the Dalit community considerably. In other words, the resources provided by reservations were effectively used by only few castes that happen to be at the top of the 'caste-ladder' within Dalit community.[74] Therefore, there arose uneven/unequal distribution of resources among Dalit community; and the primary observation of the Dandora movement was that there is an imbalance in the equality of opportunity in receiving the benefits of reservation and demanded a share in the present reservation policy based on their populations.[75] Madiga has become more assertive to the inequality that they experienced in relation to the Malas while sharing the reservation benefits.[76]

The debates and discussions that followed after the formation of MRPS between Madigas and Malas help one to have an insight into the class–caste conflict within the Dalit community.[77]

Madigas demanded categorization of SCs into four sub-groups and the 15 per cent quota allotted to the SCs as a whole should be distributed in proportion to the population of each sub-caste. And the Mala Mahanadu, which was formed in response to Madiga Dandora, strongly opposed the demand.[78] It has based its opposition on different aspects but for this analysis only three main stances are considered. They are: (a) the blame that Madigas lack in merit and does not work as hard as Malas; (b) the belief that categorization will limit competitive capabilities of the Dalits; and (c) finally the fear that categorization will destroy the unity among the Dalits.[79]

1. Merit Argument

Mala Mahanadu argued that the cornering of reservation benefits by Malas is due to their individual 'merit' and Madigas are simply not willing to do the hard work. The whole argument of 'merit' is class based, which was effectively used by the upper castes against Dalits whenever they raised the issue of uneven distribution of resources. They argued that caste should not be the criteria to decide the benefits of reservations because there are also poor people among upper caste Hindus. Therefore, class should be the deciding criteria and from among this poor people meritorious candidates should be given preference. It is unfortunate that same argument is used against the Dalits by the Dalits.[80]

2. Competency Argument

Bojja Tarakam, one of the prominent Dalit leaders, criticized the categorization demand of the Madigas in public meeting in Hyderabad by observing: 'as categorization guarantees limited but definite share in the quota of reservations for each Dalit caste, every Dalit group competes against its own members of the group for that limited share, and this potentially destroys their competing potentialities'.[81] This argument if extended, according to Gundimeda Sambaiah, could lead us to end the reservations policy itself. Apart from Sambaiah's argument, the concept of competence itself is closely linked to class. Even within the same caste, class plays a crucial role when it comes to competition. It is injustice to ask a Relli caste person to compete with a Mala or Madiga person.[82]

3. Homogeneous Class Argument

While the Madiga Dandora demanded that caste be taken as the unit of justice so that every caste in the Dalit group will have its share in reservations opportunities, the Mala Mahanadu, on the contrary, has argued that such a categorization would disturb the unity among Dalits. In other words, it has favoured class-based justice, that is, the treatment of Dalit group as one homogeneous class of people, or to be plain, it has asked for the continuation of the existing unit of the distribution of justice.

DANDORA MOVEMENT AND RADICAL LEFT PARTIES STAND

Left movement in Telangana rightly recognized the fact that Dalits constituted most of the poor agricultural labourer and they were the most exploited in all spheres of life. From the first phase, we can argue that the Communist Party did not succeed completely in realizing its goals, however through Left movement it has created sufficient awareness, among the Dalits, of the kind of oppression they are subjected to and has provided a platform to voice their rights and demands. From Karamchedu incident, Dalits rejected the Left platform to voice their grievances and Dandora movement is the manifestation of the awareness created by Left parties and Dalit movements.

Radical Left parties expressed their solidarity to the Dandora movement.[83] The demand for categorization of SC reservation into four sub-groups is aimed at stopping the dominant group from using all the benefits and thereby to new class differences within the Dalit community. Malas emerged as a new class within Dalit community.

> The role of reservations in the socio-economic development of the Dalits has been immense. They have facilitated Dalits access into educational institutions and government employment, which in turn, invariably fostered the emergence of sizeable middle class among them with guaranteed earnings, security, and the prestige that comes with government employment.[84]

They supported the Dandora movement because the demand is not in conflict with its ideology. The demand is about the equal distribution of resources among the Dalits and to neutralize the class differences that arose due to unequal distribution of reservation benefits, which is in tune with Radical Left parties' ideology.[85] But, they did not prepare any action plan to address this issue and resolve this problem among Dalit community. Because Dalits have been the driving force in the Radical Left movement.

> The sub-caste movement raised issues similar to the demand made previously by the ML movement. Both the leader of this movement, Krishna Madiga and Krupakar Madiga, were previously associated with Radical Left parties. MRPS raised the issue of 'classes within the caste groups' that got consolidated due to the disproportionate appropriation of reservation by the Mala community.[86]

Dandora movement has helped the Radical Left parties to bridge the gap created by Karamchedu and Chunduru incidents. Dandora movement is a caste-based movement with a class conflict. It is a result of Radical Left parties failure to address the caste issue and also internal caste discrimination among the Dalits. Dandora movement brought to the front the inherent link between the caste and the class in the Indian society. In India, it is the caste which decides the class, and the Radical Left parties have to recognize this fact at some point in time and Dandora Movement has forced them to reconsider their stance with regard to caste. On the other hand, Dandora movement's roots, we can daresay, lie in the consciousness and awareness given by Radical Left movement. Radical Left movement created so much awareness among Dalits about the concept of class and its relationship with the distribution and misappropriation of resources that they questioned the misappropriations of resources within themselves.

TELANGANA MOVEMENT: CASTE AND CLASS PERSPECTIVE

Ever since the formation of Andhra Pradesh, there has been discrimination against Telangana in resource allocation, development schemes, education of locals, and employment generation.[87] Injustice and discrimination are also evident in denying spaces in Telangana and Telanganites in decision-making economic, political, social, and cultural spheres. In fact, this is only a continuation of the state policy, as Telanganites could not get their share.[88]

The state of Andhra Pradesh has a distinct place in the history of social movements in India, having witnessed movements by peasants, Dalits, tribals, women, and Naxalites. The Telangana movement is not merely the demand for statehood, but also for demand for economic and cultural autonomy, from the Andhra region.[89] The rebirth of the Telangana movement in the 1990s raised the question of distribution of land, self-respect, and self-rule for an equal share in political and economic domains, along with bifurcation of the state. The movement is rooted in a historical context and development model. The regional disparities, in economic, social, and cultural spheres, are a part of reality.[90]

Telangana movement is one of very few mass movements which have witnessed participation from all sections of people. The movement gave enough hope to every section of people to come out and protest against the government. And also they brought in their own issues with them to be addressed. Telangana movement is a conglomeration of hundred demands and thousand wishes. Based on the issues, there are many perspectives to the movement, of which I will consider the most prominent ones for my analysis.

The group which belonged to dominant caste and class of the region gave first priority to the formation of separate state. They argued that if one brings in the issues related to class and caste, the movement itself would get diluted and it would become very difficult to pressurize the government to concede to the separate statehood demand. Instead they argued that once the Telangana state is realized, we can address the issues and sort out internal differences. In this demand, one can sense the desire to consolidate their dominant class and caste in the new state and also their desire to acquire power. They projected Andhra leaders and people as the enemies and the root cause of all the problems faced by Telangana people.[91]

The ML parties went for 'class analysis' and had a 'political economy perspective'. Their first priority is to fight against economic exploitation rather than the social exploitation; however, they also have taken up social and cultural issues. They argued for the equal distribution of the resources to all the sections of the society. They stand for the empowerment of all sections of the society. They are against the privatization of the resources. They are against the feudal system, imperialism of global capital, and imperialist policies of the government.

With this stand, the Radical Left parties supported a separate Telangana movement. In fact, they have put forth the demand for separate Telangana much before the birth of Telangana Rashtra Samithi (TRS) party. Way back in 1997, through their Warangal declaration document titled 'Prathyeka Telangana Udyamam—Telangana Abhivruddi', they framed their programme on separate Telangana.[92] The following are some of the important points of this document.

1. Land to the farmers
2. To solve the water (both drinking and irrigation) problems
3. Social justice for Dalits and minorities (Muslims)
4. Adivasis' rights on the forest.

Radical Left parties, though they had included Dalits and minorities issues in their programme, did not made it clear whether they consider Dalits and minorities as part of class analysis or on the basis of caste and religion. Any concrete plan of action to work with Dalit organizations and minorities is also missing. They seem to consider Dalits on the basis of resource deprivation and lack of participation in political economy of the society.

The identity groups and Radical Left parties should have come together and formed an alliance why because they have a common 'enemy'. Their main aim is to target internal and external exploitation of the poor based on class and caste, and liberate these oppressed sections in Telangana.[94] Srikrishna committee itself agreed that the subaltern communities are driving force in the recent movement.[95]

Telangana Movement: A Caste Perspective

The people who looked at Telangana from caste perspective, mainly, consisted of Dalits. In the initial stage, these agencies also fought against the discrimination and exploitation by Andhra (caste/class dominance) leaders and capitalists as everybody else. Its only late in the movement they began to question the movement on caste lines. We can see the participation of Dalits in the separate Telangana movement from the beginning to the end[96] that is, from 1956 to 2013; however, it was only from 2009 that their participation became 'visible'.[97] Most of the student union leaders from Osmania University are Dalits. The autonomous student groups emerged from Dalit movement. Left and liberal student organizations which are affiliated to the parties as front organizations on the campus already gained relative autonomy from political parties on Telangana question. The autonomous SC/ST student organization on the campus working on democratic anti-caste lines were joined by the class-oriented Left student organizations to fight for the Telangana statehood representing regional autonomous aspirations. Thus, the struggle for regional autonomy in Telangana provided a space for class and caste categories to come together without having to lose their specific nature of respective struggles, that is, Left and Dalit. Though they represented the entire Telangana people and their aspirations and worked hard for the realization of Telangana, they never undermined the caste question. Identity groups participated in Telangana movement, without having to give up their particular claims. They fought united, yet remained to hold their specificities. They never compromised with the movement and they had fought to include the question of 'social justice' into the Telangana agenda.[98]

They argued that Telangana was backward because of the existence and perpetuation of the culture of dominant castes. They have realized that both the people who are obstructing the formation of Telangana and who are leading the Telangana movement belonged to dominant castes.

The subaltern group's position therefore has been that if the caste is not addressed, then the crux of the Telangana problem would remain untouched. Because even if a separate state is obtained, benefits such as water resources, land, political power, and economy would go to the upper caste sections in the new state.[99] The Dalit issue and woman's issue cannot be separated from the Telangana movement because they are all interwoven. Therefore, the sociocultural dimension is equally important. A region cannot be seen only as a physical entity.[100]

Moreover, two demands define their political fight: the formation of separate Telangana state and equal opportunities and equal representation in the socio-political economy of the newly formed state. Movement based on the Dalit-bahujan ideology was spreading and claimed more political and economic space for the exploited and backward castes of Telangana and the recognition of their identity and culture. The objective could be seen both as a fight against the social and economic influence of the forward caste and the political influence of the rightwing organizations. There was strong hope in Telangana concerning the student movement and its ability to influence the policies of the future state as noticed by Kannabiran, 'students from oppressed classes are not only holding mainstream political formations to account in unprecedented ways, but are also providing direction to the movement'.[101]

The movement for separate statehood is a political articulation of various social identities for due share in the resources which was denied to them in the integrated state. These concerns were presented in the form of '*samajika* Telangana'. The demand for separate state was not driven by primordial loyalties. Social dynamics in Telangana clearly indicate that the struggle was driven by an urge for inclusive growth. It is in the context that the development discourse needs to be given serious consideration. Future mobilization will take place around the issue of development.

Notes

1. Inukonda Thirumali. *Against Dora and Nizam: People's Movement in Telangana 1939–1948*. New Delhi: Kaniska Publications, 2003. pp. 4–5.
2. For details see K. Srinivasulu. "Telangana Peasant Movement and Changes in the Agrarian Structures: A Case Study of Nalgonda District." Dissertation. JNU of New Delhi, 1988. pp. 219–220.
3. Gail Omvedt. *Dalits and Democratic Revolution: Dr Ambedkar and the Dalit Movement in Colonial India*. New Delhi: Sage Publications, 1994. p. 311.
4. R.M. Sarkar (Ed.). *Dalits in India: Past and Present*. New Delhi: Serials Publications, 2006. pp. 158–159.
5. Sundarayya Puchalapalli. *Telangana People's Struggle and Its Lessons*. New Delhi: Foundation Publications, 1972. pp. 167–168.
6. Barry Pavier. *The Telangana Movement 1944–51*. New Delhi: Vikas Publishing, 1981. pp. 13–14.
7. D.N. Dhanagare. "Social Origins of the Peasant Insurrection in Telangana 1946–51", *Contribution to Indian Sociology*. Delhi: Vikas Publishing, 1974. pp. 101–134.
8. As quoted in Gail Omevt's *Dalits and Democratic Revolution: Dr Ambedkar and the Dalit Movement in Colonial India*. New Delhi: Sage Publications, 1994. p. 311.
9. Inukonda Thirumali. *Against Dora and Nizam: People's Movement in Telangana 1939–48*. New Delhi: Kaniska Publications, 2003. pp. 206–207.
10. K. Ranga Rao. "Peasant Movement in Telangana". Ed. by Rao, M.S.A., *Social Movements in India: Studies in Peasant, Backward Classes, Sectarian, Tribal and Women's Movements*. New Delhi: Manohar Publications, 2002. pp. 160–162.
11. Inukonda Thirumali. *Against Dora and Nizam: People's Movement in Telangana 1939–1948*. New Delhi: Kaniska Publishers, 2003. p. 206.
12. Personal interview with K. Sreenivasulu on 7 August 2014.
13. Inukonda Thirumali. *Against Dora and Nizam: People's Movement in Telangana 1939–1948*. New Delhi: Kaniska Publishers, 2003. p. 211.
14. D.N. Dhanagare. "Social Origins of the Peasant Insurrection in Telangana 1946–51", *Contribution to Indian Sociology*. New Delhi: Vikas Publishing, 1974. pp. 101–134.

15. K. Srinivasulu. *Caste, Class and Social Articulation in Andhra Pradesh: Mapping Differential Regional Trajectories.* Working Paper 179. London: Overseas Development Institute, 2002. pp. 21–22.
16. Meganath. *Com. Tharemala Nagireddy Jivitha Sangraham.* Vijayawada: T.N. Memorial Trust, 1986. pp. 1–24.
17. Devulapalli Venkateswarrao. *Bharata Viplava Pandhanu Choopina Telangana Sayudha Poratam* (Telugu). Hyderabad: Porunela Publications, January 2014. pp. 65–70.
18. Seling S. Harrison. "Caste and the Andhra Communists", *The American Political Science Review*, Vol. 50, No. 2, June 1956. pp. 378–404.
19. *Manaku Tliyani Mana Charitra: Telangana Rythanaga Poratam lo Sthreelu*. Hyderabad: Sthri Shakthi Sangatana Publications, 1986. p. 178.
20. K. Balagopal, M. Kodandaram Reddy. "Forever 'Disturbed: Peasant Struggle of Sircilla-Vemulawada", *Economic and Political Weekly*, Vol. 17, No. 48, November 27, 1982, 1897–1901.
21. K. Srinivasulu. "CPI(ML) and the Question of Caste: Dynamics of Social Mobilisation in Anti-feudal Struggles in Telangana". Ed. by Basu, Pradip, *Discourses on Naxalite Movement 1967–2009: Insights into Radical Left Politics.* Kolkata: Setu Prakashani, February 2010. pp. 230–231.
22. *Sircilla Rythanga Poratam-Purvaparalu* (Telugu). Vijayawada: CPI (ML)-Janashakthi, Andhra Pradesh Committee Prachuranalu, 1994. pp. 18–23.
23. *Jagityal Jangil Mahal-II* (Telugu). Hyderabad: Viplava Rachithala Sangam (virasam) Prachuranalu, 2002. pp. 27–30.
24. Gaddam Krishna Reddy. *Dalit Movement and Left Practice in Andhra Pradesh: An Ideological Linkages*. 2004, p. 4.
25. K. Balagopal. "Telangana Movement Revisited', *Economic and Political Weekly*, Vol. 18, No. 18 April 30, 1983, 709–712.
26. For detailed description see Sundarayya, P. *Telangana People's Struggle and Its Lessons*. New Delhi: Foundation Publication, 1972. pp. 7–10.
27. *Jagithyala Jungle Mahal: Viplavodyama Charitraka Rachanalu.* Vol. 2. Hyderabad: Virasam Prachuranalu, 2012. pp. 98–101.
28. Thirumali Inukonda. *Against Dora and Nizam: People's Movement in 1939–1948*. New Delhi: Kaniska Publishers, 2003. pp. 17–43.
29. Ibid.

30. Balagopal, K. "Two 'Missing' Women of Karimnagar", *Economic and Political Weekly*, Vol. 26, No. 5, February 2, 1991, 201–203, 205.
31. *Sircilla Rythanaga Poratam-Porvaparalu* (Telugu). Vijayawada: Andhra Pradesh CPI (ML)-Janashakthi State Committee Prachuranalu, 1994. p. 15.
32. Ghanta Chakrapani. "Charitra Rachanalalo Anyayam: Hyderabad dhe Aasalina Vudyamam", *Samantaara* (Telugu Monthly Magazine), Vol.1, No. 2, May 2007, 23–26.
33. See Viplava Rachayithala Sangam. *Jagithyala Jungle Mahal: Viplavodyama Charitraka Rachanalu*. Hyderabad: Virasam, 2012. p. 57.
34. Personal Interview with Chalapathi Rao (leader of Rythu Cooli Sangam in Sircilla), on August 16, 2014.
35. Mallepalli Laxmaiah. "Nurella Telugu Dalitodyamam", *Samantaara*, Vol. 1, No. 2, May 2007. p. 4.
36. Sharad Patil. "Ambedkarism-Marxism". Ed. by Tarakam, Bojja, *Nalupu* (Telugu Magazine). Hyderabad: Hyderabad Book Trust Publications, Vol. 4, No. 6, August 1–15, 1992. pp. 28–32.
37. Challapalli Swaruparani. "Prathigatana Athma rakshana Dhisaga Chunduru Vudyamam, Kurnol", *Chercha* (Telugu Monthly Magazine), Vol. 2, No. 8, May/June 2007, 19–21.
38. D. Narisimha Reddy. "Karamchedu: A Dialectic without Development", *Economic and Political Weekly*, Vol. 20, No. 37, September 14, 1985, 1546–1549.
39. Katti Padmarao. "Karamchedu Oka Charitraka Malupu", Ongole: *Bahujana Kerataalu Special Issue on Karam Chedu* (Telugu Monthly Magazine on Caste, Class issues), Vol. 1, No. 4, July 2005, 5–9.
40. U. Sambashivarao. "Naxalbari Rivinism pai Poradindhi! Karamchedu Brahamanism pai Poradamandhi!!", Ongole: *Bahujana Keratalu*, Vol. 1, No. 4, July 2005, 18–22.
41. K. Balagopal. "Karamchedu Second Anniversary", *Economic and Political Weekly*, Vol. 22, No. 33, August 15, 1987, 1378–1381.
42. *Andhra Pradesh Dalita Mahasabha Pranalika*. Tenali: Dalita Mahasabha Second Anniversary Resolutions, 1986. pp. 4–6.
43. K. Balagopal. *Ear to the Ground: Selected writings on Class and Caste*. New Delhi: Navayana Publications, 2011. p. 142.
44. K. Balagopal. "Karamchedu: Second Anniversary", *Economic and Political Weekly*, Vol. 22, No. 33, August 15, 1987, 1378–1381.

45. Katti Padmarao. "Karamchedu Oka Charitraka Malupu", Ongole: *Bahujana Kerataalu Special Issue on Karam Chedu* (Telugu Monthly Magazine on Caste, Class issues), Vol. 1, No. 4, July 2005, 5–9.
46. Duddu Prabhakar. "Dalitula Atmagouravanni Dessam Nalumulala Eligetti Chatina Chunduru Dalitulu", *Kulanirmulana* (Telugu Monthly Magazine), Bulletin 4, September–November 2007, 24–27.
47. "Upper Caste Violence: Study of Chunduru Carnage", *Economic and Political Weekly,* Vol. 26, No. 36, September 7, 1991, 2079–2084.
48. *Gunturu Zilla Chunduru Dalitulapai Agrakula Durahkarula Hatyakanda pai Nija nirdhrana Nivedhika* (Fact Finding Report on Chunduru Dalit Killings), Hyderabad: Andhra Pradesh Poura Hakkula Sangam (APCLC) and Prajaswamya Hakkula Parirakshana Samasta (OPDR), August 1991, pp. 1–28.
49. K. Balagopal. "Post-Chunduru and Other Chundurus", *Economic and Political Weekly*, Vol. 26, No. 42, October 19, 1991, 2399–2401 and 2403–2405.
50. M. Shatrugana. "Guns for the Goons", *Economic and Political Weekly*, Vol. 24, No. 17, April 29, 1989, 897.
51. *Gunturu Zilla Chunduru Dalitulapai Agrakula Durahkarula Hatyakanda pai Nija nirdhrana Nivedhika* (Fact Finding Report on Chunduru Dalit Killings), Hyderabad: Andhra Pradesh Poura Hakkula Sangam (APCLC) and Prajaswamya Hakkula Parirakshana Samasta (OPDR), August 1991, pp. 1–28.
52. Andhra Pradesh Civil Liberties Committee. *The Chundur Carnage*. Vijayawada: APCLC Publications, August 6, 1991. pp. 2–6.
53. K. Murali. *Upper Caste Violence in Karamchedu, Chunduru and State Responsibility.* 1995, p. 67.
54. K. Ilaiah. *Caste or Class or Caste-Class: A Study in Dalit Bahujan Consciousness and Struggles in A P in 1980's.* New Delhi: NMML, 1995. p. 27.
55. Bojja Tarakam. (Ed.), *Nalupu*. Hyderabad: Hyderabad Book Trust, 1991. Refer Issues, May 16–31 and June 1–15, 1991.
56. *Nalupu*. op. cit., June 1–15, 1992.
57. Ibid.
58. Ajay Gudavarthy. *Maoism, Democracy and Globalisation: Cross-Currents in Indian Politics*. New Delhi: Sage Publications, 2014. pp. 44–66.

59. "Fight against the Tendencies of Economism and Revisionism", People's War Central Committee, October 1981, p. 6.
60. M. Kodandaram, Sudhakar, S. (Ed.) *Moodu Dashabdhala Naxalbari Gamyam, Gamanam* (Telugu). Hyderabad: Perspectives Publications, 1998. p. 42.
61. Azad. "Maoists in India: A Rejoinder", *Economic and Political Weekly*, Vol. 41, No. 41, October 14–20, 2006, 4379–4383.
62. "Kendra Rajakeeya Nirmana Sameeksha" (Telugu), CPI(ML)-People's War Party, 1998. p. 42.
63. K. Balagopal. "Chikati Koonalu". Ed. by Kodandaram M., Sudhakar S., *Moodu Dasabdhala Naxalbari Gamyam-Gamanam*. Hyderabad: Perspectives Publications. pp. 150–219.
64. U. Sambashivarao (Ed.). *Edureetha* (Telugu). Hyderabad: Marxist-Leninist Centre, May 1991.
65. Ibid., May 1991.
66. E.S. Ravikumar. "Maoist Party lo Saguthunna Kula Vivaksha". Ed. by Rajashekar, V.T., *Dalit Voice* (Telugu Monthly Magazine). Hyderabad: Dalita Sahitya Cultural Academy, Dalit Voice, Bulletin 12, December 2005, 23–24.
67. Katti Padmarao. "Karam Chedu Oka Charitraka Malupu", Ongole: *Bahujana Keratalu*, Vol. 1, No. 4, July 2005, 5–9.
68. Personal Interview with Bojja Tarakam on October 8, 2014.
69. Sampath Kumar. "Kulanni Chudani vaadu Marxist Ela Avuthadu", Ed. by Tarakam, Bojja, *Nalupu*. Hyderabad: Hyderabad Book Trust Publications, Vol. 4, No. 5, July 1–31, 1992. pp. 9–10.
70. Maroju Veeranna. *Indialo Emcheyyali*. Andhra Pradesh: Andhra Pradesh May 17th Comrades CPUSI (DBSV) Prachuranalu, April 2001. pp. 1–9.
71. *Dalita Samasya-Viplava Communistula Vikary: Oka Samkshipta Vivarana*", Andhra Pradesh: CPI (ML)-Janashakthi Andhra Pradesh State Committee Publications, July 1994. pp. 1–19.
72. Maroju Veeranna's group is called May 17th Comrades for which Veeranna was the leader and the document submitted by them is called May 17th Comrades Document.
73. Maroju Veeranna. *Indialo Emcheyyali*. Andhra Pradesh: Andhra Pradesh May 17th Comrades CPUSI (DBSV) Prachuranalu, April 2001. pp. 157–173.
74. Ajay Gudavarthy. *Maoism, Democracy and Globalisation: Cross-Currents in Indian Politics*. New Delhi: Sage Publications, 2014. p. 59.

75. Vadapalli Nagaraju, G. Veeranna. "SC Reservationla Vargikarana-Samajaka Nyayam". Ed. by Venugopal N., *Veekshanam* (Telugu Journal). Hyderabad: Veekshanam Publications, Vol. 6, No. 3, March 8. pp. 20–23.
76. P. Muthaiah. "Politics of Dalit Identity", *The Indian Journal of Political Science*, Vol. 65, No. 3 July–September, 2004, 385–402.
77. K. Balagopal. "Justice for Dalits among Dalits: All the Ghosts Resurface", *Economic and Political Weekly*, Vol. 40, No. 29 July16–22, 2005, 3128–3133.
78. Gouri Vara Prasad Madiga Chinthada., "Madigala Atma Gourava Poratam", Ongole: *MRPS*, May 1997, 1–9.
79. Jangam Chinnaiah. "Sub-Caste Consciousness: Challenges before Dalit Intellectuals", Ed. by Chinna Rao, Yagati, *Dividing Dalits: Writings on Sub-Categorisation of Scheduled Castes*. Jaipur: Rawat Publications, 2009. pp. 100–105.
80. Personal Interview with Krishna Madiga on July 2, 2014.
81. Personal Interview with Bojja Tarakam on October 8, 2014.
82. Gundimeda Sambaiah. "Madiga Dandora: A Social Movement for Rationalisation of Dalit Reservations". Ed. by Chinna Rao, Yagati, *Dividing Dalits: Writings on Sub-Categorisation of Scheduled Castes*. Jaipur: Rawat Publications, 2009. pp. 106–156.
83. "Kulanirmulana Lakshyamga Vargikarana Samasyanu Parishkarinchukundam". Ed. by Satyanarayana K., *Kulanirmulana* (Telugu magazine), Bulletin 4, September–November 2007, 12–16.
84. Yagati Chinna Rao (Ed.). *Dividing Dalit: Writings on Sub-Categorisation of Scheduled Castes*. Jaipur: Rawat Publications, 2009. p. 113.
85. Personal Interview with Krishna Madiga on July 2, 2014.
86. K. Balagopal. "A Tangled Web", *Economic and Political Weekly*, Vol. XXXV, No. 13, March 25, 2000, 1076.
87. Kothapalli Jayashankar. *Telangana Oka Demand*. Karimnagar: Mallepalli Rajam Memorial Trust, March 2004. pp. 34–52.
88. Keshavarao Jadhav. "Towards a History of Telangana Movement". Ed. by Simhadri S., Vishweshwar Rao P.L., *Telangana Dimensions of Underdevelopment*. Hyderabad: Centre for Telangana Studies, 1997. pp. 5–13.
89. M. Kodandaram. "Movement for Telangana: A Struggle for Autonomy", *Economic and Political Weekly*, Vol. 42, No. 2, January 13–19, 2002, 90–94.

90. Goutam Pingle. *The Fall and Rise of Telangana*. New Delhi: Orient Blackswan Publications, 2014. pp. 22–24.
91. "Surya Peta Declaration", *Telanganalo Samajika Prajarajyam*. Hyderabad: Samajaka Telangana Mahasabha, 2010. pp. 27–42.
92. U. Sambashivarao. "Bougolika Samajika Telangana", Andhra Pradesh: Andhra Jyothi (Telugu Newspaper), March 18, 2009.
93. "Prathyeka Prajaswamya Udyamanirmaanam Mana Karyakramam (Telugu)", *CPI ML-Maoist Party Document*, Letter No. 1/2008. p. 49.
94. "Maoists on Telangana", *Maoists in India: Writings and Interviews by Azad*. Hyderabad: Published by Friends of Azad, 2010. pp. 80–84.
95. *Sri Krishna Committee Report* (The Committee for Consultations on the Situation in Andhra Pradesh. Presents its report under chairmanship of Justice B.N. Krishna to the Government of India), December 30, 2010. pp. 342–367.
96. B. Shyam Sunder. "Pratyeka Telangana Oka Charithraka Avasaram" (Letter to Prime Minister on January 1973 on behalf of Scheduled Kulalu, Tegalu, Venukabadina Tharagatulu and Minorities), *Samaantara,* Vol. 3, No. 9, December 2009, 3–5.
97. "Hyderabad Declaration", Telanganalo Samajika Praja Rajyam. Hyderabad: Edureetha Publications, November 2010. pp. 5–26.
98. Gaddam Krishna Reddy. "Key Note Address" in the National Seminar on *Democracy, Development and Justice,* in Department of Political Science, Osmania University, Hyderabad, March 26–27, 2015.
99. Nagam Kumaraswamy. "Telangana-Ambedkar". Ed. by Venugopal. *Viskshanam* (Monthly Telugu Magazine), May 2007, 41–43.
100. J. Janardhan, P. Raghavendra. "Telangana: History and Political Sociology of Movement", *Social Change,* Vol. 43, No. 4, December 2013, 551–564.
101. K.G. Kannabiran. "On the Telangana Trail", *Economic and Political Weekly,* Vol. XLIX, No. 26/27, June 28, 2014, 69–82.

Conclusion

After more than half a century after independence, caste system still plagues Indian subcontinent. Even after new countries were formed with new identities and new aspirations out of Indian subcontinent, these new countries including India failed miserably in obliterating caste system. Every attempt to analyse and understand caste-based discrimination, exploitation, and practice falls short before its ability to transform and reinvent itself with every passing decade! On the surface, it seems that everybody accepts that caste system is inhuman, derogatory, and needs to be abolished, yet it is practiced in every city, town, and village and in every family. This hints at the dubious nature of the upper caste Hindus who would never let it die, because the death of caste is the death of their power and control over the society. They need the caste structure to be intact in order to maintain and perpetuate their superiority. On the other hand, Dalits who were the worst victims of the caste system needs to demolish it if they want any change in their lives and social status. And there is this continuous struggle between the conspiracy of the upper castes to maintain the caste hierarchy and Dalit's fight to destroy it and the struggle is still on. This study had made an attempt to understand caste independently (say, if that is possible) and in relation to class.

In the course of their struggle, Dalits have embraced every possible ideology and practice to confront and demolish the caste system. The significance of Dalit movement is that it had engaged and experimented with all possible political practices, as my study has pointed out in the first chapter, ranging from liberal, reformative to communist, Marxist, and Maoist movements in this modern era. Main political parties such as Congress and Communist parties did not address caste problems; most of the times they didn't even recognize caste as an issue. In their struggle for emancipation, Dalits have found a ray of hope in Radical Marxism. Radical Left parties had successfully organized and mobilized Dalits against feudal landlords with the aim of establishing an egalitarian society. Dalit youth joined radical parties in the hope that these parties might find solutions to caste and other social inequalities. This study argued that Radical Left parties failed to understand the caste equations while trying to address the social inequalities in the society.

To understand and analyse the interface between Dalit and Radical Left movement, this study has different theoretical frameworks such as Liberal, Marxist, structuralist, and post-structuralist theories.

Liberal philosophers are basically ethical individuals: they persist that individuals should be free to decide and practice their own notions of the good life. They give enormous importance to individual rights and liberties over community life and collective goods. Some of the individualist liberal thinkers even have gone to the extent of belief that one can and should account for social actions and social goods in terms of properties of the constituent individuals and individual goods. What discerns from communitarians' discussion is the transformation of cite of autonomy from individual in the liberal discourse to group or community. It becomes a basis for new mobilization politics in liberal systems to a great extent in the contemporary times.

Ambedkar philosophy was an Enlightening philosophy that could be described as of 'social liberation' combined with an emphasis on caste as a social reality; and it distinguished Ambedkar from both Marxists who saw the proletariat as revolutionary and neglected cultural and social factors, and from both the dominant and Congress Party (not to mention the Hindu Right wing), which refused to see elements of exploitation and oppression in the Hindu caste society.

Marxist structuralism is basically a theory, which theorizes the binary opposition. This proposes that there are certain theoretical and conceptual opposites, often structured in hierarchical human relations and they even permeate the common sensical language. Such binary pairs could include good/bad, rational/emotional, and true/false. Marxist especially who focussed on relative autonomy also have not succeeded in analysing the question of caste because of its class perspective and over emphasis on economic than on sociocultural aspects which are as important as economic aspects. According to Marxists of the orthodox school, the political revolution led by the proletariat or working class to capture state power would ultimately emancipate all other forms of oppression. Going by this doctrine, it followed that the emergence of Dalit consciousness and identity as a separate social movement was non-progressive and sectarian.

Neo-Marxism or New Left, which challenged the orthodox historical materialism, brought about a general renaissance of Marxist thought, led by Georg Lukacs and Antonio Gramsci. The other luminaries of the new structuralist Marxism were Louis Althusser, the Frankfurt school of critical theory led by Herbert Marcuse, Theodor Adorno, and Max Horkheimer, all of whom sought to give relevant answers to many acute problems of society and politics. They widened the political role of the working class in relation to the new social movements which are based not only on class but also on other cultural categories such as of caste, gender, culture, and ecology. Influenced by this broadened New Left thought, there emerged the phenomenon of subaltern historiography, popularly known as the Cambridge School of Indian scholars, with Ranajit Guha in the forefront. Their mode of historiography is distinctly different from the mainstream history. They wrote 'history from below'. According to the subaltern historiographers, all forms of social consciousness are an outcome of spontaneous impulse to resist imperial dominance. However, the problem with this New Left or Subaltern studies, as Kancha Ilaiah pointed out, is that they have not given due importance to caste subordination and exploitation. In order to understand the specific caste–class position of subordinated Dalit-bahujans, Ilaiah characterized them as sub-subalterns.

The study traced the history of Dalit movement in Telangana from twentieth century to present day. It started with Bhakti Movement of thirteenth century which created Brahmin and non-Brahmin division. The Bhakti poets by questioning the religious restrictions on worship, in a way directly questioned the brahmanical hegemony on religion and religious practices. By preaching all are equal before God, they created a split in the Hindu social order. They brought in Brahmin and non-Brahmin identity. Dalits who were denied entry into the temples naturally took to these people. Bhakti poets paved the way for Dalits to identify themselves as anti-brahmanical, thereby created a new non-Brahmin identity consciousness.

After Bhakti movement, it was Reform movement that furthered the Dalit cause. The Arya Samaj in Hyderabad state was founded in 1880 in Dharur Taluk of Beed district. The message propagated by Arya Samaj was of (a) Equality of all human beings, (b) Condemnation of caste system, (c) Equal opportunities of education and refinement, (d) 'Back to Vedas' and 'India for Indians'. Brahmo Samaj was established in 1828 in West Bengal by Raja Ram Mohan Roy. The Samaj aimed at reformation of the Hindu society and the religious beliefs. The samaj not only focussed on sati and child marriage, and other social issues related to dominant castes but also chalked out programmes for depressed castes. The programmes were mainly focussed on openings schools for Dalits and also supporting their amelioration.

Hence these organizations became the welcoming shelter for Dalits who tried to escape from the cruel practice of discrimination in the name of caste. Dalits believed and supported its sincere objective in building a casteless society. These movements, in fact, created space for Dalits to come out and articulate their voice. Bhagya Reddy Varma and Arige Ramaswamy were among the active Dalit workers during 1920s who initially worked with Arya Samaj and Brahmo Samaj respectively. Then they established their own Dalit organizations and began to address the more specific caste-related atrocities such as abolition of *vetti* and *jogini* practices. The leaders realized that lack of education was the main reason for Dalits deplorable condition, so they fought for the establishment of educational institutions for the enlightenment of Dalits. In this regard, the contributions of

B.S. Venkat Rao are noteworthy. He was the education minister of the then Hyderabad state and had convinced the Nizam to allot ₹ 1 crore for education of the poor. With modern education, Dalits began to assert their identity and the movement transformed into independent movement, an autonomous stage. With the entry of Dr B.R. Ambedkar into Dalit politics, the movement has taken a drastic transformation. The movement has acquired a pan-India status and began to function on Ambedkar's ideology, which in the course of time came to be called as Ambedkarism. It has also questioned the opinion of Gail Omvedt regarding Dalit participation in Telangana peasant movement. And it argued that Dalits actively participate in all the Left movements in Telangana. This study argued that Dalit movement in Telangana from 1906 to the present day has been continuous and vibrant as against the popular notion of missing decades (1950s–1980s) in the Dalit movements' historiography.

Madiga Dandora movement treaded a new path within Dalit movement opening up new lines of thought within Ambedkarism. The Dandora movement brought to the front the discrimination within Dalits and raised the curtains for sub-caste movements. Dalits began to assess the caste and class relation within the Dalit community. This study has traced back the uneasiness within the Dalits to 1930s which is when Arundathiya Mahasabha was established by Arige Ramaswamy. Till then Dalits were treated by themselves and others as more or less homogeneous group, at least in their fight against upper caste hegemony. Here it is to be noted that they are well aware of internal hierarchy that existed within Dalits. From here on, the Dalit leaders started to respond to issues such as the attacks on Dalits based on sub-castes. It forced Dalit scholars to be more critical and democratic in studying the Dalits struggle and change their methodology in studying the problems of Dalits.

Dandora movement threw focus on sub-castes which are otherwise comfortably ignored within the Dalit community. The movement has erased the gap between the rural uneducated Dalits and their leaders in urban areas. It has produced new Dalit organic leaders who are semi-literates and rural-based youth. The striking thing that Madigas leaders did was add the prefix 'Madiga' to their movement and all related activities such as

Madiga Dandora movement, Madiga Dandora rally, and Madiga Dandora meeting. Even they started suffixing their caste name to their name to assert their self-respect and confidence and to identify with their own caste men. This was a clever intentional subversion of meanings associated with certain words. The study argued that Dandora movement effectively used the elements of culture and transformed them into political tools to play it on political arena; it was a simultaneous fight both on political and cultural fronts. This has also created space for the rise of Madiga intellectuals for the first time in history of Dalit politics in erstwhile Andhra Pradesh state and present Telangana state. The study has argued that the class conscious generated by Radical Left movement has helped the Dalits to introspect and see the class differences within the Dalit communities, which in turn has led to the formation of Madiga Dandora movement.

This study also argued that Telangana Dalit movement never disassociated itself with Radical Left movement. With assumption that given the Indian specificity the caste question has to be central and integral to any Marxist understanding, it had been argued that in Indian context, one cannot completely disassociate caste from class. Thus, Dalit movement and Marxist movement are not two exclusive practices but signify a mutually influencing historical continuation. With all its shortcomings and failure to address the caste issues as promised or as expected, no other movement in Telangana has brought a change such as Left movement in rural Dalits perception of the society. It helped them to break the shackles of upper caste hegemony. The people who lived on the outskirts of the village were made members of the village committees. In a time when Dalits were not even treated as human beings, the Communist Party recognized their strength and brought them into village and some of them even rose to become prominent members of the committees.

The movement, for the first time in history, questioned openly the normative arrangements and values that legitimized oppression and marginalization of poor peasants and labourers in the social, economic, and political systems of villages. This movement provided Dalits an alternative world view and life options which equipped them ideologically to question the legitimacy of existing oppressive and exploitative socio-economic and political system of the rural society. It also united the lower castes, Dalits and tribal people, broke their isolation, and empowered them politically to fight against oppression and exploitation. The movement provided Dalits a space to articulate their issues and express their discontent against the existing forms and organization and values of the rural society. On the whole, this movement brought in the message and promise of an egalitarian society that aimed to radically change the old values, institutions, and norms of the existing society.

Naxalite movement, it is argued, was the result of state's failure to bring about any substantial change in agrarian social relations and social life in the rural areas in spite of its progressive agrarian legislations. The CPI (ML) groups established their support bases in the areas which were on the periphery of the earlier peasant struggle. In a sense, the CPI (ML) agrarian movement tried to finish the process that had remained unfinished since the 1940s.

The issues taken up in those struggles showed sensitivity to caste, though the party mobilized people using class-oriented language. We see two important changes in the CPI (ML) politics in general and the PWG in particular. One is the shift to popular mobilization by strengthening mass front organizations such as RSU, RYL, and JNM in the cultural front. Second is the clear direction to bring the subaltern social groups into the movement not in terms of class but in specific caste terms as SCs, artisans, and occupational communities. However, they did not try to engage with caste at an ideological level. The ML movement was reluctant to accept an ideological combination of Marxism with Ambedkarism. This was seen as diluting of revolution and gravitating towards reformism. More important reflection of this was the refusal to recognize Dalit movement as an independent political struggle. The Naxalite movement also strongly believed in the centrality of the armed-wing and a hierarchical relation with various mass organizations. The Dalit movement therefore could not fit into their scheme of political organization and modes of protest and mobilization.

With Karamchedu incident, Dalits rejected the Left platform to voice their grievances. As a symbolic representation of an autonomous struggle, Dalit leaders decided that only Dalits would occupy the dais and address others on the issue of Karamchedu. It was decided that no upper caste, however radical and sympathetic to the Dalit cause, would be allowed to share this space. This demand of 'only Dalits' was one of the earliest forms in which autonomy was articulated in Andhra Pradesh (erstwhile). All those Dalits who were part of the communist movement were now *discursively* re-articulated as 'Dalit communists'. Ambedkarism emerged as the guiding philosophy for an independent Dalit 'social revolution', which was later referred to as a 'New Dalit Democratic Revolution' both as a continuation and to counter the ML group's struggle for 'New Democratic Revolution'. Such alternate articulations created conditions for movements to rethink their position vis-à-vis each other.

Both Karamchedu and Chunduru incidents have brought in a set of radical changes in both Dalit and Radical Left practices. There was serious discussion between and among Dalit leaders and Naxalites on how to address the issue of caste and how to construct their future course of action. It is against this backdrop of an emerging politics of solidarity that the DMS officially launched its journal called *Nalupu* (Black) in April 1989. Its focus and purpose clearly reflected this need to evolve a broader strategy for the Dalit movement. It also reflected the need to forge solidarity with ML parties such as the PWG and yet fight for the benefits of the existing socio-legal system offered. *Nalupu* emerged as an important platform reflecting the nature of the Dalit movement and the possible directions it would take in times to come. It was to explore further possibilities of solidarity with the Naxalite movement that the Dalit writers started yet another journal called *Edureetha* (Swimming against the Tide) in May 1990. Two important Dalit leaders who were previously part of the Naxalite movement (while the editor of the journal came out of the UCCRI [ML] group, another important member of the editorial board was previously a COC member of the PWG) started it. They together also started the Marxist-Leninist Centre. Though the journal declared its perspective as 'Marxist-Leninist' and as a 'journal for revolutionary politics', none of the ML parties owned it but it was the Dalit organizations and writers who identified with it. A more explicit articulation of an ideological basis for solidarity in a synthesis of Ambedkarism and Marxism was acceptable to most of the Dalit groups, not so for many of the ML parties.

The discussions carried in *Nalupu* and *Edureetha* have led to intellectual churning in Dalit and ML parties. These discussions stressed the need for a strong ideological base, especially among CPI (ML) parties, to include and address Dalit issues. This period of ideological conflict and uncertainty led to the rise of another Dalit leader, Maroju Veeranna, from Left parties. He felt that the present communist ideology is insufficient and does not suit to Indian society. He strongly argued for the adoption of Ambedkar's ideology into Marxist ideology. Veeranna proposed that without social transformation class transformation is not possible. He proposed a new revolutionary path for India which includes Phule-Ambedkar's thoughts and prepared a document towards this end which is called May 17th Comrades Document. In 1998, Veeranna's group submitted their document titled *Indialo Emcheyyali* (What is to be done in India?) to the party for discussion on the new revolutionary path to be adopted by the party. But, the CPI (ML) party not only did not accept this document but also expelled Veeranna's group from the party.

Dandora movement has helped the Radical Left parties to bridge the gap created by Karamchedu and Chunduru incidents. Dandora movement is a caste-based movement with a class conflict. Dandora movement brought to the front the inherent link between the caste and the class in the Indian society. This study argued that in Telangana it is caste which decides the class, and Dandora movement has proved the invariable link between caste and class. And this forced the Left parties to reconsider their stance with regard to caste. Radical Left movement created so much awareness among Dalits about the concept of class and its relationship with the distribution and misappropriation of resources that they questioned the misappropriations of resources within themselves.

Finally this book focussed on Telangana movement. The Telangana movement is not merely the demand for statehood, but also the demand for political, economic, and cultural autonomy, from the Andhra region. The movement happened at the intersection of Dalit and Radical Left movement trying to consolidate their ideological positions. We can see the shades of aspirations of both the movements in Telangana movement. Both these historical movements have created space for the demand for regional autonomy to re-emerge once again.

Both the movements at their regional specifications have a long and cherished history of political struggles and in raising demands for social equality and economic freedom. Both the movements operated with a conscious aggression about their own ideological merits and hardly built any systematic dialogical relation with the other about the strategies for the defence of the oppressed sections.

However, with all these ideological differences and limitation, I have argued in this study that post Ambedkarite Dalit movements in Telangana have got its roots in Radical Left movement in this region. Left movement has successfully exposed the hegemony of upper castes on Dalits and gave Dalits a cause and reason for united struggle against the oppressive regime. This consciousness has helped the Dalit in furthering their cause and fight for the social justice. Madiga Dandora movement is a contemporary example which has shaped up and supports my arguments. Even the huge support base of Dalits and their active participation in separate Telangana state could be viewed from this perspective. In Telangana, there a solidarity between Left movement and Dalit movement which is specific to this region.

Finally a consensus, or even an agreement, between these two forces of changes can only be built if both manage to move beyond the contestations of the past and also liberate themselves from their specific ideological canons to be open to constructing new radical alternatives. Regarding caste, there does not seem to be much clarity, although there is a general recognition that the caste is an issue that needs to be consciously tackled. The factors that presses this need are: one, there is a pressure exerted from Dalit leaders such as Maroju Veeranna and Dalit cadres who constitute a majority to take a stand on caste within the Left movement; two, there is a competitive pressure on these parties to distinguish themselves because the Dalit organizations have become a significant attraction for the Dalit cadres mainly after Karamchedu incident which forced the Radical Left parties to consider the caste issue seriously. However, caste is still not recognized as the key issue in articulating successful class struggle. In any society there would be numerous issues representing as many contradictions but at a given stage only a single issue corresponding to principle contradiction dominates and needs to be resolved. Caste is such an issue but that realization is still not reflected in the understanding of any Left parties. For both the Dalits and the Marxists, there is need to rethink their theoretical model and try to formulate a new ideological base to work together without deviating from main aim of establishing an equal and egalitarian society.

Bibliography

Abbasyalu, Y.B., "Scheduled Caste Elite: A Study of Scheduled Caste Elite in Andhra Pradesh, Hyderabad", Harijan Studies Centre, Osmania University, Hyderabad, 1978.

——, "Sociology of Depressed Groups", Harijan Studies Centre, Hyderabad: Osmania University, 1979.

Acharya, K.R., "Telangana and Andhra Agitations", Ram Reddy, B.A.V. Sharma (Ed.), *State Government and Politics: Andhra Pradesh*, New Delhi: Sterling Publications, 1979.

Ajay, Gudavarthy., *Maoism, Democracy and Globalisation: Cross-Currents in Indian Politics*, New Delhi: Sage Publications, 2004.

——, "Dalit and Naxalite Movements in AP: Solidarity or Hegemony?", *Economic and Political Weekly*, Vol. 40, No. 51, December 17–23, 2005.

——, *Politics of Post-civil Society: Contemporary History of Political Movement in India*, New Delhi: Sage Publications, 2013.

Althusser, L., *For Marx*, London: Allen Lane, 1965.

Ambedkar, B.R., *The Untouchables; Who Were They and Why They Become Untouchables*, New Delhi: Amrit Books, 1948.

——, "Untouchables—Their Numbers, in Dr. Baba Saheb Ambedkar: Writings and Speeches, Vo1. 8", Bombay: Government of Maharashtra, 1989.

——, "Castes in India: Their Mechanism, Genesis and Development", Manoranjan Mohanty (Ed.), *Caste, Class Gender: Readings in Indian Government and Politics*, New Delhi: Sage Publications, 2004.

——, "Annihilation of Caste", New Delhi: Critical Quest, 2007.

——, "Gandhi and Gandhism", New Delhi: Critical Quest, 2008.

——, "Buddha or Karl Marx", New Delhi: Critical Quest, January 2014.

——, "Dr. Babasaheb Ambedkar: Writings and Speeches, Vol. 15", Bombay: Government of Maharashtra, Education Department, January 2014.

——, "Dr. Babasaheb Ambedkar: Writings and Speeches, Vol. 1", Bombay: Government of Maharashtra, Education Department, January 2014.

Aravind N. Das, "Changel: Three Centuries of an Indian Village", *The Journal of Peasant Studies*, Vol. 15, No. 1, October 1987.

——, "A Report on the Girijan Struggle by Srikakulam Comrades" *Liberation*, Vol. 2, No. 2, December 1968.

Awad, Milind, "Historical Context of the Idea of the Dalit", *Think India Quarterly*, Vol. 13, No. 3, 2002.

Babu B. Ramesh (Ed.), *From Varna to Jati: Political Economy of Caste in India Social Formation* (Commemorating Scholar and Revolutionary Martyr Yalavarthi Naveen Babu), New Delhi: Danish Books Published, September 2008.

Bailey, F.G., *Politics and Social Change: Orissa in 1959*, Berkeley and Los Angeles: University of California Press, 1963.

Balagopal, K., "Peasant Struggle and Repression in Peddapally", *Economic and Political Weekly*, Vol. 17, No. 20, May 15, 1982.

——, "Discussion Telangana Movement Revisited", *Economic and Political Weekly*, Vol. 18, No. 18, April 30, 1983.

——, "Karamchedu: Second Anniversary", *Economic and Political Weekly*, Vol. 22, No. 33, August 15, 1987.

——, *Probing in the Political Economy of Agrarian Classes and Conflicts*, Hyderabad: Perspectives, 1988.

——, "The End of Spring?", *Economic and Political Weekly*, Vol. 25, No. 34, August 25, 1990.

——, "The Man and the Times", *Economic and Political Weekly*, Vol. 34, No. 26, June 26–July 2, 1999.

——, "Maoist Movement in Andhra Pradesh", *Economic and Political Weekly*, Vol. XLI, No. 29, July 22, 2006.

——, "Physiognomy of Violence", *Economic and Political Weekly*, Vol. 41, No. 22, June 3–9, 2006.

——, "Land Unrest in Andhra Pradesh—I Ceiling Surpluses and Public Lands", *Economic and Political Weekly*, September 22, 2007.

——, *Dalitha* (in Telugu). Hyderabad: Perspectives, 2011.

Balagopal K., Kodandaram M., "Forever 'Disturbed': Peasant Struggle of Sircilla-Vemulawada", *Economic and Political Weekly*, Vol. 17, No. 48, November 27, 1982.

Bharathi, Thummapudi, *A History of Telugu Dalit Literature*, New Delhi: Kalapaz Publications, 2008.

Basu, Pradeep (Ed.), *Discourses on Naxalite Movement 1967–2009: Insights into Radical Left Politics*. Kolkata: Setu Prakashani, 2010.

Bai L. Thara, *Changing Patterns of Caste and Class Relations in South India: Social Stratification and Social Mobility*, New Delhi: Gian Publishing House, 1987.

Begari, Jagannatham, *Interrogating Democracy and Human Rights: The Telangana Peoples Movement*, Jaipur: Rawat Publications, 2014.

Beteille, A., *Caste. Class and Power*, Berkeley: University of California Press, 1965.

——, *Caste, Class and Power: Changing Patterns of Stratification in Tanjore Village* (Second Edition), New Delhi: Oxford University Press, 1996.

Bettelheim, Charles, *India Independent*, New Delhi: Khosla & Co, 1977.

Banerjee, Sumanta, *India's Simmering Revolution: The Naxalite Uprising*, New Delhi: Select Book Service Syndicate, 1984.

Bhatt, A., *Caste. Class and Politics: An Empirical Profile of Social Stratification in Modem India*, New Delhi, 1975.

Bhukya, Bhangya, *Subjugated Nomads: The Lambadas under the Rule of the Nizams*, New Delhi: Orient Blackswan, 2010

Brass, Paul R., *The Politics of India Since Independence*, New Delhi: Foundation Books, 1992.

Cantwell, Smith W., "Hyderabad Muslim Tragedy", *Journal of Middle East*, Vol. IV, No. 1, January 1950, pp. 27–51.

Carchedi, G., *On the Economic Identification of Social Classes*, London: Routledge & Kegan Paul, 1977.

Caste and Class in India, Seminar Papers Hyderabad: An All India League for Revolutionary Culture Publication (AILRC), 1988.

"Caste-Action Programme of CPI (ML)—New democracy", Andhra Pradesh State Committee, CPI (ML)—New democracy Publications, January 2003.

Chakravarti, Uma, "Conceptualising Brahminical Patriarchy in Early India: Gender, Caste, Class and State", Manoranjan Mohanty (Ed.), *Caste, Class, Gender: Readings in Indian Government and Politics*, New Delhi: Sage Publications, 2004.

Chaterjee, Partha, "Caste and Subaltern Consciousness" in Ranajit Guha (Ed.), *Subaltern Studies, IV*, New Delhi: Oxford University Press, 1989.

——, *The Partha Chatterjee Omnibus: Comprising Nationalist Thought and the Colonial World, The Nations and Its Fragments, A Possible India*, New Delhi: Oxford University Press, 1999.

Chatterjee, S.K., *The Scheduled Castes in India*, New Delhi: Gyan Publishing House, 1996.

Chinna Rao, Yagati (Ed.), *Dividing Dalits: Writings on Sub-Categorisation of Scheduled Caste*, Jaipur: Rawat Publications, 2009.

Cohin, William, "Symbol of Power: Statues in Nineteenth Century Provincial France", *Comparative Studies in Society and History*, 1987.

Desai, A.R., *Rural Sociology in India, Bombay: The Indian Society of Agricultural Economics*, 1953.

——, *State and Society in India: Essays in Dissent*. Bombay: Popular Prakashan, 1975.

——, (Ed.), *Violation of Democratic Rights in India*, Bombay: Popular Prakashan, 1986.

Dhanagare, D.N., *Peasant Movement in India, 1920–1950*, New Delhi: Oxford University Press, 1983.

——, "Social Origins of the Telangana Insurrection (1946–1951)", *Contribution of Indian Sociology*, Vol. 8, 1984.

Dharma Theertha, Swami, *History of Hindu Imperialism*, 1992.

Dube, S.C., *India's Changing Villages*, London: Routledge and Kegan Paul, 1960.

Dumont, Louis, *Homo Hierarchies: The Caste System and Its Implications*, Chicago: The University of Chicago Press, 1974.

Edwardes, M., *The Myth of the Mahatma: Gandhi, the British, and the Raj*, London: Constable, 1986.

Elliott, Carolyn M., "Caste and Faction among the Dominant Castes: The Reddy and Kummar of Andhra", Rajni Kothari (Ed.), *Caste in Indian Politics*, New Delhi: Orient Longman, 1970.

Erikson, Erik, *Gandhi's Truth*, New York: Norton, 1969.

Eswara Reddy, A., *The Lok Sabha Elections. 1977 and 1980 in Andhra Pradesh*, Madras: Tamil Nadu Academy of Political Science, 1985.

Eyerman, R., Jamiaon, A., *Social Movements: A Cognitive Approach*, Cambridge: Basil Blackwell, 1991.

Fact Finding Team, *Karamchedu*, Salalah, Hyderabad, 1985.

Fanan, Frantz, *The Wretched of the Earth*, England: Penguin Books, 1990.

Francine R. Frankel, *India's Political Economy. 1947–77: The Gradual Revolution*, Princeton: Princeton University Press, 1978.

Francine R. Frankel, "Middle Classes and Castes in India's Politics: Prospects for Political Accommodation", Atul Kohli (Ed.), *India's Democracy: An Analysis of Changing State-Society Relation*, New Delhi: Orient Longman, 1988.

Francine R. Frankel, *India's Political Economy (1947–2004): The Gradual Revolution*, New Delhi: Oxford University Press, 2005.

Front Line, Vol. 21, No. 21 (October 9–22), 2004.

Front Line, Vol. 28, No. 15 (July 16–29), 2011.

Fuches, S., *Rebellious Prophet: A Study of Messianic Movements in Indian Religion*, Bombay: Asia Publishing House, 1965.

——, *At the Bottom of Indian Society: The Harijan and Other Low Caste*, New Delhi: Munshiram Manoharlal Publications, 1981.

Gandhi, M.K., *The Removal of Untouchability*, Ahmedabad: Navajivan Publishing House, 1959.

Ghurye, G.S., *Caste and Race in India*, London: Kegan Paul, Trench, 1932.

——, *Caste and Class in India*. Bombay: Popular Prakashan, 1950.

——, "Caste and British Rule", in Ishita Banerjee-Dube (Ed.), *Caste in History: Themes in Indian History*, New Delhi: Oxford University Press, 2008.

Grigson, V., *The Challenge of Backwardness*, Hyderabad: Government Press, 1947.

Gokhale, J.B., "The evolution of Counter-Ideology: Dalit Consciousness in Maharashtra", Francine R. Frankel, Rao, M.S.A. (Ed.), *Dominance and State Power in Modem India: Decline of a Social Order*, New Delhi: Oxford University Press, 1990.

Gokhale, Jayashree, *From Concessions to Confrontation: The Politics of an Indian Untouchable Community*, Bombay: Popular Prakashan, 1993.

Gopal Guru, "Dalit Movement in Mainstream Sociology", Sandeep, P. (Ed.), *At Cross-Roads: Dalit Movement Today*, Bombay: Vikas Adhyayan Kendra, 1994.

Gore, M.S., *The Social Context of an Ideology: Ambedkar's Political and Social Thought*, New Delhi: Sage Publications, 1993.

Gough, K., and Sharma H.P., *Imperialism and Revolution in South Asia*, New York: Monthly Review Press, 1973.

Gramsci, A., *Selections from the Prison Notebooks*, Madras: Orient Longman Ltd. (Indian Edition), 1996.

Green S. Bryan, *Knowing the Poor: A Case Study in Textual Reality Construction*, London: Routledge & Kegan Paul, 1983.

Guha, Ranajit (Ed.), *Subaltern Studies: Writings on South Asian History and Society*, Volume I to 9, New Delhi: Oxford University Press, 1982.

Guru, Gopal, "Dalit Movement and Mainstream Sociology", *EPW*, Vol. XXXVIII. No. 14, April 1993.

——, "The Language of Dalit Bahujan Political Discourse", Mohanty, Manoranjan (Ed.), *Caste, Class, Gender: Reading in Indian Governments and Politics*, New Delhi: Sage Publications, 2004.

Gupta, Depankar, *Interrogating Caste: Understanding Hierarchy and Difference in Indian Society*, New Delhi: Penguin Publications, 2000.

Haberrnas, J., *Knowledge and Human Interests*, London: Heinemann, 1972.

Hanumantha Rao, G., *Caste and Poverty: A Case Study of Scheduled Caste in a Delta Village*, Malikipuram: Savithri Publication, 1977.

Hanumantha Rao, V., *Party Politics in Andhra Pradesh*, Hyderabad: ABA Publications, 1993.

Haragopal, G., "The Caste-Class Question: Some Theoretical Concerns", *Caste and Class in India*, Hyderabad: All India League for Revolutionary Culture, AILRC, 1988.

Hardtmann, Eva Maria, *The Dalit Movement in India: Local Practice, Global Connections*, New Delhi: Oxford University Press, 2009.

Harrison S. Seling., *India's Most Dangerous Decades*, New Delhi: Oxford University Press, 1968.

Hasan, Zoya (Ed.), *Forging Identities: Gender. Communities and the State*, New Delhi: Kali for Women, 1994.

Hasan, Z., *Gandhi and the Harijans*, New Delhi: Shree Publishing House, 1986.

Heberle, R., *Social Movements: An Introduction to Political Sociology*, New York: Appleton Century Crafts, 1951.

Hobsbawm, E., *Revolutionaries*, London: Journeyman Press, 1973.

Hohler, Lorraine, "A Telangana State?: An Illustrative Analysis of the Stakes in Modifying Internal Borders", *Economic and Political Weekly*, Vol. XLVIII, No. 34, August 24, 2013.

Horkheimer, Max, and Adorno, Theodor W., *Dialectic of Enlightenment*, London: Allen Lane, 1973.

Hutton, J.H., *Caste in India*, Cambridge: Cambridge University Press, 1946.

Ilaiah, K., *The State and Repressive Culture: The Andhra Experience*, Hyderabad: Swecha Prachuranalu, 1989.

——, *Why I Am Not a Hindu: A Sudra Critique of Hindutva Philosophy, Culture and Political Economy*, Calcutta: Samya, 1996.

——, "Caste or Class or Caste Class: A Study in Dalit Bahujan Consciousness and Struggles in Andhra Pradesh in 1980s", Manoranjan Mohanty (Ed.), *Class, Caste, Gender*, New Delhi: Sage Publications, 2004.

Indian Revolutionary Movements: Some Lessons. 1967–1971, Vijayawada: Red Flag Publication, 1989.

Innaiah, N., *State Government and Politics: A Study of Andhra Pradesh Politics 1885–1985*, Hyderabad: Scientific Services, 1986.

Isaacs, Horalds R., *India's Ex-untouchable*, New York: The John Day Company, 1969.

Iyengar, S. Kesava, *Economic Investigation in the Hyderabad State 1929–1930*, Vol. 5, Hyderabad-Deccan: Government Central Press, 1931–1932.

Jadhav, Narendra, *Dr. Ambedkar's Economic Thought and Philosophy*, Bombay: Popular Prakashan, 1993.

Jaffrelot, Christophe, *Dr Ambedkar and Untouchability: Analysing and Fighting Caste*, New Delhi: Permanent Black, 2005.

——, *India's Silent Revolution: The Rise of the Low Castes in North Indian Politics*, New Delhi: Permanent Black, 2003.

James, S.S. Silverberg (Ed.), *Social Mobility in the Caste System in India*, The Hague: Mouton, 1968.

Janardhan V., and Raghvendra P., "Telangana History and Political Sociology of a Movement", *Social Change*, Vol. 43, No. 4, 2013.

Jaya Sree S. Prabha, "Arya Samaj Movement in Liberation of Hyderabad-Karnataka", *Indian Streams Research Journal*, Vol. 3, No. 4, 2013.

Jeffrey, Robin, "What the Statues Tell: The Politics of Choosing Symbols in Trivandrum", *Pacific Affairs*, 1980.

Jodhka S. Surender, *Caste: Oxford India Short Introductions*, New Delhi: Oxford University Press, 2012.

Jogdand, P.G. (Ed.), *Dalit Women: Issues and Perspectives*, New Delhi: Gyan Publishing House, 1995.

John Goldthrope, *Social Mobility and Class Structure*, 1980.

Joshi, B.R., *Democracy in Search of Equally: Untouchable Politics and Indian Social Change*, New Delhi: Hindustan Publishing Corporation, 1982.

Kadam, K.N. (Ed.), *Dr. B.R. Ambedkar: The Emancipator of the Oppressed*, Bombay: Popular Prakashan, 1993.

Kamble, N.D., *Deprived Castes and Their Struggle for Equality*, New Delhi: Ashish Publishing House, 1983.

Karen, Leonard, "Hyderabad: Mulki-Non-Mulki Conflict", in Robin Jeffrey (Ed.), *People, Princes, and Paramount Power: Society and Politics in the Indian Princely States*, New Delhi: OUP, 1978.

Kannabiran, Vasantha, "Report from SSS, a Women's Group in Hyderabad, Andhra Pradesh", *Feminist Studies*, Vol. 12, No. 3, Autumn, 1986.

Kaviraj, Sudipta (Ed.), *Politics in India*, New Delhi: Oxford University Press, 1997.

Keer, Dhananjay, *Dr. Ambedkar: Life and Mission*, Bombay: Popular Prakashan, 1962.

Klass, Morton, *Caste: The Emergence of the South Asian Social System*, Philadelphia: Institute for Study of Human Issues, 1980.

Kohli, Atul, *Democracy and Discontent: India's Growing Crisis of Governability*, New York: Cambridge University Press, 1990.

Kosambi, D.O., *An Introduction to the Study of Indian History*, Bombay: Popular Book Depot (1956) 1996.

Kothari, Rajni, *Politics and The People: In Search of a Humane India*, Two Volumes, New Delhi: Ajanta Publications, 1989.

——, *Rethinking Development: In Search of Human Alternatives*, New Delhi: Ajanta Publications, 1989.

——, *State against Democracy: In Search of Humane Governance*, New Delhi: Ajanta Publications, 1989.

——, *Transformation and Survival: In Search of Human World Order*, New Delhi: Ajanta Publications, 1989.

Kshirsagar, R.K., *Dalit Movement in India and Its Leaders (1957–1956)*, New Delhi: MD Publications, 1994.

Kuber, W.N., *Ambedkar: A Critical Study*, New Delhi: People's Publishing House, 1991.

Kuhn, T., *The Structure of Scientific Revolution*, Chicago: University of Chicago Press, 1962.

Kunnat, George J., *Rebels from the Mud Houses: Dalits and the Making of Maoist Revolution in Bihar*, New Delhi: Social Science Press, 2012.

Laclau, E., *Politics and Ideology in Marxist Thought*, London: New Left, 1977.

Laclau, E., Mouffe, C., *Hegemony and Socialist Strategy*, London: Verso, 1989.

Leach, E.R. (Ed.), *Aspect of Caste in South India, Ceylon North West Pakistan*, Cambridge: Cambridge University Press, 1960.

Lenin, V.I., *Selected Works in 3 Volumes*, Moscow: Progress, 1967.

Lieten, George Kristoffel, "Caste in Class Politics", *Economic and Political Weekly*, Vol. XIV, Nos. 7/8, February 24, 1979.

Lindt, Benjamin, "Towards Comprehensive Model of Caste", *Contribution to Indian Sociology*, Vol. 47, No. 1, 2013.

Lomax, Louise E., *The Negro Revolt*, London: Hamish Hamilton, 1963.

Lukacs, G., *History and Class Consciousness*, New Delhi: Rupa and Co (Indian Print), 1993.

Lynch, Owen, M., *The Politics of Untouchability: Social Mobility and Social Change in a City of India*, New Delhi: National Publishing House, 1974.

Mahajan Gurupreet (Ed.), *Democracy Difference and Social Justices*, New Delhi: Oxford University Press, 1998.

Malcolm, X., *Autobiography*, London: Hutchinson, 1966.

Mandelbaum, D.G., *Society in India: Change and Continuity*, Two Volumes, Barkley: University of California Press, 1970.

Mann, Michael, *Consciousness and Action among the Western Working Class*, London: Macmillan, 1973.

Mao Tse-tung, *Selected Works*, Five Volumes, Peking: Foreign Languages Press, 1961.

Marguerite S. Robinson, *Local Politics: The Law of the Fishes*, New Delhi: Oxford University Press, 1988.

Masani, M.R. and Guywint, *The Communist Party of India: A Short History*, New York: MacMillan, 1959.

Mathew, Thomas, *Caste and Class Dynamics: Radical Ambedkarite Praxis*, New Delhi: dTech, 1992.

Mehrotra, Santosh (Ed.), *Countering Naxalism with Development: Challenges of Social Justices and State Security*, New Delhi: Sage Publications, 2014.

Meszaros, Istvan (Ed.), *Aspects of History and Class Consciousness*, London: Routledge and Kegan Paul, 1971.

Michael, M.J. (Ed.), *The Untouchable in Contemporary Indian*, Tuscan: University of Arizona Press.

Moffatt, M., *An Untouchable Community in South India: Structure and Consensus*, Princeton: University Press, 1979.

Mohanty, Manoranjan, (Ed.), "Conclusion: Social Movements in a Creative Society", Manoranjan Mohanty (Ed.), *Caste, Class, Gender: Readings in Indian Government and Politics*, New Delhi: Sage Publications, 2004.

——. "Challenges of Revolutionary Violence: The Naxalite Movement in Perspective", *Economic and Political Weekly*, Vol. XLI, No. 29, July 22, 2006.

Mukherjee, Subrata, Ramaswamy, Sushila, *A History of Socialist Thought: From the Precursors to the Present*, New Delhi: Sage Publications, 2000.

Mukherjee, Hirendranath, *Gandhi, Ambedkar and the Extirpation of Untouchability*, New Delhi: People's Publishing House, 1982.

Muthaiah, P., "Dandora: The Madiga Movement for Equal Identity and Social Justice in A.P.", *Social Action*, Vol. 54, April–June 2004.

——, "Politics of Dalit Identity", *The Indian Journal of Political Science*, Vol. 65, No. 3, January–September 2004.

Mukund, Kanakatha (Ed.), *Andhra Pradesh Economy in Transition*, Hyderabad: Centre for Economic and Social Studies, Hyderabad and Book Corporation, 1990.

Mouffe, Chantal, and Holdengraber, Paul Holdengraber, "Universal Abandon? The Politics of Post Modernism", *Social Text*, No. 21, 1989.

Murali, K., *Upper Caste Violence on Dalits in Karamchedu, Chunduru and State Responsibility*, Unpublished PhD Thesis, Hyderabad: Hyderabad Central University, 1995.

——, "Continuing Militancy in Telangana", *Economic and Political Weekly*, Vol. 37, No. 8, February 23–March 1, 2002.

Nagaraj, D.R., *The Flaming Feet: Dalit Movement in India*, New Delhi: Permanent Black, 2012.

Naik, D. Ramulu, *M.V. Bhagya Reddy Varma's Life and Mission: A study* (An unpublished M. Phil. Dissertation), Hyderabad: Osmania University, 1992.

Odegard, P.H., *Political Power and Social Change*, New Jersey: New Brunswick, 1966.

O'Hanlon, Rosalind, *Caste, Conflict and Ideology: Mahatma Jyoti Rao Phule and Low Caste Protest in Nineteenth Century Western India*, Hyderabad: Cambridge, 1985.

Omvedt, Gail (Ed.), *Land, Caste and Politics in Indian States*, New Delhi: Authors Guild Publications, 1975.

——, "Towards a Marxist Analysis of Caste: A Response to B.T. Ranadive", *Social Scientist*, Vol. 6, No. 11, June 1978.

——, *Reinventing Revolution: New Social Movements and the Socialist Tradition in India*, New York: An East Gate Work, 1993.

——, *Dalits and the Democratic Revolution: Dr. Ambedkar and the Dalit Movement in Colonial India*, New Delhi: Sage Publications, 1994.

——, *Dalit Visions: The anti-Caste Movement and the Construction of an Indian Identity*, New Delhi: Orient Longman Ltd., 1995.

Ommen, T.K., *Protest and Change: Studies in Social Movements*, New Delhi: Sage Publications, 1990.

Ossowski, S., *Class Structure in the Social Consciousness*, London: Routledge & Kegan Paul, 1963.

Outhwaite, W., and Bottomore, T. (Ed.), *The Blackwell Dictionary of Twentieth Century Social Thought*, Oxford: Blackwell Publications, 1993.

Pai, Sudha, *Dalit Assertion*, New Delhi: Oxford University Press, 2013.

Pandma Rao, K., *Jailu Gantalu* (Poems), Ponnur: Lokayatan Prachuranalu, 1988.

——, *Dalitula Charitra*, Part I, Ponnur: Lokayata Prachuranalu, 1991.

——, *Caste and Alternative Culture*, Madras: Gurukul Lutheran Theological College and Research institute, 1995.

——, *Sanghika Vipla Raehayiitalu: Dalit Sahitya Vimarsha* (Telugu), Ponnur: Lokayata Publishers, 1995.

——, *Dalitula Charitra,* Part 2, Ponnur: Lokayata Prachuranalu, 1996.

Parvathamma, C., *Scheduled Castes and Tribes: A Socio-Economic Survey*, New Delhi: Ashish Publishing House, 1984.

Patil, Sharad, "Dialectics of Caste and Class Conflict", *Economic and Political Weekly*, Vol. XIV, Nos. 7/8, February 24, 1979.

——, *Das-Shudra Slavery*, Volume l, New Delhi: Allied Publication, 1980.

——, *Das-Shudra Slavery*, Volume 2, Poona: Sugawa Publications, 1990.

——, "Liberals vs Left and Right", *Economic and Political Weekly*, Vol. XXXVII, No. 6, February 7, 2002.

——, "Semi-Caste Feudalism", *Economic and Political Weekly*, Vol. XXXVII, No. 47, November 23, 2002.

Patnaik, Arunkumar, "Gramsci Today", *Economic and Political Weekly*, Vol. 39, No. 11, March 13–19, 2004.

Patwardhan, Sunanda, *Change among India's Harijan*, New Delhi: Orient Longman, Asia, 1973.

Pavier, Barry, *The Telangana Movement 1944–51*, New Delhi: Vikas Publishing, 1981.

Pendre, Sandeep (Ed.), *At Crossroads: Dalit Movement Today*, Bombay: Vikas Adhyayan Kendra, 1994.

Phadke, Y.D., *Social Reform Movements in Maharashtra*, New Delhi: Maharashtra Information Centre, Government of Maharashtra, 1989.

Phule, Jotirao Govind Rao, *Slavery: Collected Works of Mahatma Jotirao Phule*. Vol. 1 and 2 (Translated by P.G. Patil), Bombay: Education Department, 1991.

Pradhan, A.C., *The Emergence of Depressed Classes*, Bhubaneswar: Book Land International, 1986.

Prasad, C.B., *The Dalit Agenda and Politics in India (1947–1995)* (Unpublished Study), 1996.

Prasad, Kalekuri, *Dalit a Sahityam* (Telugu), Vijayawada: Dalita Women Sahitya Parishad, 1996.

Prasanna Kumar, A., Linga Mukthy, V., Ravi, K., *Government and Politics in Andhra Pradesh*, New Delhi: S. Chand & Co, 1982.

Poulantzas, N., *Political Power and Social Classes*, London: New Left Books, 1973.

Purendra Prasad, N., "Agrarian Class and Caste Relation in 'United' Andhra Pradesh 1956–2014", *EPW*. Vol. L, No. 16, April 18, 2015.

Rajan, Nalini, "Left-Liberalism and Caste Politics", *Economic and Political Weekly*, Vol. 38, No. 24, June 14–20, 2003.

Raj, Sheela, *Medievalism to Modernism: Socio-Economic and Cultural History of Hyderabad 1869–1911*, Bombay: Popular Prakashan, 1987.

Ram, Nandu, "Dalit Movement in India: A Perspective from Below", *Indian Journal of Social Work*, Vol. 59, No. 1, January 1998.

Ramaswamy, Uma, "Protection and Inequality among Backward Groups", *Economic and Political Weekly*, Vol. 21, No. 9, March 1, 1986.

Rao, M.S.A. (Ed.), *Social Movements in India: Studies in Peasant, Backward Classes, Sectarian, Tribal and Women's Movements*, New Delhi: Manohar Publications, 2002.

Rao, R.S., *Towards Understanding Semi Feudal Semi Colonial Society: Perspectives Studies in Political Economy*, Hyderabad: Perspective Publications, 1995

Ray, Rabindra, *The Naxalites and Their Ideology*, New Delhi: Oxford University Press, 1988.

Rao, N. Bhaskar, *The Politics of Leadership in an Indian State: Andhra Pradesh*, Vijayawada: Bharat Publication, 1968.

Ray, Raka, Katzenstein, Mary, Fainsod (Ed.), *Social Movements in India: Poverty, Power and Politics*, New Delhi: Oxford University Press, 2005.

Reddy, G. Sudershan, "Caste Associations and Social Change in Andhra 1900–1925", M. Phil. Thesis, Hyderabad: Osmania University, 1986.

Reddy, D. Narasimha, "Karamchedu: A Dialectic with Development", *Economic and Political Weekly*, September 1985.

Reddy, G. Krishna, *Documenting Dalit Activism in Andhra Pradesh: Towards Constructing the Movement*, Centre for Economic and Social Studies and ICCSR, March 17–18, 2007.

——, "New Populism and Liberalisation", *EPW*, Vol. 37, No. 9, March 2002.

——, "Dalit Movement and Left Practice in Andhra Pradesh: An Ideological Linkages" (Unpublished Article), 2004.

——, and M. Kodandaram. "Dalit Movement and Left Practice: A View from Gramscian Perspective." *Gramsci Today*, 2004.

Reddy, G. Ram, "The Politics of Accommodation in Andhra Pradesh", Francine R. Frankel, M.S.A. Rao (Ed.), *Dominance and State Power in Modern India: Decline of Social Order*, New Delhi: Oxford University Press, 1989.

Reddy, T. Papi, *Agrarian Unrest, Peasant Struggles and Social Change: A Study Telangana in Andhra Pradesh*, Warangal: Soni Publishing House, 1990.

Rodrigues, Valerian, "Viewing Dalit Movement: Contending Perspectives", Sandeep, Pendse (Ed.), *At Cross Roads: Dalit Movement Today*, Bombay: Vikas Adhyayan Kendra, August 1994.

Roy, KumKum, "Kosambi and Questions of Caste", *Economic and Political Weekly*, Vol. 43, No. 30, July 26–August 1, 2008.

Roy, Ajit, "Human Rights Issue on the Left", *Economic and Political Weekly*, Vol. XXIX, No. 10, March 5, 1994.

Salaha, Karamchedu, *Detailed Report on Karamchedu*, Hyderabad: Hyderabad Book Trust, 1985.

Sagar, "The Spring and Its Thunder", *Economic and Political Weekly*, Vol. XLI, No. 29, July 22, 2006.

Sanjay Seth, *Marxist Theory and Nationalist Politics: The Case of Colonial India*, New Delhi: Sage Publications, 1995.

Satyanarayana, A., "Rise and Growth of Left Movement in Andhra, 1934–1939", *Social Scientist*, Vol. XIX, No. 1, 1986.

——, *Society Economy and Polity in Modern Andhra*, New Delhi: Kaniska Publishers, 2002.

——, *Dalits and Upper Caste: Essays in Social History*, New Delhi: Kaniska Publication, 2005.

Satyanarayan, A., Rajam, Venkat G., Rao, Venkateswar M. (Ed.), *Retrieving the Past: History and Culture of Telangana*, Proceedings of the Seminar, Hyderabad: Department of History, Osmania University, 2005.

Satyanarayana, G., *Changing Agrarian Structure and Labour Relations*, Jaipur: Rawat Publications, 1992.

Satyanarayana K., Susie Tharu (Ed.), *Steel Nibs Are Sprouting: New Dalit Writing from South India*, Noida: Harper Collins Publishers, 2013.

Satyashodhak (A Centre for Social Science Research) Position Paper, Hyderabad (Undated).

Sandeep, Pendse (Ed.), *At Cross-Roads: Dalit Movement Today*, Bombay: Vikas Aditya Kendra, 1994.

Sarkar, R.M. (Ed.), *Dalit in India: Past and Present*, New Delhi: Serial Publications, 2006.

Seth, D.L., "Reservation Policy Revisited", Mohanty, Manoranjan (Ed.), *Caste, Class, Gender: Readings in Indian Government and Politics*, New Delhi: Sage Publications, 2004.

Shah, Ghanashyam (Ed.), *Social Transformation in India*, Vol. 1, Jaipur: Rawat Publications, 1997.

——, (Ed.), *Caste and Democratic Politics in India: Essential Writings in Politics*, New Delhi: Permanent Black, 2002.

——, (Ed.), "Dalits and the State", Centre for Rural Studies, Lal Bahadur Shastri National Academy of Administration, Mussoorie, New Delhi: Concept Publishing Company, 2002.

——, (Ed.) *Social Movements and the State: Readings in Indian Government and Politics*, New Delhi: Sage Publications, 2002.

——, *Social Movements in India: A Review of Literature*, New Delhi: Sage Publications, 2004.

Sharma K.L., *Social Stratification and Mobility*, Jaipur: Rawat Publications, 1994.

——, (Ed.), *Caste and Class in India*, Jaipur: Rawat Publications, 1998.

Simhadri, S., Vishweshwer Rao, P.L. (Ed.), *Telangana: Dimensions of Under Development*, Hyderabad: Centre for Telangana Studies, 1997.

Simon, Roger, *Gramsci's Political Thought: An Introduction*, London: Lawrence and Wishart Limited, 1982.

Singh, Rajendra, *Social Movements, Old and New: A Post-Modernist Critique*, New Delhi: Sage Publications, 2001.

Srinivasulu, K., *Telangana Peasant Movement and Changes in the Agrarian Structure: A Case Study of Nalgonda District* (Unpublished PhD Dissertation), JNU, 1988.

——, *Caste, Class and Social Articulation in Andhra Pradesh: Mapping Differential Regional Trajectories* (Working Paper 179), Overseas Development Institute, London, September 2002.

——, "CPI (ML) and the Question of Caste: Dynamics of Social Mobilisation in Anti-feudal Struggle in Telangana", Basu, Pradeep (Ed.), *Discourses on Naxalite Movement 1967–2009: Insights into Radical Left Politics*, Kolkata: Setu Prakashani, 2010.

Srinivas, M.N., "Caste in Modern India", Mohanty, Manoranajan (Ed.), *Caste, Class, Gender: Readings in Indian Government and Politics*, New Delhi: Sage Publications, 2004.

Sumantra, Bose, *Transforming India: Changes in the World's Largest Democracy*, London: Herald University Press, 2013.

Sumanta, Banerjee, "Beyond Naxalbari", *Economic and Political Weekly*, Vol. XLI, No. 29, July 22, 2006.

Sundarayya, P., *Telangana People's Struggle and Its Lessons*, New Delhi: Foundation Books, 2006

Tarakam, Bojja, "Chunduru Theerpu: Dalita Poraata Vijayam", *Samaanthara Voice* (Monthly Magazine), Hyderabad, August 2007.

Teltumbde, Anand, *Anti-Imperialism and Annihilation of Caste*, Thane: Ramai Prakashan, 2005.

Teltumbde, Anand, Sen, Shoma (Ed.), "Scripting the Change: Selected Writings of Anuradha Ghandy", Anuradha Ghandy Memorial Committee, New Delhi: Daanish Books, 2011.

Thirumali, Inukonda, "Dora and Gadi: Manifestation of Land Lord Domination in Telangana", *Economic and Political Weekly*, Vol. 27, No. 9, February 29, 1992.

——, *Against Dora and Nizam: People's Movement in Telangana 1939–1948*, New Delhi: Kaniska Publishers, 2003.

——, *Telangana-Andhra: Castes, Regions and Politics in Andhra Pradesh*. New Delhi: Aakar Books, 2013.

Tilak D. Gupta, "Maoism in India: Ideology, Programme and Armed Struggle", *Economic and Political Weekly*, Vol. XLI, No. 29, July 22, 2006.

Veeranna, Maroju. *Indialo Emi Cheyyali*. May 17th Comrades CPUSI (Dalit Bahujan Sramika Vimukthi (Telugu). Andhra Pradesh, Hyderabad, 2005.

Venkataswamy, P.R. *Our Struggle for Emancipation*. Vol. 1 and 2, Secunderabad: Universal Art Printers, 1955.

Wankhede, S. Harish, "The Political and the Social in the Dalit Movement Today", *Economic and Political Weekly*, Vol. 43, No. 6, February 9, 2008.

——, "Class-Caste Debate Revisited", *Economic and Political Weekly*, Vol. XLVIII, Nos. 26/27, June 29, 2013.

Zelliot, Eleanor, *From Untouchable to Dalit: Essays on Ambedkar Movement*. New Delhi: Manohar Publications, 1992.

TELUGU BIBLIOGRAPHY

"Adi-Hindu Vudyama Pithamahudu-Bhagya Reddy Varma" Editorial, *Samaantara,* Vol. 2, No. 14, May 2008.

"Advitiyudu: Ambedkar Smarakopanyasalu 1986–2013", Dr. B.R. Ambedkar Memorial Trust (Ed.), Hyderabad: Hyderabad book Trust Publications, February 2014.

"Anachabadda Dalitulantha Thiragabadandi", Vijayawada: Rytucooli Sangam, Andhra Pradesh Committee, July 2012.

Andhra Pradesh lo Radical Vidyarthi Sangam (1974–92), Viplava Rachithala Sangam Prachuranalu, March 2012.

Andhra Pradesh lo Mahila Vudyama Parinam-Konni Anubhavalu, Andhra Pradesh: Sthrivimukthi Sanghatana Publications, January 2000.

Balakotaiah, Choppara, *Nenu Mala-Na Thammudu Madiga*, Vishakhapatnam: Krushi Publications, June 1998.

——, *SC Vargikarana Evariki Avasaram?* Vishakhapatnam: Krushi Publications, August 1999.

Bahujana Keratalu a Special issue on Karamchedu, Vol. 1, No. 4, July 2005.

——, "Special Issue on Telangana Movement", Ongole, November/ December 2013.

"Bharata Viplava Vyuham-Etthugadalu", 9th Congress Resolutions, CPI (ML)-Maoist Party, Central Committee, 2007.

Charcha for Democratic Values, a Monthly Magazine, Vol. 2, No. 8, Karnool, May/June 2007.

Com. Ramalingachari, Vasantha, *Srikakula Girijanodyamam: Anubhavalu-Avagahana*, Srikakulam: Com. Vasantha Ramalingachari Memorial Trust Publications, 2005.

Com. Veeranna, Maroju, *Indialo Eemee Cheyalee: Com. Veeranna Sardhyamlo Kulam pai Ambedkar Sidhanta Charcha*, Hyderabad: Jaabili Prachuranalu, 2001.

Goutam, M.B., *Bhagya Reddy Varma Jeevitadhrasham-Aacharana*, Hyderabad: Samaantara Book House Publications, December 2009.

Ilaiah, Kancha, *Kula Nirmulana-Marxist Dhrukpadham*, Hyderabad: Hyderabad Book Trust Publications, 2002.

Jagithyala Jungalmahal, Vol. 1/2, Hyderabad: Virasam Publications, 2002.

Jashuva, Gurram, *Gahbilam*, Vijayawada: Jashuva Foundation, 1996.

Jashuva, Gurram, *Naa Katha*, Vijayawada: Jashuva Foundation, 1996.

Jayashankar, Kothapalli, "Telangana Rashtram-Oka Demand", Karimnagar: Mallepalli Rajam Memorial Trust, March 2004.

"Karamchedu *Nundi Vempenttadhaka Dalitulapai Dhadulu Endhuku Jarugutunnai?" Emi Cheyyali?*, Hyderabad: Dalita Bahujana Mahajana Samithi, 1998.

Keshava P. Kumar, *Dalita Vudyamam: Velugu Needalu*, Hyderabad: Spruha Sahiti Samastha Prachuranalu, 2009.

Kranthi (Monthly Magazine), Vol. 32, No. 3, May/June 2008.

Krishnaiah B. (Ed.) *Ambedkar Ananthara Dalita Vudyamalu, Sahityam: Savallu*, Kakatiya University: Dr. B.R. Ambedkar Studies Centre (UGC), October 2011.

"Kula Nirmulana", Hyderabad: *KNPS Bulletin*, June 2, 2001.

Kula Nirmulana Porata Ssamithi (undated): *Pranalika—Nibandhanavali*, Hyderabad: KNPS Prachuranalu.

Kula Nirmulana—Oka Marxist Drukpatham, Hyderabad: Nutana Praja Swamya Vedika, 1987.

Kulanirmulana: Vidyarthi-Yuvajanulu, Vijayawada: Navayuga Samakya (NYS), Pragathi Seela Prajaswamya Vidyarthi Samstha Publications, 2007.

Kula Samasya Pai May 17th Comrades ki CPI (ML)-Janashakthi Samadahanam, Hyderabad: Janashakthi Prachuranalu, 1997.

Kumaraswamy, Nagam, "Andhra Pradesh Dalita Vudyomam-Kula Nirmulana: Vibinna Prayogaalu", *Sammantara*, Vol. 2, No. 4, July 2008.

Kumar E.S., "Maoist Partylo Saaguthunna Kulavivaksha", *Dalit Voice*, Bulletin 12, December 2005.

Lalitha, K., Kannabiran Vsanta., Melkote, Rama, Susitharu, Shtrugna Veena, Rathnamala, M., *Manakau Teliyani Mana Charithra: Telanghana Rythanga Poratamlo Sthreelu*, Hyderabad: Shakthi Sanghtana Prachuranalu, 1986.

Laxmaiah, Mallepalli, "Vuttara Telanganalo Police Rajyam", *Suprabhatam*, Vol. V, No. 8, January/February 1996.

Mahojwala Telangana Rytanaga Sayuda Poraata: Navala Sahityam Parichayaalu-Parisheelana, Hyderabad: Janasahiti Prachuranalu, May 2011.

Madiga Reservation Poratam-Oka Pariseelana, Hyderabad: Vimochana Prachuranalu, 1996.

Meghanath, "Com. Tharimela Nagi Reddy Jivitha Sangrham", Vijayawada: T.N. Memorial Trust Publications, No. 14, October 1986.

Mohiuddin, Makhdum, *Nizamlo Dhopidi Vidhanam: Muslimla Kartavyam*, Bejawada: Prajashakthi Prachuranalu, May 1947.

Nagabushnam, Mukkamala, *Nenu Communistunu Ela Ayyaanu*, Bejawada: Prajashakthi Prachuranalu, February 1946.

Nagaraju, Papani (Ed.), *Dalita Pratightana Poratala Ninaadham: Karamchedu Nundi Laximpeta Dhaaka (1985–2013)*, Hyderabad: Jaabili Prachuranalu, December 2013.

Nalupu (Monthly Magazine), 1989–1993, Hyderabad: Hyderabad Book Trust.

Narasaiah, P. *Madiga Palle (A Navel in Telugu)*, Vishakhapatnam: Books and Books Publications, 1998.

Narasimhulu, Nalla, *Telangana Saayudha Poratam Naa Anubhavaalu*, Hyderabad: Visalaandhra Publishing House, August 1989.

Naxalbary: Oka Ooru Matrame Kaadu, Oka Vudyamam! Hyderabad: Sramika Varga Prachuranalu, May 1997.

Nijanirdharana Committe Nivedhika, "Gunturu Zilla Chunduru Dalitula pai Agrakula Durahnakarula Hatyakanda", Andhra Pradesh: APCLC and OPDR, August 1991.

Praja Swetcha, Andhra Pradesh Civil Liberties Committee (APCLC), Prachuranalu, Vol. 2, No. 3/5, March/May 2004.

Prakash Rao S., "Nizam Rajyam lo Dalita Vudyama Nirmatha: P.R.Venkataswamy, *Samaantara*, Vol. 3, No. 4, July 2009.

Rajesh, K., Andhra Telangana Dalita Vudyamam: Communist Vudyama Prabhavam, *Samaantara*, Vol. 2, No. 4, July 2008.

Ramakrishna V., *Andhra Deshamlo Sanga Samskanodyamalu (1848–1919)*, Hyderabad: Hyderabad Book Trust Publications, January 1985.

Rao, U.S. (Ed.), *Edureetha*, Marxist-Leninist Centre, Hyderabad, May 1991.

——, "Patha Pata Saaxiga Kotha Pata Paduta", *Dalitha Rachayithalu, Kalakarulu, Medhavula Aikya Vedika*, Hyderabad: A.P. Publications, 1993.

Rao, Y.V. Krishna, *Andhra Pradesh lo Swatanthraniki Mundhu Rytu Porataalu, Rytu Sangaalu*, Vijayawada: Vishalandhra Publishing House, October 1981.

Rao, Prasad. Nanduri, *Andhralo Rytu Vudyamam*, Hyderabad: Praja Prachurnalayam, 1953.

Rao, Venkateswara Devulapalli, *Bharatha Viplava Panthanu Choopina Telangana Sayudha Poratam*, Hyderabad: Porunela Publications, January 2014.

Rao, Katti, Padma, *Dalitula Charitra* (Two Parts in Telugu), Ponnuru: Lokayata Publications, 1991–1994.

——, *Kulam Punadulu*, Ponnuru: Lokayata Publications, 1988.

Rao, M. L, Narasimha, *Telangana Vytalikulu*, Hyderabad: Kakatiya Vignana Samithi Publications, August 1976.

Rao, P.V., "Tholi Suryudu-Bhagya Reddy Varma", *Samaantara*, Vol. 3, No. 2, May 2009.

Reddy, Gaddam, Krishna, "Dalita Vudyamala Pratyekatha-Oka Parisheelana", *Samaantara*, Vol. 2, No. 4, July 2008.

Reddy, Kodandaram M., Sudhakar (Ed.), *Naxalbari Gamyam, Gamanam*, Hyderabad: Perspectives, 1998.

Reddy, Chandra, Pulla, *Veera Telangana Viplava Poratam*, Hyderabad: Vimochana Publications, 1968.

Samaantara (Monthly Magazine), Vol. 6, No. 2, May 2012.

Samaantara (Monthly Magazine), Vol. 3, No. 8, November 2009.

Satyanarayana, Adapa, *Andhra Pradeshlo Nurendla Dalita Vudyamaalu*, Hyderabad: Hyderabad Book Trust publications, February 2009.

Shivaprasad, Mudugonda, *Vudyama Dharshanamu*, Hyderabad: Rasagangotri Publications, March 1990.

Shyamala, Gogu, *Nene Balanni: T.N. Sadhalaxmi Batuku Katha*, Hyderabad: Hyderabad Book Trust Publications, July 2011.

"Telanganalo Samajika Prajarajyam: Hyderabad Declaration", *Samajika Telangana Mahasabha*, Hyderabad: Edureetha Publications, November 2010.

Thirumali, Inukonda, *Thiragabadda Telangana: Dhoralanu Dhincham Nizamnu Kulcham*, Hyderabad: Hyderabad Book Trust, January 2008.

"Thupaki Rjyam: Perugutunna Nirbhandam Midha Nivedhika", *Andhra Pradesh Civil Liberty Committee Report*, Vijayawada: APCLC Prachuranalu, April 1991.

"Vempenta Ghtana pai Karapatram", *Kula Nirmulana Porata Samithi* (KNPS), November 1999.

Venkatramaiah, Vemulapalli, *Bharatha Desamlo Kulavyavastha: Binna Dhrukpadhalu*, Guntur: Prajapandha Prachuranalu, 1992.

Viplava Telanagana Porata Veera Gaathalu, Vijayawada: Prajasakhti Publications, January 1984.

Viplava Rachayithala Sangam, *Jagithyala Jungalmahal-1 and 2*, Hyderabad: Virasam Publications, 2002.

"Vyavasaya Cooliretla Porata Anubhavaalu", *Andhra Pradesh Vyavasaya Karmika Sangam*, Vijayawada: Prajasakthi Prachuranalu, 1996.

INTERVIEWS

Interview with Duddu Prabhakar on 10 October 2013.

Interview with O. Sambhasiva Rao on 30 December 2013.

Interview with Devendhar alias Amar in 2014

Interview with G. Ramulu on 6 April 2014.

Interview with Chalapathi Rao on 16 August 2014.
Interview with Manda Krishna Madiga, on 16 August 2014.
Interview with Bojja Tharakam on 28 October 2014.
Interview with Gadder on 22 November 2014.
Interview with Vara Rao on 1 December 2014.
Interview with Ganta Chakrapani on 10 December 2014.
Interview with Prof Adapa Satyanarayana on 16 January 2015.
Interview with Prof K. Srinivasulu on 23 January 2015.
Interview with Mallepali Lakshmaiah on 3 May 2015.

Index